M000103309

Textbook Outlines, Highlights, and Practice Quizzes

The Legal Environment of Business

by Roger E. Meiners, 11th Edition

All "Just the Facts101" Material Written or Prepared by Cram101 Textbook Reviews

Title Page

"Just the Facts101" is a Content Technologies publication and tool designed to give you all the facts from your textbooks. Register for the full practice test for each of your chapters for virtually any of your textbooks.

Facts101 has built custom study tools specific to your textbook. We provide all of the factual testable information and unlike traditional study guides, we will never send you back to your textbook for more information.

YOU WILL NEVER HAVE TO HIGHLIGHT A BOOK AGAIN!

Facts101 StudyGuides
All of the information in this StudyGuide is written specifically for your textbook. We include the key terms, places, people, and concepts... the information you can expect on your next exam!

Facts101
Only Facts101 gives you the outlines, highlights, and PRACTICE TESTS specific to your textbook. Facts101 sister Cram101.com is an online application where you'll discover study tools designed to make the most of your limited study time.

www.Cram101.com

ISBN(s): 9781538834763. PUBI-6.20161227

STUDYING MADE EASY

This Craml0l notebook is designed to make studying easier and increase your comprehension of the textbook material. Instead of starting with a blank notebook and trying to write down everything discussed in class lectures, you can use this Craml0l textbook notebook and annotate your notes along with the lecture.

Our goal is to give you the best tools for success.

For a supreme understanding of the course, pair your notebook with our online tools at www.cram101.com

Our Online Access program is a simple way for us to keep our promise and provide you the best studying tools, regardless of where you purchased your Craml0l textbook notebook. As long as you let us know you are intereested in a free online access account we will set it up for you for 180 days.

Online Access:

SIMPLE STEPS TO GET A FREE ACCOUNT:

Email Travis.Reese@cram101.com

Include:

Order number

ISBN of Guide

Retailer where purchased

The Legal Environment of Business
Roger E. Meiners, 11th

CONTENTS

1. Today`s Business Environment: Law and Ethics

CHAPTER OUTLINE: KEY TERMS, PEOPLE, PLACES, CONCEPTS

Commission

Corruption

Discrimination

Public law

Public nuisance

Tort

Constitution

Corporation

Executive branch

Clean Water Act

Common law

Fraud

Ponzi scheme

Precedent

American Law Institute

Contract

United Nations Convention on Contracts for the International Sale of Goods

President

Private law

Misdemeanor

Procedural law

1. Today`s Business Environment: Law and Ethics

CHAPTER OUTLINE: KEY TERMS, PEOPLE, PLACES, CONCEPTS

__________ Substantive law

__________ Clayton Act

__________ Arbitration

__________ Estate

__________ Intellectual property

__________ Slavery

__________ Plaintiff

__________ Income

__________ World Bank

__________ Corporate social responsibility

__________ Social responsibility

__________ Court system

CHAPTER HIGHLIGHTS & NOTES: KEY TERMS, PEOPLE, PLACES, CONCEPTS

Commission	The payment of commission as remuneration for services rendered or products sold is a common way to reward sales people. Payments often will be calculated on the basis of a percentage of the goods sold. This is a way for firms to solve the principal-agent problem, by attempting to realign employees' interests with those of the firm.
Corruption	In philosophical, theological, or moral discussions, corruption is spiritual or moral impurity or deviation from an ideal. Corruption may include many activities including bribery and embezzlement. Government, or 'political', corruption occurs when an office-holder or other governmental employee acts in an official capacity for personal gain.

Discrimination	Discrimination is action that denies social participation or human rights to categories of people based on prejudice. This includes treatment of an individual or group based on their actual or perceived membership in a certain group or social category, 'in a way that is worse than the way people are usually treated'. It involves the group's initial reaction or interaction, influencing the individual's actual behavior towards the group or the group leader, restricting members of one group from opportunities or privileges that are available to another group, leading to the exclusion of the individual or entities based on logical or irrational decision making.
Public law	Public law is that part of law which governs relationships between individuals and the government, and those relationships between individuals which are of direct concern to the society. Public law comprises constitutional law, administrative law, tax law and criminal law, as well as all procedural law. In public law, mandatory rules (not optional) prevail.
Public nuisance	In English criminal law, public nuisance is a class of common law offence in which the injury, loss or damage is suffered by the local community as a whole rather than by individual victims.
Tort	A tort, in common law jurisdictions, is a civil wrong that unfairly causes someone else to suffer loss or harm resulting in legal liability for the person who commits the tortious act, called a tortfeasor. Although crimes may be torts, the cause of legal action is not necessarily a crime, as the harm may be due to negligence which does not amount to criminal negligence. The victim of the harm can recover their loss as damages in a lawsuit.
Constitution	A constitution is the set of regulations which govern the conduct of non-political entities, whether incorporated or not. Such entities include corporations and voluntary associations.
Corporation	A corporation is a separate legal entity that has been incorporated either directly through legislation or through a registration process established by law. Incorporated entities have legal rights and liabilities that are distinct from their employees and shareholders, and may conduct business as either a profit-seeking business or not-for-profit business. Early incorporated entities were established by charter (i.e. by an ad hoc act granted by a monarch or passed by a parliament or legislature).
Executive branch	The executive is the part of government that has sole authority and responsibility for the daily administration of the state. The executive branch executes or enforces the law. The division of power into separate branches of government is central to the idea of the separation of powers.
Clean Water Act	The Clean Water Act is a law enacted by the Legislative Assembly of Ontario, Canada. The purpose of this Act is to protect existing and future sources of drinking water. The Clean Water Act, 2006 (Bill 43) is a major part of the Ontario government's commitment to ensuring that every Ontarian has access to safe drinking water.

1. Today`s Business Environment: Law and Ethics

CHAPTER HIGHLIGHTS & NOTES: KEY TERMS, PEOPLE, PLACES, CONCEPTS

Common law

Common law is law developed by judges through decisions of courts and similar tribunals, as opposed to statutes adopted through the legislative process or regulations issued by the executive branch.

A 'common law system' is a legal system that gives great precedential weight to common law, on the principle that it is unfair to treat similar facts differently on different occasions. The body of precedent is called 'common law' and it binds future decisions.

Fraud

Fraud is a deception deliberately practiced in order to secure unfair or unlawful gain (adjectival form fraudulent; to defraud is the verb). As a legal construct, fraud is both a civil wrong (i.e., a fraud victim may sue the fraud perpetrator to avoid the fraud and/or recover monetary compensation) and a criminal wrong (i.e., a fraud perpetrator may be prosecuted and imprisoned by governmental authorities). Defrauding people or organizations of money or valuables is the usual purpose of fraud, but it sometimes instead involves obtaining benefits without actually depriving anyone of money or valuables, such as obtaining a drivers license by way of false statements made in an application for the same.

Ponzi scheme

A Ponzi scheme is a fraudulent investment operation where the operator, an individual or organization, pays returns to its investors from new capital paid to the operators by new investors, rather than from profit earned by the operator. Operators of Ponzi schemes usually entice new investors by offering higher returns than other investments, in the form of short-term returns that are either abnormally high or unusually consistent. The perpetuation of the high returns requires an ever-increasing flow of money from new investors to sustain the scheme.

Precedent

In common law legal systems, a precedent or authority is a principle or rule established in a previous legal case that is either binding on or persuasive for a court or other tribunal when deciding subsequent cases with similar issues or facts. The general principle in common law legal systems is that similar cases should be decided so as to give similar and predictable outcomes, and the principle of precedent is the mechanism by which that goal is attained. Black's Law Dictionary defines 'precedent' as a 'rule of law established for the first time by a court for a particular type of case and thereafter referred to in deciding similar cases.' Common law precedent is a third kind of law, on equal footing with statutory law (statutes and codes enacted by legislative bodies), and regulatory law (regulations promulgated by executive branch agencies).

American Law Institute

The American Law Institute was established in 1923 to promote the clarification and simplification of United States common law and its adaptation to changing social needs. The American Law Institute drafts, approves, and publishes Restatements of the Law, Principles of the Law, model codes, and other proposals for law reform. The American Law Institute is headquartered in Philadelphia, Pennsylvania, near the University of Pennsylvania Law School.

Contract	In common law legal systems, a contract is an agreement having a lawful object entered into voluntarily by two or more parties, each of whom intends to create one or more legal obligations between them. The elements of a contract are 'offer' and 'acceptance' by 'competent persons' having legal capacity who exchange 'consideration' to create 'mutuality of obligation.' Proof of some or all of these elements may be done in writing, though contracts may be made entirely orally or by conduct. The remedy for breach of contract can be 'damages' in the form of compensation of money or specific performance enforced through an injunction.
United Nations Convention on Contracts for the International Sale of Goods	The United Nations Convention on Contracts for the International Sale of Goods is a treaty that is a uniform international sales law. As of June 2014, it has been ratified by 81 countries that account for a significant proportion of world trade, making it one of the most successful international uniform laws. Congo was the most recent state to ratify the Convention, having acceded to it on 11 June 2014.
President	A President is a leader of an organization, company, community, club, trade union, university for this article. It is the legally recognized highest 'titled' corporate officer, ranking above the various Vice Presidents (e.g. Senior Vice President and Executive Vice President), however that post on its own is generally considered subordinate to the Chief Executive Officer. In a similar vein to the Chief Operating Officer, the title of corporate President as a separate position (as opposed to being combined with a 'C-Suite' designation, such as 'President and CEO' or 'President and COO') is also loosely defined.
Private law	Private law is that part of a civil law legal system which is part of the jus commune that involves relationships between individuals, such as the law of contracts or torts, and the law of obligations (as it is called in civil legal systems). It is to be distinguished from public law, which deals with relationships between both natural and artificial persons (i.e., organizations) and the state, including regulatory statutes, penal law and other law that affects the public order. In general terms, private law involves interactions between private citizens, whereas public law involves interrelations between the state and the general population.
Misdemeanor	A misdemeanor is any 'lesser' criminal act in some common law legal systems. Misdemeanors are generally punished less severely than felonies, but theoretically more so than administrative infractions (also known as minor, petty or summary offences) and regulatory offences. Many misdemeanors are punished with monetary fines.
Procedural law	Procedural law or adjective law comprises the rules by which a court hears and determines what happens in civil lawsuit, criminal or administrative proceedings. The rules are designed to ensure a fair and consistent application of due process (in the U.S). or fundamental justice (in other common law countries) to all cases that come before a court.

1. Today`s Business Environment: Law and Ethics

CHAPTER HIGHLIGHTS & NOTES: KEY TERMS, PEOPLE, PLACES, CONCEPTS

Substantive law

Substantive law is the statutory, or written law, that defines rights and duties, such as crimes and punishments, civil rights and responsibilities in civil law. It is codified in legislated statutes or can be enacted through the initiative process.

Substantive law stands in contrast to procedural law, which is the 'machinery' for enforcing those rights and duties.

Clayton Act

The Clayton Act of 1914 (Pub.L. 63-212, 38 Stat. 730, enacted October 15, 1914, codified at 15 U.S.C. §§ 12-27, 29 U.S.C. §§ 52-53), was a part of United States antitrust law with the goal of adding further substance to the U.S. antitrust law regime; the Clayton Act sought to prevent anticompetitive practices in their incipiency. That regime started with the Sherman Antitrust Act of 1890, the first Federal law outlawing practices considered harmful to consumers (monopolies, cartels, and trusts). The Clayton Act specified particular prohibited conduct, the three-level enforcement scheme, the exemptions, and the remedial measures.

Arbitration

Arbitration, a form of alternative dispute resolution, is a technique for the resolution of disputes outside the courts. The parties to a dispute refer it to arbitration by one or more persons (the 'arbitrators', 'arbiters' or 'arbitral tribunal'), and agree to be bound by the arbitration decision (the 'award'). A third party reviews the evidence in the case and imposes a decision that is legally binding on both sides and enforceable in the courts.

Estate

An estate comprises the houses and outbuildings and supporting farmland and woods that surround the gardens and grounds of a very large property, such as a country house or mansion. It is the modern term for a manor, but lacks the latter's now abolished jurisdictional authority. It is an 'estate' because the profits from its produce and rents are sufficient to support the household in the house at its center, formerly known as the manor house.

Intellectual property

Intellectual property rights are the legally recognized exclusive rights to creations of the mind. Under intellectual property law, owners are granted certain exclusive rights to a variety of intangible assets, such as musical, literary, and artistic works; discoveries and inventions; and words, phrases, symbols, and designs. Common types of intellectual property rights include copyright, trademarks, patents, industrial design rights, trade dress, and in some jurisdictions trade secrets.

Slavery

Slavery is a system under which people are treated as property to be bought and sold, and are forced to work. Slaves can be held against their will from the time of their capture, purchase or birth, and deprived of the right to leave, to refuse to work, or to demand compensation. Historically, slavery was institutionally recognized by most societies; in more recent times, slavery has been outlawed in all countries, but it continues through the practices of debt bondage, indentured servitude, serfdom, domestic servants kept in captivity, certain adoptions in which children are forced to work as slaves, child soldiers, and forced marriage.

Plaintiff	A plaintiff, also known as a claimant or complainant, is the term used in some jurisdictions for the party who initiates a lawsuit (also known as an action) before a court. By doing so, the plaintiff seeks a legal remedy, and if successful, the court will issue judgment in favor of the plaintiff and make the appropriate court order (e.g., an order for damages). In some jurisdictions the commencement of a lawsuit is done by filing a summons, claim form and/or a complaint.
Income	Income is the consumption and savings opportunity gained by an entity within a specified timeframe, which is generally expressed in monetary terms. However, for households and individuals, 'income is the sum of all the wages, salaries, profits, interests payments, rents and other forms of earnings received... in a given period of time.' In the field of public economics, the term may refer to the accumulation of both monetary and non-monetary consumption ability, with the former (monetary) being used as a proxy for total income.
World Bank	The World Bank is a United Nations international financial institution that provides loans to developing countries for capital programs. The World Bank is a component of the World Bank Group, and a member of the United Nations Development Group. The World Bank's official goal is the reduction of poverty.
Corporate social responsibility	Corporate social responsibility is a form of corporate self-regulation integrated into a business model. Corporate social responsibility policy functions as a built-in, self-regulating mechanism whereby a business monitors and ensures its active compliance with the spirit of the law, ethical standards, and international norms. In some models, a firm's implementation of Corporate social responsibility goes beyond compliance and engages in 'actions that appear to further some social good, beyond the interests of the firm and that which is required by law.' Corporate social responsibility is a process with the aim to embrace responsibility for the company's actions and encourage a positive impact through its activities on the environment, consumers, employees, communities, stakeholders and all other members of the public sphere who may also be considered stakeholders.
Social responsibility	Social responsibility is an ethical theory that an entity, be it an organization or individual, has an obligation to act to benefit society at large. Social responsibility is a duty every individual has to perform so as to maintain a balance between the economy and the ecosystems. A trade-off may exist between economic development, in the material sense, and the welfare of the society and environment.
Court system	The judiciary' (also known as the judicial system or 'court system) is the system of courts that interprets and applies the law in the name of the state. The judiciary also provides a mechanism for the resolution of disputes.

1. Today`s Business Environment: Law and Ethics

CHAPTER QUIZ: KEY TERMS, PEOPLE, PLACES, CONCEPTS

1. The _________ is a treaty that is a uniform international sales law. As of June 2014, it has been ratified by 81 countries that account for a significant proportion of world trade, making it one of the most successful international uniform laws. Congo was the most recent state to ratify the Convention, having acceded to it on 11 June 2014.

   a. United Nations Convention on Contracts for the International Sale of Goods
   b. Cynthia Cooper
   c. Financial scandal in the Orthodox Church in America
   d. HP Autonomy

2. In English criminal law, _________ is a class of common law offence in which the injury, loss or damage is suffered by the local community as a whole rather than by individual victims.

   a. Public nuisance
   b. Class Action Fairness Act
   c. Family Entertainment and Copyright Act
   d. Breach of contract

3. A _________ is any 'lesser' criminal act in some common law legal systems. _________s are generally punished less severely than felonies, but theoretically more so than administrative infractions (also known as minor, petty or summary offences) and regulatory offences. Many _________s are punished with monetary fines.

   a. Small Business Liability Relief and Brownfields Revitalization Act
   b. Chartered Secretaries Australia
   c. Chartered Secretaries New Zealand
   d. Misdemeanor

4. The _________ of 1914 (Pub.L. 63-212, 38 Stat. 730, enacted October 15, 1914, codified at 15 U.S.C. §§ 12-27, 29 U.S.C. §§ 52-53), was a part of United States antitrust law with the goal of adding further substance to the U.S. antitrust law regime; the _________ sought to prevent anticompetitive practices in their incipiency. That regime started with the Sherman Antitrust Act of 1890, the first Federal law outlawing practices considered harmful to consumers (monopolies, cartels, and trusts). The _________ specified particular prohibited conduct, the three-level enforcement scheme, the exemptions, and the remedial measures.

   a. Sherman Act
   b. Sherman Antitrust
   c. Clayton Antitrust Act
   d. Clayton Act

5. . The payment of _________ as remuneration for services rendered or products sold is a common way to reward sales people. Payments often will be calculated on the basis of a percentage of the goods sold. This is a way for firms to solve the principal-agent problem, by attempting to realign employees' interests with those of the firm.

   a. Beneficial interest
   b. Big boy letter

c. Bonus clause
d. Commission

ANSWER KEY

1. Today`s Business Environment: Law and Ethics

---

1. a
2. a
3. d
4. d
5. d

---

2. The Court Systems

CHAPTER OUTLINE: KEY TERMS, PEOPLE, PLACES, CONCEPTS

Contract

Corporation

Deposit insurance

Federal Circuit

Insurance

Appellate

Appellate jurisdiction

Jurisdiction

Original Jurisdiction

Appellate Court

Madrid system

Federal district

Bankruptcy

Income

Trade

Bankruptcy court

En banc

Duty

Excuse

Amendment

Commission

2. The Court Systems

CHAPTER OUTLINE: KEY TERMS, PEOPLE, PLACES, CONCEPTS

- Plea
- Superfund
- Court system
- General jurisdiction
- Superior Court
- Supreme Court
- Federal Rules of Civil Procedure
- Plaintiff
- Private law
- Diversity
- Subject-matter jurisdiction
- Default judgment
- Personal jurisdiction
- Defendant
- Constitution
- Exclusive jurisdiction
- Concurrent jurisdiction
- Federal question
- Swift v. Tyson
- Tortfeasor
- Alliance

CHAPTER OUTLINE: KEY TERMS, PEOPLE, PLACES, CONCEPTS

Change of venue

CHAPTER HIGHLIGHTS & NOTES: KEY TERMS, PEOPLE, PLACES, CONCEPTS

Contract

In common law legal systems, a contract is an agreement having a lawful object entered into voluntarily by two or more parties, each of whom intends to create one or more legal obligations between them. The elements of a contract are 'offer' and 'acceptance' by 'competent persons' having legal capacity who exchange 'consideration' to create 'mutuality of obligation.'

Proof of some or all of these elements may be done in writing, though contracts may be made entirely orally or by conduct. The remedy for breach of contract can be 'damages' in the form of compensation of money or specific performance enforced through an injunction.

Corporation

A corporation is a separate legal entity that has been incorporated either directly through legislation or through a registration process established by law. Incorporated entities have legal rights and liabilities that are distinct from their employees and shareholders, and may conduct business as either a profit-seeking business or not-for-profit business. Early incorporated entities were established by charter (i.e. by an ad hoc act granted by a monarch or passed by a parliament or legislature).

Deposit insurance

Explicit deposit insurance is a measure implemented in many countries to protect bank depositors, in full or in part, from losses caused by a bank's inability to pay its debts when due. Deposit insurance systems are one component of a financial system safety net that promotes financial stability.

Federal Circuit

The United States Court of Appeals for the Federal Circuit is a United States court of appeals headquartered in Washington, D.C.. The court was created by Congress with passage of the Federal Courts Improvement Act of 1982, which merged the United States Court of Customs and Patent Appeals and the appellate division of the United States Court of Claims, making the judges of the former courts into circuit judges. The Federal Circuit is particularly known for its decisions on patent law, as it is the only appellate-level court with the jurisdiction to hear patent case appeals.

Insurance

Insurance is the equitable transfer of the risk of a loss, from one entity to another in exchange for payment. It is a form of risk management primarily used to hedge against the risk of a contingent, uncertain loss.

2. The Court Systems

CHAPTER HIGHLIGHTS & NOTES: KEY TERMS, PEOPLE, PLACES, CONCEPTS

According to study texts of The Chartered Insurance Institute, there are the following categories of risk:•Financial risks which means that the risk must have financial measurement.•Pure risks which means that the risk must be real and not related to gambling•Particular risks which means that these risks are not widespread in their effect, for example such as earthquake risk for the region prone to it.

It is commonly accepted that only financial, pure and particular risks are insurable.

Appellate	In law, an appeal is the process in which cases are reviewed, where parties request a formal change to an official decision. Appeals function both as a process for error correction as well as a process of clarifying and interpreting law. Although appellate courts have existed for thousands of years, common law countries did not incorporate an affirmative right to appeal into their jurisprudence until the 19th century.
Appellate jurisdiction	Appellate jurisdiction is the power of a court to review decisions and change outcomes of decisions of lower courts. Most appellate jurisdiction is legislatively created, and may consist of appeals by leave of the appellate court or by right. Depending on the type of case and the decision below, appellate review primarily consists of: an entirely new hearing (a non trial de novo); a hearing where the appellate court gives deference to factual findings of the lower court; or review of particular legal rulings made by the lower court (an appeal on the record).
Jurisdiction	Jurisdiction is the practical authority granted to a formally constituted legal body or to a political leader to deal with and make pronouncements on legal matters and, by implication, to administer justice within a defined area of responsibility. The term is also used to denote the geographical area or subject-matter to which such authority applies. Areas of jurisdiction apply to local, state, and federal levels.
Original Jurisdiction	The original jurisdiction of a court is the power to hear a case for the first time, as opposed to appellate jurisdiction, when a court has the power to review a lower court's decision.
Appellate Court	An appellate court, commonly called an appeals court or court of appeals or appeal court (British English) or court of second instance or second instance court, is any court of law that is empowered to hear an appeal of a trial court or other lower tribunal. In most jurisdictions, the court system is divided into at least three levels: the trial court, which initially hears cases and reviews evidence and testimony to determine the facts of the case; at least one intermediate appellate court; and a supreme court (or court of last resort) which primarily reviews the decisions of the intermediate courts. A jurisdiction's supreme court is that jurisdiction's highest appellate court.
Madrid system	The Madrid system is the primary international system for facilitating the registration of trademarks in multiple jurisdictions around the world.

Its legal basis is the multilateral treaty Madrid Agreement Concerning the International Registration of Marks of 1891, as well as the Protocol Relating to the Madrid Agreement (1989).

The Madrid system provides a centrally administered system of obtaining a bundle of trademark registrations in separate jurisdictions.

Federal district

A federal district is a type of administrative division of a federation, under the direct control of a federal government. Federal districts often include capital districts, and they exist in various countries and states all over the world.

Bankruptcy

Bankruptcy is a legal status of a person or other entity that cannot repay the debts it owes to creditors. In most jurisdictions, bankruptcy is imposed by a court order, often initiated by the debtor.

Bankruptcy is not the only legal status that an insolvent person or other entity may have, and the term bankruptcy is therefore not a synonym for insolvency.

Income

Income is the consumption and savings opportunity gained by an entity within a specified timeframe, which is generally expressed in monetary terms. However, for households and individuals, 'income is the sum of all the wages, salaries, profits, interests payments, rents and other forms of earnings received... in a given period of time.'

In the field of public economics, the term may refer to the accumulation of both monetary and non-monetary consumption ability, with the former (monetary) being used as a proxy for total income.

Trade

In professional sports, a trade is a sports league transaction involving an exchange of players' contracts or draft picks between sports clubs. Cash is another commodity that may be packaged together with contracts or draft picks to complete a trade. Typically, trades are completed between two clubs, but there are instances where trades are consummated between three or more clubs.

Bankruptcy court

United States bankruptcy courts are courts created under Article I of the United States Constitution. They function as units of the district courts and have subject-matter jurisdiction over bankruptcy cases. The federal district courts have original and exclusive jurisdiction over all cases arising under the bankruptcy code and bankruptcy cases cannot be filed in state court.

En banc

In law, an en banc session is a session where a case is heard before all the judges of a court - in other words, before the entire bench - rather than by a panel selected from them. The equivalent terms in banc, in banco or in bank are also sometimes seen.

En banc is often used for unusually complex cases or cases considered to be of greater importance.

Duty

Duty is a term that conveys a sense of moral commitment or obligation to someone or something.

	The moral commitment should result in action; it is not a matter of passive feeling or mere recognition. When someone recognizes a duty, that person theoretically commits themself to its fulfillment without considering their own self-interest.
Excuse	In jurisprudence, an excuse or justification is a defense to criminal charges that is distinct from an exculpation. Exculpation is related concept which reduces or extinguishes a person's culpability and therefore a person's liability to pay compensation to the victim of a tort in the civil law. The 'excuse' provides a mitigating factor for a group of persons sharing a common characteristic.
Amendment	An amendment is a formal or official change made to a law, contract, constitution, or other legal document. It is based on the verb to amend, which means to change. Amendments can add, remove, or update parts of these agreements.
Commission	The payment of commission as remuneration for services rendered or products sold is a common way to reward sales people. Payments often will be calculated on the basis of a percentage of the goods sold. This is a way for firms to solve the principal-agent problem, by attempting to realign employees' interests with those of the firm.
Plea	In legal terms, a plea is simply an answer to a claim made by someone in a criminal case under common law using the adversarial system. Colloquially, a plea has come to mean the assertion by a defendant at arraignment, or otherwise in response to a criminal charge, whether that person pleaded guilty, not guilty, no contest or (in the United States) Alford plea. The concept of the plea is one of the major differences between criminal procedure under common law and procedure under the civil law system.
Superfund	Superfund or Comprehensive Environmental Response, Compensation, and Liability Act of 1980 is a United States federal law designed to clean up sites contaminated with hazardous substances as well as broadly defined 'pollutants or contaminants'. Superfund also gives authority to federal natural resource agencies, states and Native American tribes to recover natural resource damages caused by releases of hazardous substances, and it created the Agency for Toxic Substances and Disease Registry .•A section 104..
Court system	The judiciary' (also known as the judicial system or 'court system) is the system of courts that interprets and applies the law in the name of the state. The judiciary also provides a mechanism for the resolution of disputes. Under the doctrine of the separation of powers, the judiciary generally does not make law (that is, in a plenary fashion, which is the responsibility of the legislature) or enforce law (which is the responsibility of the executive), but rather interprets law and applies it to the facts of each case.

Superior Court	In common law systems, a superior court is a court of general competence which typically has unlimited jurisdiction with regard to civil and criminal legal cases. A superior court is 'superior' relative to a court with limited jurisdiction, which is restricted to civil cases involving monetary amounts with a specific limit, or criminal cases involving offenses of a less serious nature. A superior court may hear appeals from lower courts .
Supreme Court	A supreme court is the highest court within the hierarchy of many legal jurisdictions. Other descriptions for such courts include court of last resort, instance court, judgment court, apex court, and highest court of appeal. Broadly speaking, the decisions of a supreme court are not subject to further review by any other court.
Federal Rules of Civil Procedure	The Federal Rules of Civil Procedure govern civil procedure (i.e. for civil lawsuits) in United States district (federal) courts. The FRCP are promulgated by the United States Supreme Court pursuant to the Rules Enabling Act, and then the United States Congress has 7 months to veto the rules promulgated or they become part of the FRCP. The Court's modifications to the rules are usually based upon recommendations from the Judicial Conference of the United States, the federal judiciary's internal policy-making body. Although federal courts are required to apply the substantive law of the states as rules of decision in cases where state law is in question, the federal courts almost always use the FRCP as their rules of procedure.
Plaintiff	A plaintiff, also known as a claimant or complainant, is the term used in some jurisdictions for the party who initiates a lawsuit (also known as an action) before a court. By doing so, the plaintiff seeks a legal remedy, and if successful, the court will issue judgment in favor of the plaintiff and make the appropriate court order (e.g., an order for damages). In some jurisdictions the commencement of a lawsuit is done by filing a summons, claim form and/or a complaint.
Private law	Private law is that part of a civil law legal system which is part of the jus commune that involves relationships between individuals, such as the law of contracts or torts, and the law of obligations (as it is called in civil legal systems). It is to be distinguished from public law, which deals with relationships between both natural and artificial persons (i.e., organizations) and the state, including regulatory statutes, penal law and other law that affects the public order. In general terms, private law involves interactions between private citizens, whereas public law involves interrelations between the state and the general population.
Diversity	The 'business case for diversity' stem from the progression of the models of diversity within the workplace since the 1960s. The original model for diversity was situated around affirmative action drawing strength from the law and a need to comply with equal opportunity employment objectives. This compliance-based model gave rise to the idea that tokenism was the reason an individual was hired into a company when they differed from the dominant group.

2. The Court Systems

CHAPTER HIGHLIGHTS & NOTES: KEY TERMS, PEOPLE, PLACES, CONCEPTS

Subject-matter jurisdiction

Subject-matter jurisdiction is the authority of a court to hear cases of a particular type or cases relating to a specific subject matter. For instance, bankruptcy court only has the authority to hear bankruptcy cases.

Subject-matter jurisdiction must be distinguished from personal jurisdiction, which is the power of a court to render a judgment against a particular defendant, and territorial jurisdiction, which is the power of the court to render a judgment concerning events that have occurred within a well-defined territory.

Default judgment

Default judgment is a binding judgment in favor of either party based on some failure to take action by the other party. Most often, it is a judgment in favor of a plaintiff when the defendant has not responded to a summons or has failed to appear before a court of law. The failure to take action is the default.

Personal jurisdiction

Personal jurisdiction refers to a court's jurisdiction over the parties to a lawsuit, as opposed to subject-matter jurisdiction, which is jurisdiction over the law and facts involved in the suit. If a court does not have personal jurisdiction over a party, its rulings or decrees cannot be enforced upon that party, except by comity, that is, to the extent the sovereign that does have jurisdiction over the party allows the court to enforce them upon that party. A court that has personal jurisdiction has both the authority to rule on the law and facts of a suit and the power to enforce its decision upon a party to the suit.

Defendant

A defendant is a person or entity accused of a crime in criminal prosecution or a person or entity against whom some type of civil relief is being sought in a civil case.

Terminology varies from one jurisdiction to another. For example, Scots law does not use the term 'defendant'; the terms 'accused' or 'panel' are used instead in criminal proceedings, and 'defender' in civil proceedings.

Constitution

A constitution is the set of regulations which govern the conduct of non-political entities, whether incorporated or not. Such entities include corporations and voluntary associations.

Exclusive jurisdiction

In civil procedure, exclusive jurisdiction exists where one court has the power to adjudicate a case to the exclusion of all other courts. It is the opposite situation from concurrent jurisdiction or non exclusive jurisdiction, in which more than one court may take jurisdiction over the case.

Exclusive jurisdiction is typically defined in terms of subject matter.

Concurrent jurisdiction

Concurrent jurisdiction exists where two or more courts from different systems simultaneously have jurisdiction over a specific case. This situation leads to forum shopping, as parties will try to have their civil or criminal case heard in the court that they perceive will be most favorable to them.

Federal question	In United States law, federal-question jurisdiction is the subject-matter jurisdiction of United States federal courts to hear a civil case because the plaintiff has alleged a violation of the United States Constitution, federal law, or a treaty to which the United States is a party. Article III of the United States Constitution permits federal courts to hear such cases, so long as the United States Congress passes a statute to that effect. However, when Congress passed the Judiciary Act of 1789, which authorized the newly created federal courts to hear such cases, it initially chose not to allow the lower federal courts to possess federal question jurisdiction for fear that it would make the courts too powerful.
Swift v. Tyson	Swift v. Tyson, 41 U.S. 1 (1842), was a case brought in diversity in the Circuit Court for the Southern District of New York on a bill of Exchange accepted in New York in which the Supreme Court of the United States determined that United States federal courts hearing cases brought under their diversity jurisdiction pursuant to the Judiciary Act of 1789 must apply the statutory law of the states when the state legislature of the state in question had spoken on the issue but did not have to apply the state's common law in those cases in which that state's legislature had not spoken on the issue. The Court's ruling meant that the federal courts, when deciding matters not specifically addressed by the state legislature, had the authority to develop a federal common law.
Tortfeasor	A tort, in common law jurisdictions, is a civil wrong that unfairly causes someone else to suffer loss or harm resulting in legal liability for the person who commits the tortious act, called a tortfeasor. Although crimes may be torts, the cause of legal action is not necessarily a crime, as the harm may be due to negligence which does not amount to criminal negligence. The victim of the harm can recover their loss as damages in a lawsuit.
Alliance	An alliance is a pact, coalition or friendship between two or more parties, made in order to advance common goals and to secure common interests. It is a Political agreement between countries to support each other in disputes with other countries. See also military alliance, treaty, contract, coalition (disambiguation) and business alliance.
Change of venue	A change of venue is the legal term for moving a trial to a new location. In high-profile matters, a change of venue may occur to move a jury trial away from a location where a fair and impartial jury may not be possible due to widespread publicity about a crime and its defendant(s) to another community in order to obtain jurors who can be more objective in their duties. This change may be to different towns, and across the other sides of states or, in some extremely high-profile federal cases, to other states.

2. The Court Systems

CHAPTER QUIZ: KEY TERMS, PEOPLE, PLACES, CONCEPTS

1. The payment of _________ as remuneration for services rendered or products sold is a common way to reward sales people. Payments often will be calculated on the basis of a percentage of the goods sold. This is a way for firms to solve the principal-agent problem, by attempting to realign employees' interests with those of the firm.

   a. Commission
   b. Big boy letter
   c. Bonus clause
   d. Breach of contract

2. In common law legal systems, a _________ is an agreement having a lawful object entered into voluntarily by two or more parties, each of whom intends to create one or more legal obligations between them. The elements of a _________ are 'offer' and 'acceptance' by 'competent persons' having legal capacity who exchange 'consideration' to create 'mutuality of obligation.'

   Proof of some or all of these elements may be done in writing, though _________s may be made entirely orally or by conduct. The remedy for breach of _________ can be 'damages' in the form of compensation of money or specific performance enforced through an injunction.

   a. Beneficial interest
   b. Big boy letter
   c. Bonus clause
   d. Contract

3. _________ is a legal status of a person or other entity that cannot repay the debts it owes to creditors. In most jurisdictions, _________ is imposed by a court order, often initiated by the debtor.

   _________ is not the only legal status that an insolvent person or other entity may have, and the term _________ is therefore not a synonym for insolvency.

   a. Cynthia Cooper
   b. Financial scandal in the Orthodox Church in America
   c. Bankruptcy
   d. James Henry Ting Wei

4. A _________ is the set of regulations which govern the conduct of non-political entities, whether incorporated or not. Such entities include corporations and voluntary associations.

   a. Benihana of Tokyo, Inc. v. Benihana, Inc.
   b. Bonus share
   c. Constitution
   d. Caltec Citrus Company

5. . In jurisprudence, an _________ or justification is a defense to criminal charges that is distinct from an exculpation.

Exculpation is related concept which reduces or extinguishes a person's culpability and therefore a person's liability to pay compensation to the victim of a tort in the civil law.

The '_________' provides a mitigating factor for a group of persons sharing a common characteristic.

a. Beneficial interest
b. Big boy letter
c. Bonus clause
d. Excuse

ANSWER KEY
2. The Court Systems

---

1. a
2. d
3. c
4. c
5. d

You can take the complete Online Interactive Chapter Practice Test

for 2. The Court Systems
on all key terms, persons, places, and concepts.

No Additional Costs

http://www.Cram101.com

Register, send an email request to Travis.Reese@Cram101.com to get your user Id and password.

Include your customer order number, and ISBN number from your studyguide Retailer.

3. Trials and Resolving Disputes

CHAPTER OUTLINE: KEY TERMS, PEOPLE, PLACES, CONCEPTS

- Public law
- Adversary system
- Complaint
- Plaintiff
- Lanham Act
- Affirmative defense
- Demurrer
- Reinsurance
- Default judgment
- Indemnity
- Bargaining
- President
- Substantive law
- Summary judgment
- Duty
- Excuse
- Jurisdiction
- Jury Trial
- Voir dire
- Commission
- OPEC

3. Trials and Resolving Disputes

CHAPTER OUTLINE: KEY TERMS, PEOPLE, PLACES, CONCEPTS

- Red flag
- Cross-examination
- Direct examination
- Opening statement
- Redirect examination
- Building
- Arbitration
- Persuasion
- Verdict
- Rehabilitation
- Rehabilitation Act
- Specific performance
- Trade
- Injunction
- Intellectual property
- General contractor
- Income
- Madrid system
- Appellate
- Appellate Court
- Oral argument

3. Trials and Resolving Disputes

CHAPTER OUTLINE: KEY TERMS, PEOPLE, PLACES, CONCEPTS

______	Garnishment
______	Writ
______	Alternate dispute resolution
______	Federal Arbitration Act
______	Uniform Arbitration Act
______	Pollution
______	Mediation
______	Summary jury trial

CHAPTER HIGHLIGHTS & NOTES: KEY TERMS, PEOPLE, PLACES, CONCEPTS

Public law

Public law is that part of law which governs relationships between individuals and the government, and those relationships between individuals which are of direct concern to the society. Public law comprises constitutional law, administrative law, tax law and criminal law, as well as all procedural law. In public law, mandatory rules (not optional) prevail.

Adversary system

The adversarial system (or adversary system) is a legal system used in the common law countries where two advocates represent their parties' positions before an impartial person or group of people, usually a jury or judge, who attempt to determine the truth of the case. It is in contrast to the inquisitorial system used in some civil law systems (i.e. those deriving from Roman law or the Napoleonic code) where a judge, or group of judges investigates the case.

The adversarial system is the two-sided structure under which criminal trial courts operate that pits the prosecution against the defense.

Complaint

In legal terminology, a complaint is any formal legal document that sets out the facts and legal reasons that the filing party or parties (the plaintiff(s)) believes are sufficient to support a claim against the party or parties against whom the claim is brought (the defendant(s)) that entitles the plaintiff(s) to a remedy (either money damages or injunctive relief)]).

For example, the Federal Rules of Civil Procedure (FRCP) that govern civil litigation in United States courts provide that a civil action is commenced with the filing or service of a pleading called a complaint. Civil court rules in states that have incorporated the Federal Rules of Civil Procedure use the same term for the same pleading.

Plaintiff

A plaintiff, also known as a claimant or complainant, is the term used in some jurisdictions for the party who initiates a lawsuit (also known as an action) before a court. By doing so, the plaintiff seeks a legal remedy, and if successful, the court will issue judgment in favor of the plaintiff and make the appropriate court order (e.g., an order for damages).

In some jurisdictions the commencement of a lawsuit is done by filing a summons, claim form and/or a complaint.

Lanham Act

The Lanham Act (Pub.L. 79-489, 60 Stat. 427, enacted July 5, 1946, codified at 15 U.S.C. § 1051 et seq. (15 U.S.C. ch. 22)) is the primary federal trademark statute of law in the United States. The Act prohibits a number of activities, including trademark infringement, trademark dilution, and false advertising.

Affirmative defense

An affirmative defense to a civil lawsuit or criminal charge is a fact or set of facts other than those alleged by the plaintiff or prosecutor which, if proven by the defendant, defeats or mitigates the legal consequences of the defendant's otherwise unlawful conduct. In civil lawsuits, affirmative defenses include the statute of limitations, the statute of frauds, and waiver. In criminal prosecutions, examples of affirmative defenses are self defense, insanity, and the statute of limitations.

Demurrer

A demurrer is a pleading in a lawsuit that objects to or challenges a pleading filed by an opposing party. The word demur means 'to object'; a demurrer is the document that makes the objection. Lawyers informally define a demurrer as a defendant saying, 'So what?' to the pleading.

Reinsurance

Reinsurance is insurance that is purchased by an insurance company from one or more other insurance companies (the 'reinsurer') directly or through a broker as a means of risk management, sometimes in practice including tax mitigation and other reasons described below. The ceding company and the reinsurer enter into a reinsurance agreement which details the conditions upon which the reinsurer would pay a share of the claims incurred by the ceding company. The reinsurer is paid a 'reinsurance premium' by the ceding company, which issues insurance policies to its own policyholders.

Default judgment

Default judgment is a binding judgment in favor of either party based on some failure to take action by the other party. Most often, it is a judgment in favor of a plaintiff when the defendant has not responded to a summons or has failed to appear before a court of law. The failure to take action is the default.

Indemnity

An indemnity is a sum paid by party A to party B by way of compensation for a particular loss suffered by B. The indemnitor (A) may or may not be responsible for the loss suffered by the indemnitee (B). Forms of indemnity include cash payments, repairs, replacement, and reinstatement.

Bargaining

Bargaining or haggling is a type of negotiation in which the buyer and seller of a good or service dispute the price which will be paid and the exact nature of the transaction that will take place, and eventually come to an agreement. Bargaining is an alternative pricing strategy to fixed prices. Optimally, if it costs the retailer nothing to engage and allow bargaining, he can divine the buyer's willingness to spend.

President

A President is a leader of an organization, company, community, club, trade union, university for this article. It is the legally recognized highest 'titled' corporate officer, ranking above the various Vice Presidents (e.g. Senior Vice President and Executive Vice President), however that post on its own is generally considered subordinate to the Chief Executive Officer. In a similar vein to the Chief Operating Officer, the title of corporate President as a separate position (as opposed to being combined with a 'C-Suite' designation, such as 'President and CEO' or 'President and COO') is also loosely defined.

Substantive law

Substantive law is the statutory, or written law, that defines rights and duties, such as crimes and punishments, civil rights and responsibilities in civil law. It is codified in legislated statutes or can be enacted through the initiative process.

Substantive law stands in contrast to procedural law, which is the 'machinery' for enforcing those rights and duties.

Summary judgment

In law, a summary judgment is a judgment entered by a court for one party and against another party summarily, i.e., without a full trial. Such a judgment may be issued on the merits of an entire case, or on discrete issues in that case.

In common-law systems, questions about what the law actually is in a particular case are decided by judges; in rare cases jury nullification of the law may act to contravene or complement the instructions or orders of the judge, or other officers of the court.

Duty

Duty is a term that conveys a sense of moral commitment or obligation to someone or something. The moral commitment should result in action; it is not a matter of passive feeling or mere recognition. When someone recognizes a duty, that person theoretically commits themself to its fulfillment without considering their own self-interest.

Excuse

In jurisprudence, an excuse or justification is a defense to criminal charges that is distinct from an exculpation. Exculpation is related concept which reduces or extinguishes a person's culpability and therefore a person's liability to pay compensation to the victim of a tort in the civil law.

3. Trials and Resolving Disputes

CHAPTER HIGHLIGHTS & NOTES: KEY TERMS, PEOPLE, PLACES, CONCEPTS

Jurisdiction	Jurisdiction is the practical authority granted to a formally constituted legal body or to a political leader to deal with and make pronouncements on legal matters and, by implication, to administer justice within a defined area of responsibility. The term is also used to denote the geographical area or subject-matter to which such authority applies. Areas of jurisdiction apply to local, state, and federal levels.
Jury Trial	A jury trial or trial by jury is a legal proceeding in which a jury either makes a decision or makes findings of fact, which then direct the actions of a judge. It is distinguished from a bench trial, in which a judge or panel of judges make all decisions. Jury trials are used in a significant share of serious criminal cases in almost all common law legal systems, and juries or lay judges have been incorporated into the legal systems of many civil law countries for criminal cases.
Voir dire	Voir dire is a legal phrase that refers to a variety of procedures connected with jury trials. It originally referred to an oath taken by jurors to tell the truth, i.e., to say what is true, what is objectively accurate or subjectively honest, or both. It comes from the Anglo-Norman language.
Commission	The payment of commission as remuneration for services rendered or products sold is a common way to reward sales people. Payments often will be calculated on the basis of a percentage of the goods sold. This is a way for firms to solve the principal-agent problem, by attempting to realign employees' interests with those of the firm.
OPEC	OPEC is an international organization and economic cartel whose mission is to coordinate the policies of the oil-producing countries. The goal is to secure a steady income to the member states and to collude in influencing world oil prices through economic means. OPEC is an intergovernmental organization that was created at the Baghdad Conference on 10-14 September 1960, by Iraq, Kuwait, Iran, Saudi Arabia and Venezuela.
Red flag	In politics, a red flag is a symbol of Socialism, or Communism, or sometimes left-wing politics in general. It has been associated with left-wing politics since the French Revolution. Socialists adopted the symbol during the Revolutions of 1848 and it became a symbol of communism as a result of its use by the Paris Commune of 1871. The flags of several communist states, including China, Vietnam and the Soviet Union, are explicitly based on the original red flag.
Cross-examination	In law, cross-examination is the interrogation of a witness called by one's opponent. It is preceded by direct examination (in the United Kingdom, Australia, Canada, South Africa, India and Pakistan known as examination-in-chief) and may be followed by a redirect (re-examination in England, Scotland, Australia, Canada, South Africa, India, Hong Kong, and Pakistan).

Direct examination	The Direct Examination or Examination-in-Chief is one stage in the process of adducing evidence from witnesses in a court of law. Direct examination is the questioning of a witness by the party who called him or her, in a trial. Direct examination is usually performed to elicit evidence in support of facts which will satisfy a required element of a party's claim or defense.
Opening statement	An opening statement is generally the first occasion that the trier of fact has to hear from a lawyer in a trial, aside possibly from questioning during voir dire. The opening statement is generally constructed to serve as a 'road map' for the fact-finder. This is especially essential, in many jury trials, since jurors (at least theoretically) know nothing at all about the case before the trial, (or if they do, they are strictly instructed by the judge to put preconceived notions aside).
Redirect examination	Redirect examination is the trial process by which the party who offered the witness has a chance to explain or otherwise qualify any damaging or accusing testimony brought out by the opponent during cross-examination. Redirect examination may question only those areas brought out on cross-examination and may not stray beyond that boundary. In Australia, Canada and South Africa the process is called re-examination.
Building	A building is a man-made structure with a roof and walls standing more or less permanently in one place. Buildings come in a variety of shapes, sizes and functions, and have been adapted throughout history for a wide number of factors, from building materials available, to weather conditions, to land prices, ground conditions, specific uses and aesthetic reasons. To better understand the term building compare the list of nonbuilding structures.
Arbitration	Arbitration, a form of alternative dispute resolution, is a technique for the resolution of disputes outside the courts. The parties to a dispute refer it to arbitration by one or more persons (the 'arbitrators', 'arbiters' or 'arbitral tribunal'), and agree to be bound by the arbitration decision (the 'award'). A third party reviews the evidence in the case and imposes a decision that is legally binding on both sides and enforceable in the courts.
Persuasion	Persuasion is an umbrella term of influence. Persuasion can attempt to influence a person's beliefs, attitudes, intentions, motivations, or behaviors. In business, persuasion is a process aimed at changing a person's (or a group's) attitude or behavior toward some event, idea, object, or other person(s), by using written or spoken words to convey information, feelings, or reasoning, or a combination thereof.
Verdict	In law, a verdict is the formal finding of fact made by a jury on matters or questions submitted to the jury by a judge. The term, from the Latin veredictum, literally means 'to say the truth' and is derived from Middle English verdit, from Anglo-Norman: a compound of ver ('true,' from the Latin verus) and dit ('speech,' from the Latin dictum, the neuter past participle of dicere, to say).

3. Trials and Resolving Disputes

CHAPTER HIGHLIGHTS & NOTES: KEY TERMS, PEOPLE, PLACES, CONCEPTS

Rehabilitation	Rehabilitation of sensory and cognitive function typically involves methods for retraining neural pathways or training new neural pathways to regain or improve neurocognitive functioning that has been diminished by disease or trauma. Three common neuropsychological problems treatable with rehabilitation are attention deficit/hyperactivity disorder (ADHD), concussion, and spinal cord injury. Rehabilitation research and practices are a fertile area for clinical neuropsychologists and others.
Rehabilitation Act	The Rehabilitation Act of 1973, (Pub.L. 93-112, 87 Stat. 355, enacted September 26, 1973), is a federal law, codified as 29 U.S.C. § 701. The principal sponsor of the bill was Rep. John Brademas [IN-3]. The Rehabilitation Act of 1973 replaces the Vocational Rehabilitation Act, to extend and revise the authorization of grants to States for vocational rehabilitation services, with special emphasis on services to those with the most severe disabilities, to expand special Federal responsibilities and research and training programs with respect to individuals with disabilities, to establish special responsibilities in the Secretary of Health, Education, and Welfare for coordination of all programs with respect to individuals with disabilities within the Department of Health, Education, and Welfare, and for other purposes.
Specific performance	Specific performance is an order of a court which requires a party to perform a specific act, usually what is stated in a contract. It is an alternative to awarding damages, and is classed as an equitable remedy commonly used in the form of injunctive relief concerning confidential information or real property. While specific performance can be in the form of any type of forced action, it is usually used to complete a previously established transaction, thus being the most effective remedy in protecting the expectation interest of the innocent party to a contract.
Trade	In professional sports, a trade is a sports league transaction involving an exchange of players' contracts or draft picks between sports clubs. Cash is another commodity that may be packaged together with contracts or draft picks to complete a trade. Typically, trades are completed between two clubs, but there are instances where trades are consummated between three or more clubs.
Injunction	An injunction is an equitable remedy in the form of a court order that requires a party to do or refrain from doing specific acts. A party that fails to comply with an injunction faces criminal or civil penalties, including possible monetary sanctions and even imprisonment.
Intellectual property	Intellectual property rights are the legally recognized exclusive rights to creations of the mind. Under intellectual property law, owners are granted certain exclusive rights to a variety of intangible assets, such as musical, literary, and artistic works; discoveries and inventions; and words, phrases, symbols, and designs. Common types of intellectual property rights include copyright, trademarks, patents, industrial design rights, trade dress, and in some jurisdictions trade secrets.
General contractor	A general contractor is responsible for the day-to-day oversight of a construction site, management of vendors and trades, and communication of information to involved parties throughout the course of a building project.

Income

Income is the consumption and savings opportunity gained by an entity within a specified timeframe, which is generally expressed in monetary terms. However, for households and individuals, 'income is the sum of all the wages, salaries, profits, interests payments, rents and other forms of earnings received... in a given period of time.'

In the field of public economics, the term may refer to the accumulation of both monetary and non-monetary consumption ability, with the former (monetary) being used as a proxy for total income.

Madrid system

The Madrid system is the primary international system for facilitating the registration of trademarks in multiple jurisdictions around the world. Its legal basis is the multilateral treaty Madrid Agreement Concerning the International Registration of Marks of 1891, as well as the Protocol Relating to the Madrid Agreement (1989).

The Madrid system provides a centrally administered system of obtaining a bundle of trademark registrations in separate jurisdictions.

Appellate

In law, an appeal is the process in which cases are reviewed, where parties request a formal change to an official decision. Appeals function both as a process for error correction as well as a process of clarifying and interpreting law. Although appellate courts have existed for thousands of years, common law countries did not incorporate an affirmative right to appeal into their jurisprudence until the 19th century.

Appellate Court

An appellate court, commonly called an appeals court or court of appeals or appeal court (British English) or court of second instance or second instance court, is any court of law that is empowered to hear an appeal of a trial court or other lower tribunal. In most jurisdictions, the court system is divided into at least three levels: the trial court, which initially hears cases and reviews evidence and testimony to determine the facts of the case; at least one intermediate appellate court; and a supreme court (or court of last resort) which primarily reviews the decisions of the intermediate courts. A jurisdiction's supreme court is that jurisdiction's highest appellate court.

Oral argument

Oral arguments are spoken to a judge or appellate court by a lawyer of the legal reasons why they should prevail. Oral argument at the appellate level accompanies written briefs, which also advance the argument of each party in the legal dispute. Oral arguments can also occur during motion practice when one of the parties presents a motion to the court for consideration before trial, such as when the case is to be dismissed on a point of law, or when summary judgment may lie because there are no factual issues in dispute.

Garnishment

Garnishment is an American legal order for collecting a monetary judgment on behalf of a plaintiff from a defendant. The money can come directly from the defendant (the garnishee) or - at a court's discretion - from a third party. Jurisdiction law may allow for collection - without a judgment or other court order - in the case of collecting for taxes.

3. Trials and Resolving Disputes

CHAPTER HIGHLIGHTS & NOTES: KEY TERMS, PEOPLE, PLACES, CONCEPTS

Writ	In common law, a writ is a formal written order issued by a body with administrative or judicial jurisdiction; in modern usage, this body is generally a court. Warrants, prerogative writs and subpoenas are common types of writs but there are many others.
Alternate dispute resolution	Alternative dispute resolution includes dispute resolution processes and techniques that act as a means for disagreeing parties to come to an agreement short of litigation. It is a collective term for the ways that parties can settle disputes, with (or without) the help of a third party. Despite historic resistance to Alternate dispute resolution by many popular parties and their advocates, Alternate dispute resolution has gained widespread acceptance among both the general public and the legal profession in recent years.
Federal Arbitration Act	The Federal Arbitration Act. is an act of Congress that provides for judicial facilitation of private dispute resolution through arbitration. It applies in both state courts and federal courts, as was held in Southland Corp.
Uniform Arbitration Act	The Uniform Arbitration Act is one of the uniform acts that attempt to harmonize the law in force in the fifty U.S. states. The 'Uniform Arbitration Act', is a statute that was adopted by Congress in 2000 and requires states to adopt their own version of it.
Pollution	Pollution is the introduction of contaminants into the natural environment that cause adverse change. Pollution can take the form of chemical substances or energy, such as noise, heat or light. Pollutants, the components of pollution, can be either foreign substances/energies or naturally occurring contaminants.
Mediation	Mediation, as used in law, is a form of alternative dispute resolution, a way of resolving disputes between two or more parties with concrete effects. Typically, a third party, the mediator, assists the parties to negotiate a settlement. Disputants may mediate disputes in a variety of domains, such as commercial, legal, diplomatic, workplace, community and family matters.
Summary jury trial	Summary jury trial is an alternative dispute resolution technique, increasingly being used in civil disputes in the United States. In essence, a mock trial is held: a jury is selected and, in some cases, presented with the evidence that would be used at a real trial. The parties are required to attend the proceeding and hear the verdict that the jury brings in.

1. _________ rights are the legally recognized exclusive rights to creations of the mind. Under _________ law, owners are granted certain exclusive rights to a variety of intangible assets, such as musical, literary, and artistic works; discoveries and inventions; and words, phrases, symbols, and designs. Common types of _________ rights include copyright, trademarks, patents, industrial design rights, trade dress, and in some jurisdictions trade secrets.

   a. Barriers to exit
   b. Bilateral monopoly
   c. Intellectual property
   d. Competition Commission

2. A _________ is responsible for the day-to-day oversight of a construction site, management of vendors and trades, and communication of information to involved parties throughout the course of a building project.

   a. 3D floor plan
   b. 999-year lease
   c. 99-year lease
   d. General contractor

3. The _________ of 1973, (Pub.L. 93-112, 87 Stat. 355, enacted September 26, 1973), is a federal law, codified as 29 U.S.C. § 701. The principal sponsor of the bill was Rep. John Brademas [IN-3]. The _________ of 1973 replaces the Vocational _________, to extend and revise the authorization of grants to States for vocational rehabilitation services, with special emphasis on services to those with the most severe disabilities, to expand special Federal responsibilities and research and training programs with respect to individuals with disabilities, to establish special responsibilities in the Secretary of Health, Education, and Welfare for coordination of all programs with respect to individuals with disabilities within the Department of Health, Education, and Welfare, and for other purposes.

   a. Small Business Liability Relief and Brownfields Revitalization Act
   b. Canadian model of occupational performance and engagement
   c. Rehabilitation Act
   d. Goniometer

4. In law, a _________ is a judgment entered by a court for one party and against another party summarily, i.e., without a full trial. Such a judgment may be issued on the merits of an entire case, or on discrete issues in that case.

   In common-law systems, questions about what the law actually is in a particular case are decided by judges; in rare cases jury nullification of the law may act to contravene or complement the instructions or orders of the judge, or other officers of the court.

   a. Summary judgment
   b. Verdict
   c. Merger clause
   d. Plain meaning

5. _________ is an American legal order for collecting a monetary judgment on behalf of a plaintiff from a defendant. The money can come directly from the defendant (the garnishee) or - at a court's discretion - from a third party. Jurisdiction law may allow for collection - without a judgment or other court order - in the case of collecting for taxes.

a. Beneficial interest
b. Big boy letter
c. Bonus clause
d. Garnishment

ANSWER KEY
3. Trials and Resolving Disputes

---

1. c
2. d
3. c
4. a
5. d

---

4. The Constitution: Focus on Application to Business

CHAPTER OUTLINE: KEY TERMS, PEOPLE, PLACES, CONCEPTS

- Amendment
- First Amendment
- Ratification
- Pollution
- Commerce Clause
- Superfund
- Supremacy Clause
- Madrid system
- Civil procedure
- Portland Cement
- Income
- Intellectual property
- Freedom of speech
- Landlord
- Contract
- Plaintiff
- Communications Decency Act
- Commission
- Commercial speech
- Central Hudson
- Corporation

4. The Constitution: Focus on Application to Business

CHAPTER OUTLINE: KEY TERMS, PEOPLE, PLACES, CONCEPTS

- Constitution
- Administration
- Exclusionary rule
- Self-incrimination
- Duty
- Eminent domain
- Excuse
- Just compensation
- President
- Equal protection

CHAPTER HIGHLIGHTS & NOTES: KEY TERMS, PEOPLE, PLACES, CONCEPTS

Amendment

An amendment is a formal or official change made to a law, contract, constitution, or other legal document. It is based on the verb to amend, which means to change. Amendments can add, remove, or update parts of these agreements.

First Amendment

The First Amendment to the United States Constitution prohibits the making of any law respecting an establishment of religion, impeding the free exercise of religion, abridging the freedom of speech, infringing on the freedom of the press, interfering with the right to peaceably assemble or prohibiting the petitioning for a governmental redress of grievances. It was adopted on December 15, 1791, as one of the ten amendments that constitute the Bill of Rights.

The Bill of Rights was originally proposed as a measure to assuage Anti-Federalist opposition to Constitutional ratification.

Ratification

Ratification is a principal's approval of an act of its agent where the agent lacked authority to legally bind the principal.

The term applies to private contract law, international treaties, and constitutions in federations such as the United States and Canada.

Pollution

Pollution is the introduction of contaminants into the natural environment that cause adverse change. Pollution can take the form of chemical substances or energy, such as noise, heat or light. Pollutants, the components of pollution, can be either foreign substances/energies or naturally occurring contaminants.

Commerce Clause

The Commerce Clause describes an enumerated power listed in the United States Constitution . The clause states that the United States Congress shall have power 'To regulate Commerce with foreign Nations, and among the several States, and with the Indian Tribes.' Courts and commentators have tended to discuss each of these three areas of commerce as a separate power granted to Congress. It is common to see the individual components of the Commerce Clause referred to under specific terms: The Foreign Commerce Clause, the Interstate Commerce Clause, and the Indian Commerce Clause.

Superfund

Superfund or Comprehensive Environmental Response, Compensation, and Liability Act of 1980 is a United States federal law designed to clean up sites contaminated with hazardous substances as well as broadly defined 'pollutants or contaminants'. Superfund also gives authority to federal natural resource agencies, states and Native American tribes to recover natural resource damages caused by releases of hazardous substances, and it created the Agency for Toxic Substances and Disease Registry .•A section 104..

Supremacy Clause

The Supremacy Clause is the provision in Article Six, Clause 2 of the U.S. Constitution that establishes the U.S. Constitution, federal statutes, and U.S. treaties as 'the supreme law of the land'. It provides that these are the highest form of law in the U.S. legal system, and mandates that all state judges must follow federal law when a conflict arises between federal law and either the state constitution or state law of any state.

The supremacy of federal law over state law only applies if Congress is acting in pursuance of its constitutionally authorized powers.

Madrid system

The Madrid system is the primary international system for facilitating the registration of trademarks in multiple jurisdictions around the world. Its legal basis is the multilateral treaty Madrid Agreement Concerning the International Registration of Marks of 1891, as well as the Protocol Relating to the Madrid Agreement (1989).

The Madrid system provides a centrally administered system of obtaining a bundle of trademark registrations in separate jurisdictions.

Civil procedure

Civil procedure is the body of law that sets out the rules and standards that courts follow when adjudicating civil lawsuits .

These rules govern how a lawsuit or case may be commenced, what kind of service of process (if any) is required, the types of pleadings or statements of case, motions or applications, and orders allowed in civil cases, the timing and manner of depositions and discovery or disclosure, the conduct of trials, the process for judgment, various available remedies, and how the courts and clerks must function.

Portland Cement

Portland cement is the most common type of cement in general use around the world, used as a basic ingredient of concrete, mortar, stucco, and most non-speciality grout. It developed from other types of hydraulic lime in England in the mid 19th century and usually originates from limestone. It is a fine powder produced by heating materials in a kiln to form what is called clinker, grinding the clinker, and adding small amounts of other materials.

Income

Income is the consumption and savings opportunity gained by an entity within a specified timeframe, which is generally expressed in monetary terms. However, for households and individuals, 'income is the sum of all the wages, salaries, profits, interests payments, rents and other forms of earnings received... in a given period of time.'

In the field of public economics, the term may refer to the accumulation of both monetary and non-monetary consumption ability, with the former (monetary) being used as a proxy for total income.

Intellectual property

Intellectual property rights are the legally recognized exclusive rights to creations of the mind. Under intellectual property law, owners are granted certain exclusive rights to a variety of intangible assets, such as musical, literary, and artistic works; discoveries and inventions; and words, phrases, symbols, and designs. Common types of intellectual property rights include copyright, trademarks, patents, industrial design rights, trade dress, and in some jurisdictions trade secrets.

Freedom of speech

Freedom of speech is the political right to communicate one's opinions and ideas using one's body and property to anyone who is willing to receive them. The term freedom of expression is sometimes used synonymously, but includes any act of seeking, receiving and imparting information or ideas, regardless of the medium used.

Every government restricts speech to some degree.

Landlord

A landlord is the owner of a house, apartment, condominium, land or real estate which is rented or leased to an individual or business, who is called a tenant . When a juristic person is in this position, the term landlord is used. Other terms include lessor and owner.

Contract

In common law legal systems, a contract is an agreement having a lawful object entered into voluntarily by two or more parties, each of whom intends to create one or more legal obligations between them. The elements of a contract are 'offer' and 'acceptance' by 'competent persons' having legal capacity who exchange 'consideration' to create 'mutuality of obligation.'

Proof of some or all of these elements may be done in writing, though contracts may be made entirely orally or by conduct. The remedy for breach of contract can be 'damages' in the form of compensation of money or specific performance enforced through an injunction.

Plaintiff

A plaintiff, also known as a claimant or complainant, is the term used in some jurisdictions for the party who initiates a lawsuit (also known as an action) before a court. By doing so, the plaintiff seeks a legal remedy, and if successful, the court will issue judgment in favor of the plaintiff and make the appropriate court order (e.g., an order for damages).

In some jurisdictions the commencement of a lawsuit is done by filing a summons, claim form and/or a complaint.

Communications Decency Act

The Communications Decency Act of 1996, also known by some legislators as the 'Great Cyberporn Panic of 1995', was the first notable attempt by the United States Congress to regulate pornographic material on the Internet. In 1997, in the landmark cyberlaw case of Reno v. ACLU, the United States Supreme Court struck the anti-indecency provisions of the Act.

The Act was Title V of the Telecommunications Act of 1996. It was introduced to the Senate Committee of Commerce, Science, and Transportation by Senators James Exon (D-NE) and Slade Gorton (R-WA) in 1995. The amendment that became the Communications Decency Act was added to the Telecommunications Act in the Senate by an 84-16 vote on June 14, 1995.

Commission

The payment of commission as remuneration for services rendered or products sold is a common way to reward sales people. Payments often will be calculated on the basis of a percentage of the goods sold. This is a way for firms to solve the principal-agent problem, by attempting to realign employees' interests with those of the firm.

Commercial speech

Commercial speech is speech done on behalf of a company or individual for the intent of making a profit. It is economic in nature and usually has the intent of convincing the audience to partake in a particular action, often purchasing a specific product. Generally, the United States Supreme Court defines commercial speech as speech that 'proposes a commercial transaction.' Additionally, the Court developed a three factor inquiry in determining whether speech is commercial in Bolger v. Youngs Drug Products; however, those factors have yet to be utilized in any other Supreme Court case dealing with commercial speech.

Central Hudson

Central Hudson Gas & Electric Corp. v. Public Service Commission, 447 U.S. 557 (1980), was an important case decided by the United States Supreme Court that laid out a four-part test for determining when restrictions on commercial speech violated the First Amendment of the United States Constitution. Justice Powell wrote the opinion of the court.

4. The Constitution: Focus on Application to Business

CHAPTER HIGHLIGHTS & NOTES: KEY TERMS, PEOPLE, PLACES, CONCEPTS

Corporation	A corporation is a separate legal entity that has been incorporated either directly through legislation or through a registration process established by law. Incorporated entities have legal rights and liabilities that are distinct from their employees and shareholders, and may conduct business as either a profit-seeking business or not-for-profit business. Early incorporated entities were established by charter (i.e. by an ad hoc act granted by a monarch or passed by a parliament or legislature).
Constitution	A constitution is the set of regulations which govern the conduct of non-political entities, whether incorporated or not. Such entities include corporations and voluntary associations.
Administration	As a legal concept, administration is a procedure under the insolvency laws of a number of common law jurisdictions. It functions as a rescue mechanism for insolvent entities and allows them to carry on running their business. The process - an alternative to liquidation - is often known as going into administration.
Exclusionary rule	The exclusionary rule is a legal principle in the United States, under constitutional law, which holds that evidence collected or analyzed in violation of the defendant's constitutional rights is sometimes inadmissible for a criminal prosecution in a court of law. This may be considered an example of a prophylactic rule formulated by the judiciary in order to protect a constitutional right. The exclusionary rule may also, in some circumstances at least, be considered to follow directly from the constitutional language, such as the Fifth Amendment's command that no person 'shall be compelled in any criminal case to be a witness against himself' and that no person 'shall be deprived of life, liberty or property without due process of law'.
Self-incrimination	Self-incrimination is the act of exposing oneself 'to an accusation or charge of crime; to involve oneself or another [person] in a criminal prosecution or the danger thereof.' Self-incrimination can occur either directly or indirectly: directly, by means of interrogation where information of a self-incriminatory nature is disclosed; or indirectly, when information of a self-incriminatory nature is disclosed voluntarily without pressure from another person. In many legal systems, accused criminals cannot be compelled to incriminate themselves--they may choose to speak to police or other authorities, but they cannot be punished for refusing to do so. The precise details of this right of the accused vary between different countries, and some countries do not recognize such a right at all.
Duty	Duty is a term that conveys a sense of moral commitment or obligation to someone or something. The moral commitment should result in action; it is not a matter of passive feeling or mere recognition. When someone recognizes a duty, that person theoretically commits themself to its fulfillment without considering their own self-interest.

Eminent domain	Eminent domain, compulsory purchase (United Kingdom, New Zealand, Ireland), resumption (Hong Kong), resumption/compulsory acquisition (Australia), or expropriation (South Africa, Canada) is the power to take private property for public use, by a state or a national government. However, it can be legislatively delegated by the state to municipalities, government subdivisions, or even private persons or corporations, when they are authorized to exercise the functions of public character. The property may be taken either for government use or by delegation to third parties, who will devote it to public or civic use or, in some cases, to economic development.
Excuse	In jurisprudence, an excuse or justification is a defense to criminal charges that is distinct from an exculpation. Exculpation is related concept which reduces or extinguishes a person's culpability and therefore a person's liability to pay compensation to the victim of a tort in the civil law. The 'excuse' provides a mitigating factor for a group of persons sharing a common characteristic.
Just compensation	Just Compensation is required to be paid by the Fifth Amendment to the U.S. Constitution (and counterpart state constitutions) when private property is taken (or in some states, damaged then Inverse Condemnation is the relevant description of eminent domain) for public use. For reasons of expedience, courts have been generally using fair market value as the measure of just compensation, reasoning that this is the amount that a willing seller would accept in a voluntary sales transaction and therefore it should also be payable in an involuntary one. However, the U.S. Supreme Court has repeatedly acknowledged that 'fair market value' as defined by it falls short of what sellers would demand and receive in voluntary transactions.
President	A President is a leader of an organization, company, community, club, trade union, university for this article. It is the legally recognized highest 'titled' corporate officer, ranking above the various Vice Presidents (e.g. Senior Vice President and Executive Vice President), however that post on its own is generally considered subordinate to the Chief Executive Officer. In a similar vein to the Chief Operating Officer, the title of corporate President as a separate position (as opposed to being combined with a 'C-Suite' designation, such as 'President and CEO' or 'President and COO') is also loosely defined.
Equal protection	The Equal Protection Clause is part of the Fourteenth Amendment to the United States Constitution. The clause, which took effect in 1868, provides that no state shall deny to any person within its jurisdiction 'the equal protection of the laws'. A primary motivation for this clause was to validate and perpetuate the equality provisions contained in the Civil Rights Act of 1866, which guaranteed that all people would have rights equal to those of white citizens.

4. The Constitution: Focus on Application to Business

CHAPTER QUIZ: KEY TERMS, PEOPLE, PLACES, CONCEPTS

1. _________ is a principal's approval of an act of its agent where the agent lacked authority to legally bind the principal. The term applies to private contract law, international treaties, and constitutions in federations such as the United States and Canada.

   a. Statute of repose
   b. Ratification
   c. Statutory Law
   d. Small Business Liability Relief and Brownfields Revitalization Act

2. An _________ is a formal or official change made to a law, contract, constitution, or other legal document. It is based on the verb to amend, which means to change. _________s can add, remove, or update parts of these agreements.

   a. Cynthia Cooper
   b. Financial scandal in the Orthodox Church in America
   c. Amendment
   d. James Henry Ting Wei

3. _________ or Comprehensive Environmental Response, Compensation, and Liability Act of 1980 is a United States federal law designed to clean up sites contaminated with hazardous substances as well as broadly defined 'pollutants or contaminants'. _________ also gives authority to federal natural resource agencies, states and Native American tribes to recover natural resource damages caused by releases of hazardous substances, and it created the Agency for Toxic Substances and Disease Registry .•A section 104..

   a. Superfund
   b. Full Faith and Credit Clause
   c. Class Action Fairness Act
   d. Cynthia Cooper

4. The _________ is the primary international system for facilitating the registration of trademarks in multiple jurisdictions around the world. Its legal basis is the multilateral treaty Madrid Agreement Concerning the International Registration of Marks of 1891, as well as the Protocol Relating to the Madrid Agreement (1989).

   The _________ provides a centrally administered system of obtaining a bundle of trademark registrations in separate jurisdictions.

   a. Madrid system
   b. Brand piracy
   c. Certification mark
   d. Chartered mark

5. . The _________ to the United States Constitution prohibits the making of any law respecting an establishment of religion, impeding the free exercise of religion, abridging the freedom of speech, infringing on the freedom of the press, interfering with the right to peaceably assemble or prohibiting the petitioning for a governmental redress of grievances.

It was adopted on December 15, 1791, as one of the ten amendments that constitute the Bill of Rights.

The Bill of Rights was originally proposed as a measure to assuage Anti-Federalist opposition to Constitutional ratification.

a. First Amendment
b. Financial scandal in the Orthodox Church in America
c. HP Autonomy
d. James Henry Ting Wei

ANSWER KEY
4. The Constitution: Focus on Application to Business

---

1. b

2. c

3. a

4. a

5. a

---

5. Criminal Law and Business

CHAPTER OUTLINE: KEY TERMS, PEOPLE, PLACES, CONCEPTS

Blackacre

Misdemeanor

Madrid system

White-collar crime

Reinsurance

Mens rea

Negligence

Corporation

Lanham Act

Affirmative defense

Amendment

Income

Arbitration

Entrapment

Exclusionary rule

Indictment

Private law

Probable cause

Commission

Arraignment

Nolo contendere

5. Criminal Law and Business

CHAPTER OUTLINE: KEY TERMS, PEOPLE, PLACES, CONCEPTS

______ Disclaimer

______ Plaintiff

______ Plea

______ Warranty

______ Clayton Act

______ Sherman Act

______ CARD Act

______ Bankruptcy

______ Bankruptcy court

______ Credit card fraud

______ Fraud

______ Economic espionage

______ Embezzlement

______ Insider

______ Insider trading

______ Insurance

______ Insurance fraud

______ Money laundering

______ Racketeering

______ Indemnity

______ Intellectual property

5. Criminal Law and Business

CHAPTER OUTLINE: KEY TERMS, PEOPLE, PLACES, CONCEPTS

____________	Trade
____________	Wire fraud
____________	Ponzi scheme
____________	Constitution
____________	Bank Secrecy Act
____________	Know your customer
____________	Criminal law
____________	Tortfeasor

CHAPTER HIGHLIGHTS & NOTES: KEY TERMS, PEOPLE, PLACES, CONCEPTS

Blackacre

Blackacre, Whiteacre, Greenacre, Brownacre, and variations are the placeholder names used for fictitious estates in land.

The names are used by professors of law in common law jurisdictions, particularly in the area of real property and occasionally in contracts, to discuss the rights of various parties to a piece of land. A typical law school or bar exam question on real property might say:

Adam, owner of a fee simple in Blackacre, conveyed the property 'to Bill for life, remainder to Charles, provided that if any person should consume alcohol on the property before the first born son of Charles turns twenty-one, then the property shall go to Dwight in fee simple.' Assume that neither Bill, Charles, or Dwight is an heir of Adam, and that Adam's only heir is his son, Edward.

Misdemeanor

A misdemeanor is any 'lesser' criminal act in some common law legal systems. Misdemeanors are generally punished less severely than felonies, but theoretically more so than administrative infractions (also known as minor, petty or summary offences) and regulatory offences. Many misdemeanors are punished with monetary fines.

Madrid system

The Madrid system is the primary international system for facilitating the registration of trademarks in multiple jurisdictions around the world.

5. Criminal Law and Business

Its legal basis is the multilateral treaty Madrid Agreement Concerning the International Registration of Marks of 1891, as well as the Protocol Relating to the Madrid Agreement (1989).

The Madrid system provides a centrally administered system of obtaining a bundle of trademark registrations in separate jurisdictions.

White-collar crime

White-collar crime refers to financially motivated nonviolent crime committed by business and government professionals. Within criminology, it was first defined by sociologist Edwin Sutherland in 1939 as 'a crime committed by a person of respectability and high social status in the course of his occupation.' Typical white-collar crimes include fraud, bribery, Ponzi schemes, insider trading, embezzlement, cybercrime, copyright infringement, money laundering, identity theft, and forgery.

Reinsurance

Reinsurance is insurance that is purchased by an insurance company from one or more other insurance companies (the 'reinsurer') directly or through a broker as a means of risk management, sometimes in practice including tax mitigation and other reasons described below. The ceding company and the reinsurer enter into a reinsurance agreement which details the conditions upon which the reinsurer would pay a share of the claims incurred by the ceding company. The reinsurer is paid a 'reinsurance premium' by the ceding company, which issues insurance policies to its own policyholders.

Mens rea

Mens rea is Latin for 'guilty mind'. In criminal law, it is viewed as one of the necessary elements of some crimes. The standard common law test of criminal liability is usually expressed in the Latin phrase, actus non facit reum nisi mens sit rea, which means 'the act is not culpable unless the mind is guilty'.

Negligence

Negligence is a failure to exercise the care that a reasonably prudent person would exercise in like circumstances. The area of tort law known as negligence involves harm caused by carelessness, not intentional harm.

According to Jay M. Feinman of the Rutgers University School of Law;

'those who go personally or bring property where they know that they or it may come into collision with the persons or property of others have by law a duty cast upon them to use reasonable care and skill to avoid such a collision.' Fletcher v Rylands (LR 1 Ex 265)

Through civil litigation, if an injured person proves that another person acted negligently to cause their injury, they can recover damages to compensate for their harm.

Corporation

A corporation is a separate legal entity that has been incorporated either directly through legislation or through a registration process established by law. Incorporated entities have legal rights and liabilities that are distinct from their employees and shareholders, and may conduct business as either a profit-seeking business or not-for-profit business.

	Early incorporated entities were established by charter (i.e. by an ad hoc act granted by a monarch or passed by a parliament or legislature).
Lanham Act	The Lanham Act (Pub.L. 79-489, 60 Stat. 427, enacted July 5, 1946, codified at 15 U.S.C. § 1051 et seq. (15 U.S.C. ch. 22)) is the primary federal trademark statute of law in the United States. The Act prohibits a number of activities, including trademark infringement, trademark dilution, and false advertising.
Affirmative defense	An affirmative defense to a civil lawsuit or criminal charge is a fact or set of facts other than those alleged by the plaintiff or prosecutor which, if proven by the defendant, defeats or mitigates the legal consequences of the defendant's otherwise unlawful conduct. In civil lawsuits, affirmative defenses include the statute of limitations, the statute of frauds, and waiver. In criminal prosecutions, examples of affirmative defenses are self defense, insanity, and the statute of limitations.
Amendment	An amendment is a formal or official change made to a law, contract, constitution, or other legal document. It is based on the verb to amend, which means to change. Amendments can add, remove, or update parts of these agreements.
Income	Income is the consumption and savings opportunity gained by an entity within a specified timeframe, which is generally expressed in monetary terms. However, for households and individuals, 'income is the sum of all the wages, salaries, profits, interests payments, rents and other forms of earnings received... in a given period of time.' In the field of public economics, the term may refer to the accumulation of both monetary and non-monetary consumption ability, with the former (monetary) being used as a proxy for total income.
Arbitration	Arbitration, a form of alternative dispute resolution, is a technique for the resolution of disputes outside the courts. The parties to a dispute refer it to arbitration by one or more persons (the 'arbitrators', 'arbiters' or 'arbitral tribunal'), and agree to be bound by the arbitration decision (the 'award'). A third party reviews the evidence in the case and imposes a decision that is legally binding on both sides and enforceable in the courts.
Entrapment	In criminal law, entrapment is a practice whereby a law enforcement agent induces a person to commit a criminal offense that the person would have otherwise been unlikely to commit. It is a type of conduct that is generally frowned upon, and thus in many jurisdictions is a possible defense against criminal liability. Depending on the law in the jurisdiction, the prosecution may be required to prove beyond a reasonable doubt that the defendant was not entrapped or the defendant may be required to prove that they were entrapped as an affirmative defense.

5. Criminal Law and Business

CHAPTER HIGHLIGHTS & NOTES: KEY TERMS, PEOPLE, PLACES, CONCEPTS

Exclusionary rule

The exclusionary rule is a legal principle in the United States, under constitutional law, which holds that evidence collected or analyzed in violation of the defendant's constitutional rights is sometimes inadmissible for a criminal prosecution in a court of law. This may be considered an example of a prophylactic rule formulated by the judiciary in order to protect a constitutional right. The exclusionary rule may also, in some circumstances at least, be considered to follow directly from the constitutional language, such as the Fifth Amendment's command that no person 'shall be compelled in any criminal case to be a witness against himself' and that no person 'shall be deprived of life, liberty or property without due process of law'.

Indictment

An indictment in the common law system, is a formal accusation that a person has committed a crime. In jurisdictions that maintain the concept of felonies, the most serious criminal offence is a felony; jurisdictions that lack the concept of felonies often use that of an indictable offence--an offence that requires an indictment.

Historically, in most common law jurisdictions, an indictment was handed up by a grand jury, which returned a 'true bill' if it found cause to make the charge, or 'no bill' if it did not find cause.

Private law

Private law is that part of a civil law legal system which is part of the jus commune that involves relationships between individuals, such as the law of contracts or torts, and the law of obligations (as it is called in civil legal systems). It is to be distinguished from public law, which deals with relationships between both natural and artificial persons (i.e., organizations) and the state, including regulatory statutes, penal law and other law that affects the public order. In general terms, private law involves interactions between private citizens, whereas public law involves interrelations between the state and the general population.

Probable cause

In United States criminal law, probable cause is the standard by which police authorities have reason to obtain a warrant for the arrest of a suspected criminal. The standard also applies to personal or property searches.

Probable cause, in conjunction with a preponderance of the evidence, also refers to the standard by which a grand jury believes that a crime has been committed.

Commission

The payment of commission as remuneration for services rendered or products sold is a common way to reward sales people. Payments often will be calculated on the basis of a percentage of the goods sold. This is a way for firms to solve the principal-agent problem, by attempting to realign employees' interests with those of the firm.

Arraignment

Arraignment is a formal reading of a criminal charging document in the presence of the defendant to inform the defendant of the charges against him or her. In response to arraignment, the accused is expected to enter a plea.

Nolo contendere

Nolo contendere is a legal term that comes from the Latin for 'I do not wish to contend.' It is also referred to as a plea of no contest. In criminal trials in certain U.S. jurisdictions, it is a plea where the defendant neither admits nor disputes a charge, serving as an alternative to a pleading of guilty or not guilty. A no-contest plea, while not technically a guilty plea, has the same immediate effect as a guilty plea, and is often offered as a part of a plea bargain.

Disclaimer

A disclaimer is generally any statement intended to specify or delimit the scope of rights and obligations that may be exercised and enforced by parties in a legally recognized relationship. In contrast to other terms for legally operative language, the term disclaimer usually implies situations that involve some level of uncertainty, waiver, or risk.

A disclaimer may specify mutually agreed and privately arranged terms and conditions as part of a contract; or may specify warnings or expectations to the general public (or some other class of persons) in order to fulfill a duty of care owed to prevent unreasonable risk of harm or injury.

Plaintiff

A plaintiff, also known as a claimant or complainant, is the term used in some jurisdictions for the party who initiates a lawsuit (also known as an action) before a court. By doing so, the plaintiff seeks a legal remedy, and if successful, the court will issue judgment in favor of the plaintiff and make the appropriate court order (e.g., an order for damages).

In some jurisdictions the commencement of a lawsuit is done by filing a summons, claim form and/or a complaint.

Plea

In legal terms, a plea is simply an answer to a claim made by someone in a criminal case under common law using the adversarial system. Colloquially, a plea has come to mean the assertion by a defendant at arraignment, or otherwise in response to a criminal charge, whether that person pleaded guilty, not guilty, no contest or (in the United States) Alford plea.

The concept of the plea is one of the major differences between criminal procedure under common law and procedure under the civil law system.

Warranty

In contract law, a warranty has various meanings but generally means a guarantee or promise which provides assurance by one party to the other party that specific facts or conditions are true or will happen. This factual guarantee may be enforced regardless of materiality which allows for a legal remedy if that promise is not true or followed.

Although a warranty is in its simplest form an element of a contract, some warranties run with a product so that a manufacturer makes the warranty to a consumer with which the manufacturer has no direct contractual relationship.

Clayton Act

The Clayton Act of 1914 (Pub.L. 63-212, 38 Stat. 730, enacted October 15, 1914, codified at 15 U.S.C. §§ 12-27, 29 U.S.C.

§§ 52-53), was a part of United States antitrust law with the goal of adding further substance to the U.S. antitrust law regime; the Clayton Act sought to prevent anticompetitive practices in their incipiency. That regime started with the Sherman Antitrust Act of 1890, the first Federal law outlawing practices considered harmful to consumers (monopolies, cartels, and trusts). The Clayton Act specified particular prohibited conduct, the three-level enforcement scheme, the exemptions, and the remedial measures.

Sherman Act

The Sherman Antitrust Act (Sherman Act,26 Stat. 209, 15 U.S.C. §§ 1-7) is a landmark federal statute in the history of United States antitrust law (or 'competition law') passed by Congress in 1890. It prohibits certain business activities that federal government regulators deem to be anti-competitive, and requires the federal government to investigate and pursue trusts.

It has since, more broadly, been used to oppose the combination of entities that could potentially harm competition, such as monopolies or cartels.

According to its authors, it was not intended to impact market gains obtained by honest means, by benefiting the consumers more than the competitors.

CARD Act

The Credit Card Accountability Responsibility and Disclosure Act of 2009 or Credit CARD Act of 2009 is a federal statute passed by the United States Congress and signed by President Barack Obama on May 22, 2009. It is comprehensive credit card reform legislation that aims '...to establish fair and transparent practices relating to the extension of credit under an open end consumer credit plan, and for other purposes.' The bill was passed with bipartisan support by both the House of Representatives and the Senate.

Bankruptcy

Bankruptcy is a legal status of a person or other entity that cannot repay the debts it owes to creditors. In most jurisdictions, bankruptcy is imposed by a court order, often initiated by the debtor.

Bankruptcy is not the only legal status that an insolvent person or other entity may have, and the term bankruptcy is therefore not a synonym for insolvency.

Bankruptcy court

United States bankruptcy courts are courts created under Article I of the United States Constitution. They function as units of the district courts and have subject-matter jurisdiction over bankruptcy cases. The federal district courts have original and exclusive jurisdiction over all cases arising under the bankruptcy code and bankruptcy cases cannot be filed in state court.

Credit card fraud

Credit card fraud is a wide-ranging term for theft and fraud committed using or involving a payment card, such as a credit card or debit card, as a fraudulent source of funds in a transaction. The purpose may be to obtain goods without paying, or to obtain unauthorized funds from an account. Credit card fraud is also an adjunct to identity theft.

Fraud	Fraud is a deception deliberately practiced in order to secure unfair or unlawful gain (adjectival form fraudulent; to defraud is the verb). As a legal construct, fraud is both a civil wrong (i.e., a fraud victim may sue the fraud perpetrator to avoid the fraud and/or recover monetary compensation) and a criminal wrong (i.e., a fraud perpetrator may be prosecuted and imprisoned by governmental authorities). Defrauding people or organizations of money or valuables is the usual purpose of fraud, but it sometimes instead involves obtaining benefits without actually depriving anyone of money or valuables, such as obtaining a drivers license by way of false statements made in an application for the same.
Economic espionage	Industrial espionage, economic espionage or corporate espionage is a form of espionage conducted for commercial purposes instead of purely national security. Economic espionage is conducted or orchestrated by governments and is international in scope, while industrial or corporate espionage is more often national and occurs between companies or corporations.
Embezzlement	Embezzlement is the act of dishonestly withholding assets for the purpose of conversion of such assets by one or more individuals to whom such assets have been entrusted, to be held and/or used for other purposes. Embezzlement is a kind of financial fraud. For instance, a lawyer could embezzle funds from clients' trust accounts, a financial advisor could embezzle funds from investors, or a person could embezzle funds from his or her spouse.
Insider	An insider is a member of any group of people of limited number and generally restricted access. The term is used in the context of secret, privileged, hidden or otherwise esoteric information or knowledge: an insider is a 'member of the gang' and as such knows things only people in the gang know. In our complicated and information-rich world, the concept of insider knowledge is popular and pervasive, as a source of direct and useful guidance.
Insider trading	Insider trading is the trading of a public company's stock or other securities by individuals with access to non-public information about the company. In various countries, insider trading based on inside information is illegal. This is because it is seen as unfair to other investors who do not have access to the information.
Insurance	Insurance is the equitable transfer of the risk of a loss, from one entity to another in exchange for payment. It is a form of risk management primarily used to hedge against the risk of a contingent, uncertain loss.

5. Criminal Law and Business

According to study texts of The Chartered Insurance Institute, there are the following categories of risk:•Financial risks which means that the risk must have financial measurement.•Pure risks which means that the risk must be real and not related to gambling•Particular risks which means that these risks are not widespread in their effect, for example such as earthquake risk for the region prone to it.

It is commonly accepted that only financial, pure and particular risks are insurable.

Insurance fraud

Insurance fraud occurs when any act is committed with the intent to fraudulently obtain some benefit or advantage to which they are not otherwise entitled or someone knowingly denies some benefit that is due and to which someone is entitled. According to the United States Federal Bureau of Investigation the most common schemes include: Premium Diversion, Fee Churning, Asset Diversion and Workers Compensation Fraud. The perpetrators in these schemes can be both insurance company employees and claimants.

Money laundering

Money laundering is the process whereby the proceeds of crime are transformed into ostensibly legitimate money or other assets. However in a number of legal and regulatory system the term money laundering has become conflated with other forms of financial crime, and sometimes used more generally to include misuse of the financial system (involving things such as securities, digital currencies such as bitcoin, credit cards, and traditional currency), including terrorism financing, tax evasion and evading of international sanctions. Most anti-money laundering laws openly conflate money laundering with terrorism financing (which is concerned with destination of funds) when regulating the financial system.

Racketeering

A racket is a service that is fraudulently offered to solve a problem, such as for a problem that does not actually exist, that will not be put into effect, or that would not otherwise exist if the racket did not exist. Conducting a racket is racketeering. Particularly, the potential problem may be caused by the same party that offers to solve it, although that fact may be concealed, with the specific intent to engender continual patronage for this party.

Indemnity

An indemnity is a sum paid by party A to party B by way of compensation for a particular loss suffered by B. The indemnitor (A) may or may not be responsible for the loss suffered by the indemnitee (B). Forms of indemnity include cash payments, repairs, replacement, and reinstatement.

Intellectual property

Intellectual property rights are the legally recognized exclusive rights to creations of the mind. Under intellectual property law, owners are granted certain exclusive rights to a variety of intangible assets, such as musical, literary, and artistic works; discoveries and inventions; and words, phrases, symbols, and designs. Common types of intellectual property rights include copyright, trademarks, patents, industrial design rights, trade dress, and in some jurisdictions trade secrets.

Trade

In professional sports, a trade is a sports league transaction involving an exchange of players' contracts or draft picks between sports clubs. Cash is another commodity that may be packaged together with contracts or draft picks to complete a trade. Typically, trades are completed between two clubs, but there are instances where trades are consummated between three or more clubs.

Wire fraud

In the United States, mail and wire fraud is any fraudulent scheme to intentionally deprive another of property or honest services via mail or wire communication. It has been a federal crime in the United States since 1872.

Ponzi scheme

A Ponzi scheme is a fraudulent investment operation where the operator, an individual or organization, pays returns to its investors from new capital paid to the operators by new investors, rather than from profit earned by the operator. Operators of Ponzi schemes usually entice new investors by offering higher returns than other investments, in the form of short-term returns that are either abnormally high or unusually consistent. The perpetuation of the high returns requires an ever-increasing flow of money from new investors to sustain the scheme.

Constitution

A constitution is the set of regulations which govern the conduct of non-political entities, whether incorporated or not. Such entities include corporations and voluntary associations.

Bank Secrecy Act

The Bank Secrecy Act of 1970 requires financial institutions in the United States to assist U.S. government agencies to detect and prevent money laundering. Specifically, the act requires financial institutions to keep records of cash purchases of negotiable instruments, and file reports of cash purchases of these negotiable instruments of more than $10,000 : Each person (including a bank) subject to the jurisdiction of the United States having an interest in, signature or other authority over, one or more bank, securities, or other financial accounts in a foreign country must file an FBAR if the aggregate value of such accounts at any point in a calendar year exceeds $10,000. A recent District Court case in the 10th Circuit has significantly expanded the definition of 'interest in' and 'other Authority'.•Treasury Department Form 90-22.47 and OCC Form 8010-9, 8010-1 Suspicious Activity Report (SAR): Banks must file a SAR for any suspicious transaction relevant to a possible violation of law or regulation.•FinCEN Form 110 Designation of Exempt Person: Banks must file this form to designate an exempt customer for the purpose of CTR reporting under the Bank Secrecy Act. In addition, banks use this form biennially (every two years) to renew exemptions for eligible non-listed business and payroll customers.

It also requires any business receiving one or more related cash payments totalling $10,000 or more to file IRS/FinCEN Form 8300.

Know your customer

Know your customer is the process used by a business to verify the identity of their clients. The term is also used to refer to the bank regulation which governs these activities. Know Your Customer processes are also employed by companies of all sizes for the purpose of ensuring their proposed agents', consultants' or distributors' anti-bribery compliance.

5. Criminal Law and Business

CHAPTER HIGHLIGHTS & NOTES: KEY TERMS, PEOPLE, PLACES, CONCEPTS

Criminal law	Criminal law is the body of law that relates to crime. It regulates social conduct and proscribes whatever is threatening, harmful, or otherwise endangering to the property, health, safety, and moral welfare of people. It includes the punishment of people who violate these laws.
Tortfeasor	A tort, in common law jurisdictions, is a civil wrong that unfairly causes someone else to suffer loss or harm resulting in legal liability for the person who commits the tortious act, called a tortfeasor. Although crimes may be torts, the cause of legal action is not necessarily a crime, as the harm may be due to negligence which does not amount to criminal negligence. The victim of the harm can recover their loss as damages in a lawsuit.

CHAPTER QUIZ: KEY TERMS, PEOPLE, PLACES, CONCEPTS

1. _________ refers to financially motivated nonviolent crime committed by business and government professionals. Within criminology, it was first defined by sociologist Edwin Sutherland in 1939 as 'a crime committed by a person of respectability and high social status in the course of his occupation.' Typical _________s include fraud, bribery, Ponzi schemes, insider trading, embezzlement, cybercrime, copyright infringement, money laundering, identity theft, and forgery.

   a. Bullshit Detector
   b. White-collar crime
   c. Crust punk
   d. Geekfest

2. A _________ is any 'lesser' criminal act in some common law legal systems. _________s are generally punished less severely than felonies, but theoretically more so than administrative infractions (also known as minor, petty or summary offences) and regulatory offences. Many _________s are punished with monetary fines.

   a. Misdemeanor
   b. Bargain and sale deed
   c. Betterment
   d. Cynthia Cooper

3. . _________ is the process whereby the proceeds of crime are transformed into ostensibly legitimate money or other assets. However in a number of legal and regulatory system the term _________ has become conflated with other forms of financial crime, and sometimes used more generally to include misuse of the financial system (involving things such as securities, digital currencies such as bitcoin, credit cards, and traditional currency), including terrorism financing, tax evasion and evading of international sanctions. Most anti-_________ laws openly conflate _________ with terrorism financing (which is concerned with destination of funds) when regulating the financial system.

   a. 2008 Liechtenstein tax affair

b. Cartel
c. Money laundering
d. Clearstream

4. The _________ is the primary international system for facilitating the registration of trademarks in multiple jurisdictions around the world. Its legal basis is the multilateral treaty Madrid Agreement Concerning the International Registration of Marks of 1891, as well as the Protocol Relating to the Madrid Agreement (1989).

   The _________ provides a centrally administered system of obtaining a bundle of trademark registrations in separate jurisdictions.

   a. Madrid system
   b. Brand piracy
   c. Certification mark
   d. Chartered mark

5. _________ is the body of law that relates to crime. It regulates social conduct and proscribes whatever is threatening, harmful, or otherwise endangering to the property, health, safety, and moral welfare of people. It includes the punishment of people who violate these laws.

   a. Mala in se
   b. Criminal law
   c. Small Business Liability Relief and Brownfields Revitalization Act
   d. Basel Committee on Banking Supervision

ANSWER KEY
5. Criminal Law and Business

---

1. b
2. a
3. c
4. a
5. b

---

6. Elements of Torts

CHAPTER OUTLINE: KEY TERMS, PEOPLE, PLACES, CONCEPTS

- Pollution
- Tort
- Causation
- Duty
- Duty of care
- Res ipsa
- Proximate cause
- Superfund
- Superseding cause
- Negligence
- Corporation
- Assumption of risk
- Comparative negligence
- Contributory negligence
- Intellectual property
- Risk
- Principal
- Waiver
- Bargaining
- Private law
- Reinsurance

6. Elements of Torts

CHAPTER OUTLINE: KEY TERMS, PEOPLE, PLACES, CONCEPTS

______	Arbitration
______	Discrimination
______	False imprisonment
______	President
______	Defamation
______	Landlord
______	Cyberbullying
______	Absolute privilege
______	Actual malice

CHAPTER HIGHLIGHTS & NOTES: KEY TERMS, PEOPLE, PLACES, CONCEPTS

Pollution	Pollution is the introduction of contaminants into the natural environment that cause adverse change. Pollution can take the form of chemical substances or energy, such as noise, heat or light. Pollutants, the components of pollution, can be either foreign substances/energies or naturally occurring contaminants.
Tort	A tort, in common law jurisdictions, is a civil wrong that unfairly causes someone else to suffer loss or harm resulting in legal liability for the person who commits the tortious act, called a tortfeasor. Although crimes may be torts, the cause of legal action is not necessarily a crime, as the harm may be due to negligence which does not amount to criminal negligence. The victim of the harm can recover their loss as damages in a lawsuit.
Causation	Causation is the 'causal relationship between conduct and result'. That is to say that causation provides a means of connecting conduct with a resulting effect, typically an injury. In criminal law, it is defined as the actus reus (an action) from which the specific injury or other effect arose and is combined with mens rea (a state of mind) to comprise the elements of guilt.
Duty	Duty is a term that conveys a sense of moral commitment or obligation to someone or something.

The moral commitment should result in action; it is not a matter of passive feeling or mere recognition. When someone recognizes a duty, that person theoretically commits themself to its fulfillment without considering their own self-interest.

Duty of care	In United States corporation and business association law, a duty of care is part of the fiduciary duty owed to a corporation by its directors. The other aspects of fiduciary duty are a director's Duty of Loyalty and (possibly) duty of good faith. Put simply, a director owes a duty to exercise good business judgment and to use ordinary care and prudence in the operation of the business.
Res ipsa	In the common law of negligence, the doctrine of res ipsa loquitur states that the elements of duty of care and breach can sometimes be inferred from the very nature of an accident or other outcome, even without direct evidence of how any defendant behaved. Although modern formulations differ by jurisdiction, the common law originally stated that the accident must satisfy the necessary conditions of negligence.
Proximate cause	In the law, a proximate cause is an event sufficiently related to a legally recognizable injury to be held to be the cause of that injury. There are two types of causation in the law: cause-in-fact, and proximate (or legal) cause. Cause-in-fact is determined by the 'but for' test: But for the action, the result would not have happened.
Superfund	Superfund or Comprehensive Environmental Response, Compensation, and Liability Act of 1980 is a United States federal law designed to clean up sites contaminated with hazardous substances as well as broadly defined 'pollutants or contaminants'. Superfund also gives authority to federal natural resource agencies, states and Native American tribes to recover natural resource damages caused by releases of hazardous substances, and it created the Agency for Toxic Substances and Disease Registry .•A section 104..
Superseding cause	An intervening cause is an event that occurs after a tortfeasor's initial act of negligence and causes injury/harm to a victim. An intervening cause will generally absolve the tortfeasor of liability for the victim's injury only if the event is deemed a superseding cause. A superseding cause is an unforeseeable intervening cause.
Negligence	Negligence is a failure to exercise the care that a reasonably prudent person would exercise in like circumstances. The area of tort law known as negligence involves harm caused by carelessness, not intentional harm. According to Jay M. Feinman of the Rutgers University School of Law;

'those who go personally or bring property where they know that they or it may come into collision with the persons or property of others have by law a duty cast upon them to use reasonable care and skill to avoid such a collision.' Fletcher v Rylands (LR 1 Ex 265)

Through civil litigation, if an injured person proves that another person acted negligently to cause their injury, they can recover damages to compensate for their harm.

Corporation

A corporation is a separate legal entity that has been incorporated either directly through legislation or through a registration process established by law. Incorporated entities have legal rights and liabilities that are distinct from their employees and shareholders, and may conduct business as either a profit-seeking business or not-for-profit business. Early incorporated entities were established by charter (i.e. by an ad hoc act granted by a monarch or passed by a parliament or legislature).

Assumption of risk

Assumption of risk is a defense in the law of torts, which bars or reduces a plaintiff's right to recovery against a negligent tortfeasor if the defendant can demonstrate that the plaintiff voluntarily and knowingly assumed the risks at issue inherent to the dangerous activity in which he was participating at the time of his injury.

What is usually meant by assumption of risk is more precisely termed primary or 'express' assumption of risk. It occurs when the plaintiff has either expressly or implicitly relieved the defendant of the duty to mitigate or relieve the risk causing the injury from which the cause of action arises.

Comparative negligence

Comparative negligence, or non-absolute contributory negligence outside of the United States, is a partial legal defense that reduces the amount of damages that a plaintiff can recover in a negligence-based claim based upon the degree to which the plaintiff's own negligence contributed to cause the injury. When the defense is asserted, the fact-finder, usually a jury, must decide the degree to which the plaintiff's negligence versus the combined negligence of all other relevant actors contributed to cause the plaintiff's damages. It is a modification of the doctrine of contributory negligence which disallows any recovery by a plaintiff whose negligence contributed, even minimally, to causing the damages.

Contributory negligence

Contributory negligence in common-law jurisdictions is generally a defense to a claim based on negligence, an action in Tort. This principle is relevant to the determination of liability and is applicable when plaintiffs/claimants have, through their own negligence, contributed to the harm they suffered. It can also be applied by the Court in a Tort matter irrespective of whether it was pleaded as a defence.

Intellectual property

Intellectual property rights are the legally recognized exclusive rights to creations of the mind.

6. Elements of Torts

Under intellectual property law, owners are granted certain exclusive rights to a variety of intangible assets, such as musical, literary, and artistic works; discoveries and inventions; and words, phrases, symbols, and designs. Common types of intellectual property rights include copyright, trademarks, patents, industrial design rights, trade dress, and in some jurisdictions trade secrets.

Risk

Risk is the potential of losing something of value, weighed against the potential to gain something of value. Values (such as physical health, social status, emotional well being or financial wealth) can be gained or lost when taking risk resulting from a given action, activity and/or inaction, foreseen or unforeseen. Risk can also be defined as the intentional interaction with uncertainty.

Principal

In commercial law, a principal is a person, legal or natural, who authorizes an agent to act to create one or more legal relationships with a third party. This branch of law is called agency and relies on the common law proposition qui facit per alium, facit per se (Latin 'he who acts through another, acts personally').

It is a parallel concept to vicarious liability and strict liability (in which one person is held liable for the acts or omissions of another) in criminal law or torts.

Waiver

A waiver is the voluntary relinquishment or surrender of some known right or privilege.

Regulatory agencies or governments may issue waivers to exempt companies from certain regulations. For example, a United States law restricted the size of banks, but when banks exceeded these sizes, they obtained waivers.

Bargaining

Bargaining or haggling is a type of negotiation in which the buyer and seller of a good or service dispute the price which will be paid and the exact nature of the transaction that will take place, and eventually come to an agreement. Bargaining is an alternative pricing strategy to fixed prices. Optimally, if it costs the retailer nothing to engage and allow bargaining, he can divine the buyer's willingness to spend.

Private law

Private law is that part of a civil law legal system which is part of the jus commune that involves relationships between individuals, such as the law of contracts or torts, and the law of obligations (as it is called in civil legal systems). It is to be distinguished from public law, which deals with relationships between both natural and artificial persons (i.e., organizations) and the state, including regulatory statutes, penal law and other law that affects the public order. In general terms, private law involves interactions between private citizens, whereas public law involves interrelations between the state and the general population.

Reinsurance

Reinsurance is insurance that is purchased by an insurance company from one or more other insurance companies (the 'reinsurer') directly or through a broker as a means of risk management, sometimes in practice including tax mitigation and other reasons described below.

The ceding company and the reinsurer enter into a reinsurance agreement which details the conditions upon which the reinsurer would pay a share of the claims incurred by the ceding company. The reinsurer is paid a 'reinsurance premium' by the ceding company, which issues insurance policies to its own policyholders.

Arbitration	Arbitration, a form of alternative dispute resolution, is a technique for the resolution of disputes outside the courts. The parties to a dispute refer it to arbitration by one or more persons (the 'arbitrators', 'arbiters' or 'arbitral tribunal'), and agree to be bound by the arbitration decision (the 'award'). A third party reviews the evidence in the case and imposes a decision that is legally binding on both sides and enforceable in the courts.
Discrimination	Discrimination is action that denies social participation or human rights to categories of people based on prejudice. This includes treatment of an individual or group based on their actual or perceived membership in a certain group or social category, 'in a way that is worse than the way people are usually treated'. It involves the group's initial reaction or interaction, influencing the individual's actual behavior towards the group or the group leader, restricting members of one group from opportunities or privileges that are available to another group, leading to the exclusion of the individual or entities based on logical or irrational decision making.
False imprisonment	False imprisonment is a restraint of a person in a bounded area without justification or consent. False imprisonment is a common-law felony and a tort. It applies to private as well as governmental detention.
President	A President is a leader of an organization, company, community, club, trade union, university for this article. It is the legally recognized highest 'titled' corporate officer, ranking above the various Vice Presidents (e.g. Senior Vice President and Executive Vice President), however that post on its own is generally considered subordinate to the Chief Executive Officer. In a similar vein to the Chief Operating Officer, the title of corporate President as a separate position (as opposed to being combined with a 'C-Suite' designation, such as 'President and CEO' or 'President and COO') is also loosely defined.
Defamation	Defamation--also called calumny, vilification, or traducement--is the communication of a false statement that harms the reputation of an individual, business, product, group, government, religion, or nation. Most jurisdictions allow legal action to deter various kinds of defamation and retaliate against groundless criticism. It is usually regarded as irrational unprovoked criticism which has little or no factual basis and can be compared to hate speech, which is discrimination against a particular organisation, individual, nation, corporation or other political, social, cultural or commercial entity which has been entrenched in the practitioner by old prejudice and xenophobia.
Landlord	A landlord is the owner of a house, apartment, condominium, land or real estate which is rented or leased to an individual or business, who is called a tenant . When a juristic person is in this position, the term landlord is used.

6. Elements of Torts

CHAPTER HIGHLIGHTS & NOTES: KEY TERMS, PEOPLE, PLACES, CONCEPTS

Cyberbullying	Cyberbullying is the use of information technology to repeatedly harm or harass other people in a deliberate manner. According to U.S. Legal Definitions, Cyber-bullying could be limited to posting rumors or gossips about a person in the internet bringing about hatred in other's minds; or it may go to the extent of personally identifying victims and publishing materials severely defaming and humiliating them. With the increase in use of these technologies, cyberbullying has become increasingly common, especially among teenagers.
Absolute privilege	Parliamentary privilege (also absolute privilege) is a legal immunity enjoyed by members of certain legislatures, in which legislators are granted protection against civil or criminal liability for actions done or statements made in the course of their legislative duties. It is common in countries whose constitutions are based on the Westminster system. A similar mechanism is known as parliamentary immunity.
Actual malice	Actual malice in United States law is a condition required to establish libel against public officials or public figures and is defined as 'knowledge that the information was false' or that it was published 'with reckless disregard of whether it was false or not.' Reckless disregard does not encompass mere neglect in following professional standards of fact checking. The publisher must entertain actual doubt as to the statement's truth. This is the definition in only the United States and came from the landmark 1964 lawsuit New York Times Co. v. Sullivan, which ruled that public officials needed to prove actual malice in order to recover damages for libel.

CHAPTER QUIZ: KEY TERMS, PEOPLE, PLACES, CONCEPTS

1. _________ is the use of information technology to repeatedly harm or harass other people in a deliberate manner. According to U.S. Legal Definitions, Cyber-bullying could be limited to posting rumors or gossips about a person in the internet bringing about hatred in other's minds; or it may go to the extent of personally identifying victims and publishing materials severely defaming and humiliating them.

   With the increase in use of these technologies, _________ has become increasingly common, especially among teenagers.

   a. Cyberbullying
   b. 999-year lease
   c. 99-year lease
   d. Blockbusting

2. . _________ in common-law jurisdictions is generally a defense to a claim based on negligence, an action in Tort. This principle is relevant to the determination of liability and is applicable when plaintiffs/claimants have, through their own negligence, contributed to the harm they suffered.

It can also be applied by the Court in a Tort matter irrespective of whether it was pleaded as a defence.

a. Mutual mistake
b. Contributory negligence
c. Proximate cause
d. Res ipsa loquitur

3. _________ is the introduction of contaminants into the natural environment that cause adverse change. _________ can take the form of chemical substances or energy, such as noise, heat or light. Pollutants, the components of _________, can be either foreign substances/energies or naturally occurring contaminants.

a. Bioconcentration
b. Pollution
c. Modes of Toxic Action
d. Cynthia Cooper

4. In commercial law, a _________ is a person, legal or natural, who authorizes an agent to act to create one or more legal relationships with a third party. This branch of law is called agency and relies on the common law proposition qui facit per alium, facit per se (Latin 'he who acts through another, acts personally').

It is a parallel concept to vicarious liability and strict liability (in which one person is held liable for the acts or omissions of another) in criminal law or torts.

a. Bulk sale
b. Business license
c. Principal
d. Business valuation

5. A _________, in common law jurisdictions, is a civil wrong that unfairly causes someone else to suffer loss or harm resulting in legal liability for the person who commits the tortious act, called a tortfeasor. Although crimes may be _________s, the cause of legal action is not necessarily a crime, as the harm may be due to negligence which does not amount to criminal negligence. The victim of the harm can recover their loss as damages in a lawsuit.

a. Malicious prosecution
b. Tort
c. Nuisance
d. Trespasser

ANSWER KEY
6. Elements of Torts

---

1. a
2. b
3. b
4. c
5. b

---

7. Business Torts and Product Liability

CHAPTER OUTLINE: KEY TERMS, PEOPLE, PLACES, CONCEPTS

Environmental Protection

Fraud

Intellectual property

Material fact

Misdemeanor

Tort

Causation

Private law

Proximate cause

Scienter

Commission

Estate

Real estate

Reinsurance

Procedural law

Pollution

Caveat emptor

Negligence

Reasonable care

Contract

Product liability

7. Business Torts and Product Liability

CHAPTER OUTLINE: KEY TERMS, PEOPLE, PLACES, CONCEPTS

________ Asbestos

________ Hazard

________ Assumption of risk

________ Risk

________ Building

________ Cape

________ Landlord

________ OPEC

________ User

CHAPTER HIGHLIGHTS & NOTES: KEY TERMS, PEOPLE, PLACES, CONCEPTS

Environmental Protection	Environmental protection is a practice of protecting the natural environment on individual, organizational or governmental levels, for the benefit of both the natural environment and humans. Due to the pressures of population and technology, the biophysical environment is being degraded, sometimes permanently. This has been recognized, and governments have begun placing restraints on activities that cause environmental degradation.
Fraud	Fraud is a deception deliberately practiced in order to secure unfair or unlawful gain (adjectival form fraudulent; to defraud is the verb). As a legal construct, fraud is both a civil wrong (i.e., a fraud victim may sue the fraud perpetrator to avoid the fraud and/or recover monetary compensation) and a criminal wrong (i.e., a fraud perpetrator may be prosecuted and imprisoned by governmental authorities). Defrauding people or organizations of money or valuables is the usual purpose of fraud, but it sometimes instead involves obtaining benefits without actually depriving anyone of money or valuables, such as obtaining a drivers license by way of false statements made in an application for the same.
Intellectual property	Intellectual property rights are the legally recognized exclusive rights to creations of the mind.

Under intellectual property law, owners are granted certain exclusive rights to a variety of intangible assets, such as musical, literary, and artistic works; discoveries and inventions; and words, phrases, symbols, and designs. Common types of intellectual property rights include copyright, trademarks, patents, industrial design rights, trade dress, and in some jurisdictions trade secrets.

Material fact

A material fact is a fact that would be to a reasonable person germane to the decision to be made as distinguished from an insignificant, trivial or unimportant detail. In other words, it is a fact which expression (concealment) would reasonably result in a different decision.

Falsification of a material fact in such a manner that, had the insurance company known the truth, it would not have insured the risk.

Misdemeanor

A misdemeanor is any 'lesser' criminal act in some common law legal systems. Misdemeanors are generally punished less severely than felonies, but theoretically more so than administrative infractions (also known as minor, petty or summary offences) and regulatory offences. Many misdemeanors are punished with monetary fines.

Tort

A tort, in common law jurisdictions, is a civil wrong that unfairly causes someone else to suffer loss or harm resulting in legal liability for the person who commits the tortious act, called a tortfeasor. Although crimes may be torts, the cause of legal action is not necessarily a crime, as the harm may be due to negligence which does not amount to criminal negligence. The victim of the harm can recover their loss as damages in a lawsuit.

Causation

Causation is the 'causal relationship between conduct and result'. That is to say that causation provides a means of connecting conduct with a resulting effect, typically an injury. In criminal law, it is defined as the actus reus (an action) from which the specific injury or other effect arose and is combined with mens rea (a state of mind) to comprise the elements of guilt.

Private law

Private law is that part of a civil law legal system which is part of the jus commune that involves relationships between individuals, such as the law of contracts or torts, and the law of obligations (as it is called in civil legal systems). It is to be distinguished from public law, which deals with relationships between both natural and artificial persons (i.e., organizations) and the state, including regulatory statutes, penal law and other law that affects the public order. In general terms, private law involves interactions between private citizens, whereas public law involves interrelations between the state and the general population.

Proximate cause

In the law, a proximate cause is an event sufficiently related to a legally recognizable injury to be held to be the cause of that injury. There are two types of causation in the law: cause-in-fact, and proximate (or legal) cause. Cause-in-fact is determined by the 'but for' test: But for the action, the result would not have happened.

Scienter

Scienter is a legal term that refers to intent or knowledge of wrongdoing.

This means that an offending party has knowledge of the 'wrongness' of an act or event prior to committing it. For example, if a man sells a car with brakes that do not work to his friend, but the seller does not know about the brake problem, then the seller has no scienter.

Commission

The payment of commission as remuneration for services rendered or products sold is a common way to reward sales people. Payments often will be calculated on the basis of a percentage of the goods sold. This is a way for firms to solve the principal-agent problem, by attempting to realign employees' interests with those of the firm.

Estate

An estate comprises the houses and outbuildings and supporting farmland and woods that surround the gardens and grounds of a very large property, such as a country house or mansion. It is the modern term for a manor, but lacks the latter's now abolished jurisdictional authority. It is an 'estate' because the profits from its produce and rents are sufficient to support the household in the house at its center, formerly known as the manor house.

Real estate

Real estate is "property consisting of land and the buildings on it, along with its natural resources such as crops, minerals, or water; immovable property of this nature; an interest vested in this; an item of real property; (more generally) buildings or housing in general. Also: the business of real estate; the profession of buying, selling, or renting land, buildings or housing."

It is a legal term used in jurisdictions such as the United States, United Kingdom, Canada, Nigeria, Australia, and New Zealand.

Reinsurance

Reinsurance is insurance that is purchased by an insurance company from one or more other insurance companies (the 'reinsurer') directly or through a broker as a means of risk management, sometimes in practice including tax mitigation and other reasons described below. The ceding company and the reinsurer enter into a reinsurance agreement which details the conditions upon which the reinsurer would pay a share of the claims incurred by the ceding company. The reinsurer is paid a 'reinsurance premium' by the ceding company, which issues insurance policies to its own policyholders.

Procedural law

Procedural law or adjective law comprises the rules by which a court hears and determines what happens in civil lawsuit, criminal or administrative proceedings. The rules are designed to ensure a fair and consistent application of due process (in the U.S). or fundamental justice (in other common law countries) to all cases that come before a court.

Pollution

Pollution is the introduction of contaminants into the natural environment that cause adverse change. Pollution can take the form of chemical substances or energy, such as noise, heat or light. Pollutants, the components of pollution, can be either foreign substances/energies or naturally occurring contaminants.

Caveat emptor

Caveat emptor is Latin for 'Let the buyer beware' .

Generally, caveat emptor is the contract law principle that controls the sale of real property after the date of closing, but may also apply to sales of other goods.

The phrase caveat emptor arises from the fact that buyers often have less information about the good or service they are purchasing, while the seller has more information.

Negligence

Negligence is a failure to exercise the care that a reasonably prudent person would exercise in like circumstances. The area of tort law known as negligence involves harm caused by carelessness, not intentional harm.

According to Jay M. Feinman of the Rutgers University School of Law;

'those who go personally or bring property where they know that they or it may come into collision with the persons or property of others have by law a duty cast upon them to use reasonable care and skill to avoid such a collision.' Fletcher v Rylands (LR 1 Ex 265)

Through civil litigation, if an injured person proves that another person acted negligently to cause their injury, they can recover damages to compensate for their harm.

Reasonable care

In tort law, a duty of care is a legal obligation, which is imposed on an individual requiring adherence to a standard of reasonable care while performing any acts that could foreseeably harm others. It is the first element that must be established to proceed with an action in negligence. The claimant must be able to show a duty of care imposed by law which the defendant has breached.

Contract

In common law legal systems, a contract is an agreement having a lawful object entered into voluntarily by two or more parties, each of whom intends to create one or more legal obligations between them. The elements of a contract are 'offer' and 'acceptance' by 'competent persons' having legal capacity who exchange 'consideration' to create 'mutuality of obligation.'

Proof of some or all of these elements may be done in writing, though contracts may be made entirely orally or by conduct. The remedy for breach of contract can be 'damages' in the form of compensation of money or specific performance enforced through an injunction.

Product liability

Product liability is the area of law in which manufacturers, distributors, suppliers, retailers, and others who make products available to the public are held responsible for the injuries those products cause. Although the word 'product' has broad connotations, product liability as an area of law is traditionally limited to products in the form of tangible personal property.

Asbestos

Asbestos is a set of six naturally occurring silicate minerals which all have in common their eponymous asbestiform habit: long (roughly 1:20 aspect ratio), thin fibrous crystals.

Asbestos mining began more than 4,000 years ago, but did not start large-scale until the end of the 19th century when manufacturers and builders used asbestos because of its desirable physical properties: sound absorption, average tensile strength, its resistance to fire, heat, electrical and chemical damage, and affordability. It was used in such applications as electrical insulation for hotplate wiring and in building insulation.

Hazard

A hazard is any biological, chemical, mechanical, environmental or physical agent that is reasonably likely to cause harm or damage to humans, other organisms, or the environment in the absence of its control. This can include, but is not limited to: asbestos, electricity, microbial pathogens, motor vehicles, nuclear power plants, pesticides, vaccines, and X-rays. Identification of hazards is the first step in performing a risk assessment and in some cases risk assessment may not even be necessary.

Assumption of risk

Assumption of risk is a defense in the law of torts, which bars or reduces a plaintiff's right to recovery against a negligent tortfeasor if the defendant can demonstrate that the plaintiff voluntarily and knowingly assumed the risks at issue inherent to the dangerous activity in which he was participating at the time of his injury.

What is usually meant by assumption of risk is more precisely termed primary or 'express' assumption of risk. It occurs when the plaintiff has either expressly or implicitly relieved the defendant of the duty to mitigate or relieve the risk causing the injury from which the cause of action arises.

Risk

Risk is the potential of losing something of value, weighed against the potential to gain something of value. Values (such as physical health, social status, emotional well being or financial wealth) can be gained or lost when taking risk resulting from a given action, activity and/or inaction, foreseen or unforeseen. Risk can also be defined as the intentional interaction with uncertainty.

Building

A building is a man-made structure with a roof and walls standing more or less permanently in one place. Buildings come in a variety of shapes, sizes and functions, and have been adapted throughout history for a wide number of factors, from building materials available, to weather conditions, to land prices, ground conditions, specific uses and aesthetic reasons. To better understand the term building compare the list of nonbuilding structures.

Cape

In old British law, a cape was a judicial writ concerning a plea of lands and tenements; so called, as most writs are, from the word which carried the chief intention of the writ.

The writ was divided into cape magnum, or the grand cape, and cape parvum, or the petit cape.

7. Business Torts and Product Liability

CHAPTER HIGHLIGHTS & NOTES: KEY TERMS, PEOPLE, PLACES, CONCEPTS

Landlord	A landlord is the owner of a house, apartment, condominium, land or real estate which is rented or leased to an individual or business, who is called a tenant . When a juristic person is in this position, the term landlord is used. Other terms include lessor and owner.
OPEC	OPEC is an international organization and economic cartel whose mission is to coordinate the policies of the oil-producing countries. The goal is to secure a steady income to the member states and to collude in influencing world oil prices through economic means. OPEC is an intergovernmental organization that was created at the Baghdad Conference on 10-14 September 1960, by Iraq, Kuwait, Iran, Saudi Arabia and Venezuela.
User	A user of a system is a person who interacts with the system, to enable its operation or to utilize its function.

CHAPTER QUIZ: KEY TERMS, PEOPLE, PLACES, CONCEPTS

1. _________ rights are the legally recognized exclusive rights to creations of the mind. Under _________ law, owners are granted certain exclusive rights to a variety of intangible assets, such as musical, literary, and artistic works; discoveries and inventions; and words, phrases, symbols, and designs. Common types of _________ rights include copyright, trademarks, patents, industrial design rights, trade dress, and in some jurisdictions trade secrets.

   a. Intellectual property
   b. Bilateral monopoly
   c. Chamberlinian monopolistic competition
   d. Competition Commission

2. _________ is a practice of protecting the natural environment on individual, organizational or governmental levels, for the benefit of both the natural environment and humans. Due to the pressures of population and technology, the biophysical environment is being degraded, sometimes permanently. This has been recognized, and governments have begun placing restraints on activities that cause environmental degradation.

   a. Electronic Signatures in Global and National Commerce Act
   b. Environmental Protection
   c. Ethical culture
   d. American Federation of Labor

3. . A _________ is a man-made structure with a roof and walls standing more or less permanently in one place.

_________s come in a variety of shapes, sizes and functions, and have been adapted throughout history for a wide number of factors, from _________ materials available, to weather conditions, to land prices, ground conditions, specific uses and aesthetic reasons. To better understand the term _________ compare the list of non_________ structures.

a. 3D floor plan
b. Building
c. 99-year lease
d. Blockbusting

4. _________ is a deception deliberately practiced in order to secure unfair or unlawful gain (adjectival form fraudulent; to de_________ is the verb). As a legal construct, _________ is both a civil wrong (i.e., a _________ victim may sue the _________ perpetrator to avoid the _________ and/or recover monetary compensation) and a criminal wrong (i.e., a _________ perpetrator may be prosecuted and imprisoned by governmental authorities). Defrauding people or organizations of money or valuables is the usual purpose of _________, but it sometimes instead involves obtaining benefits without actually depriving anyone of money or valuables, such as obtaining a drivers license by way of false statements made in an application for the same.

a. Big Tobacco
b. Fraud
c. Big Oil
d. Big Media

5. A _________ is a fact that would be to a reasonable person germane to the decision to be made as distinguished from an insignificant, trivial or unimportant detail. In other words, it is a fact which expression (concealment) would reasonably result in a different decision.

Falsification of a _________ in such a manner that, had the insurance company known the truth, it would not have insured the risk.

a. Small Business Liability Relief and Brownfields Revitalization Act
b. Bilateral monopoly
c. Chamberlinian monopolistic competition
d. Material fact

ANSWER KEY
7. Business Torts and Product Liability

---

1. a
2. b
3. b
4. b
5. d

---

8. Real and Personal Property

CHAPTER OUTLINE: KEY TERMS, PEOPLE, PLACES, CONCEPTS

Deed

Quitclaim deed

Warranty

Warranty deed

Commission

Trade

Estate

Fee simple

Insurance

Lien

Principal

Title insurance

Tort

Mineral rights

Blackacre

Grantor

Life estate

Settlor

Trust

Condominium

Adverse possession

8. Real and Personal Property

CHAPTER OUTLINE: KEY TERMS, PEOPLE, PLACES, CONCEPTS

- Easement
- Procedural law
- Plea
- Landlord
- Constitution
- Uniform Residential Landlord and Tenant Act
- Constructive discharge
- Constructive eviction
- Eviction
- Lease
- Building
- Eminent domain
- Plaintiff
- Zoning
- Trespass
- Private law
- Public law
- Public nuisance
- Misappropriation
- Invitee
- Premises

8. Real and Personal Property

CHAPTER OUTLINE: KEY TERMS, PEOPLE, PLACES, CONCEPTS

	Premises liability

CHAPTER HIGHLIGHTS & NOTES: KEY TERMS, PEOPLE, PLACES, CONCEPTS

Deed	A deed is any legal instrument in writing which passes, affirms or confirms an interest, right, or property and that is signed, attested, delivered, and in some jurisdictions sealed. It is commonly associated with transferring title to property. The deed has a greater presumption of validity and is less rebuttable than an instrument signed by the party to the deed.
Quitclaim deed	A quitclaim deed is a legal instrument by which the owner of a piece of real property, called the grantor, transfers any interest to a recipient, called the grantee. The owner/grantor terminates ("quits") any right and claim to the property, thereby allowing claim to transfer to the recipient/grantee. Unlike most other property deeds, a quitclaim deed contains no title covenant and thus, offers the grantee no warranty as to the status of the property title; the grantee is entitled only to whatever interest the grantor actually possesses at the time the transfer occurs.
Warranty	In contract law, a warranty has various meanings but generally means a guarantee or promise which provides assurance by one party to the other party that specific facts or conditions are true or will happen. This factual guarantee may be enforced regardless of materiality which allows for a legal remedy if that promise is not true or followed. Although a warranty is in its simplest form an element of a contract, some warranties run with a product so that a manufacturer makes the warranty to a consumer with which the manufacturer has no direct contractual relationship.
Warranty deed	A warranty deed is a type of deed where the grantor guarantees that he or she holds clear title to a piece of real estate and has a right to sell it to the grantee (buyer). This is in contrast to a quitclaim deed, where the seller does not guarantee that he or she holds title to a piece of real estate. A general warranty deed protects the grantee against title defects arising at any point in time, extending back to the property's origins.
Commission	The payment of commission as remuneration for services rendered or products sold is a common way to reward sales people. Payments often will be calculated on the basis of a percentage of the goods sold.

Trade

In professional sports, a trade is a sports league transaction involving an exchange of players' contracts or draft picks between sports clubs. Cash is another commodity that may be packaged together with contracts or draft picks to complete a trade. Typically, trades are completed between two clubs, but there are instances where trades are consummated between three or more clubs.

Estate

An estate comprises the houses and outbuildings and supporting farmland and woods that surround the gardens and grounds of a very large property, such as a country house or mansion. It is the modern term for a manor, but lacks the latter's now abolished jurisdictional authority. It is an 'estate' because the profits from its produce and rents are sufficient to support the household in the house at its center, formerly known as the manor house.

Fee simple

In English law, a fee simple is an estate in land, a form of freehold ownership. It is the way that real estate is owned in common law countries, and is the highest ownership interest possible that can be had in real property. Allodial title is reserved to governments under a civil law structure.

Insurance

Insurance is the equitable transfer of the risk of a loss, from one entity to another in exchange for payment. It is a form of risk management primarily used to hedge against the risk of a contingent, uncertain loss.

According to study texts of The Chartered Insurance Institute, there are the following categories of risk:•Financial risks which means that the risk must have financial measurement.•Pure risks which means that the risk must be real and not related to gambling•Particular risks which means that these risks are not widespread in their effect, for example such as earthquake risk for the region prone to it.

It is commonly accepted that only financial, pure and particular risks are insurable.

Lien

In law, a lien is a form of security interest granted over an item of property to secure the payment of a debt or performance of some other obligation. The owner of the property, who grants the lien, is referred to as the lieneeand the person who has the benefit of the lien is referred to as the lienor or lien holder.

The etymological root is Anglo-French lien, loyen 'bond', 'restraint', from Latin ligamen, from ligare 'to bind'.

Principal

In commercial law, a principal is a person, legal or natural, who authorizes an agent to act to create one or more legal relationships with a third party. This branch of law is called agency and relies on the common law proposition qui facit per alium, facit per se (Latin 'he who acts through another, acts personally').

8. Real and Personal Property

CHAPTER HIGHLIGHTS & NOTES: KEY TERMS, PEOPLE, PLACES, CONCEPTS

Title insurance	Title insurance is a form of indemnity insurance predominantly found in the United States which insures against financial loss from defects in title to real property and from the invalidity or unenforceability of mortgage loans. Title insurance is principally a product developed and sold in the United States as a result of an alleged comparative deficiency of the U.S. land records laws. It is meant to protect an owner's or a lender's financial interest in real property against loss due to title defects, liens or other matters.
Tort	A tort, in common law jurisdictions, is a civil wrong that unfairly causes someone else to suffer loss or harm resulting in legal liability for the person who commits the tortious act, called a tortfeasor. Although crimes may be torts, the cause of legal action is not necessarily a crime, as the harm may be due to negligence which does not amount to criminal negligence. The victim of the harm can recover their loss as damages in a lawsuit.
Mineral rights	Mineral Rights are property rights to exploit an area for the minerals it harbors. Mineral rights can be separate from property ownership.
Blackacre	Blackacre, Whiteacre, Greenacre, Brownacre, and variations are the placeholder names used for fictitious estates in land. The names are used by professors of law in common law jurisdictions, particularly in the area of real property and occasionally in contracts, to discuss the rights of various parties to a piece of land. A typical law school or bar exam question on real property might say: Adam, owner of a fee simple in Blackacre, conveyed the property 'to Bill for life, remainder to Charles, provided that if any person should consume alcohol on the property before the first born son of Charles turns twenty-one, then the property shall go to Dwight in fee simple.' Assume that neither Bill, Charles, or Dwight is an heir of Adam, and that Adam's only heir is his son, Edward.
Grantor	A grant, in law, is a transfer of property, generally from a person or other entity giving the property (the grantor) to a person or entity receiving the property . Historically, a grant was a transfer by deed of that which could not be passed by livery, an act evidenced by letters patent under the Great Seal, granting something from the king to a subject, and a technical term made use of in deeds of conveyance of lands to import a transfer. Though the word 'grant' was originally made use of, in treating of conveyances of interests in lands, to denote a transfer by deed of that which could not be passed by livery, and was applied only to incorporeal hereditaments, it became a generic term, applicable to the transfer of all classes of real property.
Life estate	In common law and statutory law, a life estate is the ownership of land for the duration of a person's life.

In legal terms it is an estate in real property that ends at death when ownership of the property may revert to the original owner, or it may pass to another person. The owner of a life estate is called a 'life tenant'.

Settlor

In law a settlor is a person who settles property on trust law for the benefit of beneficiaries. In some legal systems, a settlor is also referred to as a trustor, or occasionally, a grantor or donor. Where the trust is a testamentary trust, the settlor is usually referred to as the testator.

Trust

A 'trust,' or 'corporate trust' is a large business. Originally, it was Standard Oil, which was already the largest corporation in the world

Condominium

A condominium, or condo, is the form of housing tenure and other real property where a specified part of a piece of real estate is individually owned. Use of and access to common facilities in the piece such as hallways, heating system, elevators, and exterior areas are executed under legal rights associated with the individual ownership. These rights are controlled by the association of owners that jointly represent ownership of the whole piece.

Adverse possession

Adverse possession is a method of acquiring title to real property by possession for a statutory period under certain conditions, viz: proof of non-permissive use which is actual, open and notorious, exclusive, adverse, and continuous for the statutory period. It is governed by statute concerning the title to real property (land and the fixed structures built upon it). By adverse possession, title to another's real property can be acquired without compensation, by holding the property in a manner that conflicts with the true owner's rights for a specified period.

Easement

An easement is a non-possessory right of use and/or entry onto the real property of another without possessing it. It is 'best typified in the right of way which one landowner, A, may enjoy over the land of another, B'. It is similar to real covenants and equitable servitudes; in the United States, the Restatement (Third) of Property takes steps to merge these concepts as servitudes.

Procedural law

Procedural law or adjective law comprises the rules by which a court hears and determines what happens in civil lawsuit, criminal or administrative proceedings. The rules are designed to ensure a fair and consistent application of due process (in the U.S). or fundamental justice (in other common law countries) to all cases that come before a court.

Plea

In legal terms, a plea is simply an answer to a claim made by someone in a criminal case under common law using the adversarial system. Colloquially, a plea has come to mean the assertion by a defendant at arraignment, or otherwise in response to a criminal charge, whether that person pleaded guilty, not guilty, no contest or (in the United States) Alford plea.

The concept of the plea is one of the major differences between criminal procedure under common law and procedure under the civil law system.

8. Real and Personal Property

CHAPTER HIGHLIGHTS & NOTES: KEY TERMS, PEOPLE, PLACES, CONCEPTS

Landlord	A landlord is the owner of a house, apartment, condominium, land or real estate which is rented or leased to an individual or business, who is called a tenant . When a juristic person is in this position, the term landlord is used. Other terms include lessor and owner.
Constitution	A constitution is the set of regulations which govern the conduct of non-political entities, whether incorporated or not. Such entities include corporations and voluntary associations.
Uniform Residential Landlord and Tenant Act	The Uniform Residential Landlord and Tenant Act, also known as Uniform Residential Landlord Tenant Act, is a sample law governing residential landlord and tenant interactions, created in 1972 by the National Conference of Commissioners on Uniform State Laws in the United States. Many states have adopted all or part of this Act.
Constructive discharge	In employment law, constructive dismissal, also called constructive discharge, occurs when an employee resigns as a result of the employer creating a hostile work environment. Since the resignation was not truly voluntary, it is in effect a termination. For example, when an employer makes life extremely difficult for an employee, to attempt to have the employee resign, rather than outright firing the employee, the employer is trying to effect a constructive discharge.
Constructive eviction	Constructive eviction is a term used in the law of real property to describe a circumstance in which a landlord either does something or fails to do something that he has a legal duty to provide, rendering the property uninhabitable. A tenant who is constructively evicted may terminate the lease and seek damages. To maintain an action for damages, the tenant must show that:•the uninhabitable conditions (substantial interferences) were a result of the landlord's actions (not the actions of some third party) and•that the tenant vacated the premises in a reasonable time. A tenant who suffers from a constructive eviction can claim all of the legal remedies available to a tenant who was actually told to leave.
Eviction	Eviction is the removal of a tenant from rental property by the landlord. In some jurisdictions it may also involve the removal of persons from premises that were foreclosed by a mortgagee (often, the prior owners who defaulted on a mortgage). Depending on the laws of the jurisdiction, eviction may also be known as unlawful detainer, summary possession, summary dispossess, summary process, forcible detainer, ejectment, and repossession, among other terms.
Lease	A lease is a contractual arrangement calling for the lessee to pay the lessor (owner) for use of an asset.

The narrower term rental agreement can be used to describe a lease in which the asset is tangible property. Language used is that the user rents the land or goods let or rented out by the owner.

Building

A building is a man-made structure with a roof and walls standing more or less permanently in one place. Buildings come in a variety of shapes, sizes and functions, and have been adapted throughout history for a wide number of factors, from building materials available, to weather conditions, to land prices, ground conditions, specific uses and aesthetic reasons. To better understand the term building compare the list of nonbuilding structures.

Eminent domain

Eminent domain, compulsory purchase (United Kingdom, New Zealand, Ireland), resumption (Hong Kong), resumption/compulsory acquisition (Australia), or expropriation (South Africa, Canada) is the power to take private property for public use, by a state or a national government. However, it can be legislatively delegated by the state to municipalities, government subdivisions, or even private persons or corporations, when they are authorized to exercise the functions of public character.

The property may be taken either for government use or by delegation to third parties, who will devote it to public or civic use or, in some cases, to economic development.

Plaintiff

A plaintiff, also known as a claimant or complainant, is the term used in some jurisdictions for the party who initiates a lawsuit (also known as an action) before a court. By doing so, the plaintiff seeks a legal remedy, and if successful, the court will issue judgment in favor of the plaintiff and make the appropriate court order (e.g., an order for damages).

In some jurisdictions the commencement of a lawsuit is done by filing a summons, claim form and/or a complaint.

Zoning

Zoning is a device of land-use planning used by local governments in most developed countries.

Zoning may be use-based (regulating the uses to which land may be put, also called functional zoning), or it may regulate building height, lot coverage (density), and similar characteristics, or some combination of these.

Similar urban planning methods have dictated the use of various areas for particular purposes in many cities from ancient times.

Trespass

Trespass is an area of tort law broadly divided into three groups: trespass to the person, trespass to chattels and trespass to land.

Trespass to the person historically involved six separate trespasses: threats, assault, battery, wounding, mayhem, and maiming.

8. Real and Personal Property

Through the evolution of the common law in various jurisdictions, and the codification of common law torts, most jurisdictions now broadly recognize three trespasses to the person: assault, which is 'any act of such a nature as to excite an apprehension of battery'; battery, 'any intentional and unpermitted contact with the plaintiff's person or anything attached to it and practically identified with it'; and false imprisonment, the 'unlaw[ful] obstruct[ion] or depriv[ation] of freedom from restraint of movement'.

Private law

Private law is that part of a civil law legal system which is part of the jus commune that involves relationships between individuals, such as the law of contracts or torts, and the law of obligations (as it is called in civil legal systems). It is to be distinguished from public law, which deals with relationships between both natural and artificial persons (i.e., organizations) and the state, including regulatory statutes, penal law and other law that affects the public order. In general terms, private law involves interactions between private citizens, whereas public law involves interrelations between the state and the general population.

Public law

Public law is that part of law which governs relationships between individuals and the government, and those relationships between individuals which are of direct concern to the society. Public law comprises constitutional law, administrative law, tax law and criminal law, as well as all procedural law. In public law, mandatory rules (not optional) prevail.

Public nuisance

In English criminal law, public nuisance is a class of common law offence in which the injury, loss or damage is suffered by the local community as a whole rather than by individual victims.

Misappropriation

In law, misappropriation can be both a criminal and a civil violation. In civil law in the United States, many states define misappropriation as the unauthorized use of another's name, likeness, or identity without that person's permission, resulting in harm to that person.

Invitee

In the law of torts, an invitee is a person who is invited to land by the possessor of the land as a member of the public or one who is invited to the land for the purpose of business dealings with the possessor of the land. The status of a visitor as an invitee defines the legal rights of the visitor if they are injured due to the negligence of the property owner. However, the case of Rowlands v. Christian sought to eliminate the distinction between business invitee and licensee in regards to a land occupier owing a duty to act as a 'reasonable man' in rendering the property safe for others.

Premises

Premises are land and buildings together considered as a property. This usage arose from property owners finding the word in their title deeds, where it originally correctly meant 'the aforementioned; what this document is about', from Latin prae-missus = 'placed before'.

In this sense, the word is always used in the plural, but singular in construction.

Premises liability

Premises liability is the liability for a landowner for certain torts that occur on the real property.

CHAPTER HIGHLIGHTS & NOTES: KEY TERMS, PEOPLE, PLACES, CONCEPTS

This can range from things from 'injuries caused by a variety of hazardous conditions, including open excavations, uneven pavement, standing water, crumbling curbs, wet floors, uncleared snow, icy walks, falling objects, inadequate security, insufficient lighting, concealed holes, improperly secured mats, or defects in chairs or benches'. In sum:

Premises liability law is the body of law which makes the person who is in possession of land or premises responsible for certain injuries suffered by persons who are present on the premises.

CHAPTER QUIZ: KEY TERMS, PEOPLE, PLACES, CONCEPTS

1. _________ is a form of indemnity insurance predominantly found in the United States which insures against financial loss from defects in title to real property and from the invalidity or unenforceability of mortgage loans. _________ is principally a product developed and sold in the United States as a result of an alleged comparative deficiency of the U.S. land records laws. It is meant to protect an owner's or a lender's financial interest in real property against loss due to title defects, liens or other matters.

   a. Small Business Liability Relief and Brownfields Revitalization Act
   b. Title insurance
   c. Business method patent
   d. Business valuation

2. _________ is the liability for a landowner for certain torts that occur on the real property. This can range from things from 'injuries caused by a variety of hazardous conditions, including open excavations, uneven pavement, standing water, crumbling curbs, wet floors, uncleared snow, icy walks, falling objects, inadequate security, insufficient lighting, concealed holes, improperly secured mats, or defects in chairs or benches'. In sum:'

   _________ law is the body of law which makes the person who is in possession of land or premises responsible for certain injuries suffered by persons who are present on the premises.'

   a. 3D floor plan
   b. Premises liability
   c. 99-year lease
   d. Blockbusting

3. . In English law, a _________ is an estate in land, a form of freehold ownership. It is the way that real estate is owned in common law countries, and is the highest ownership interest possible that can be had in real property. Allodial title is reserved to governments under a civil law structure.

a. 72-hour clause
b. Bargain and sale deed
c. Betterment
d. Fee simple

4. _________ is that part of a civil law legal system which is part of the jus commune that involves relationships between individuals, such as the law of contracts or torts, and the law of obligations (as it is called in civil legal systems). It is to be distinguished from public law, which deals with relationships between both natural and artificial persons (i.e., organizations) and the state, including regulatory statutes, penal law and other law that affects the public order. In general terms, _________ involves interactions between private citizens, whereas public law involves interrelations between the state and the general population.

a. Small Business Liability Relief and Brownfields Revitalization Act
b. Bargain and sale deed
c. Private law
d. Blackacre

5. A _________ is the owner of a house, apartment, condominium, land or real estate which is rented or leased to an individual or business, who is called a tenant . When a juristic person is in this position, the term _________ is used. Other terms include lessor and owner.

a. 3D floor plan
b. Landlord
c. 99-year lease
d. Blockbusting

ANSWER KEY
8. Real and Personal Property

---

1. b
2. b
3. d
4. c
5. b

You can take the complete Online Interactive Chapter Practice Test

for 8. Real and Personal Property
on all key terms, persons, places, and concepts.

No Additional Costs

http://www.Cram101.com

9. Intellectual Property

CHAPTER OUTLINE: KEY TERMS, PEOPLE, PLACES, CONCEPTS

- Copyright
- Intellectual property
- Patent
- Lanham Act
- Arbitration
- Madrid system
- Generic trademark
- Substantive law
- Corporation
- Cybersquatting
- Trade
- Trade dress
- Amendment
- Certification
- Certification mark
- Collective mark
- Service mark
- Clayton Act
- Fair use
- Federal Circuit
- Tortfeasor

9. Intellectual Property

CHAPTER OUTLINE: KEY TERMS, PEOPLE, PLACES, CONCEPTS

______________ Economic espionage

CHAPTER HIGHLIGHTS & NOTES: KEY TERMS, PEOPLE, PLACES, CONCEPTS

Copyright

Copyright is a legal concept, enacted by most governments, that grants the creator of an original work exclusive rights to its use and distribution, usually for a limited time, with the intention of enabling the creator of intellectual wealth to receive compensation for their work and be able to financially support themselves.

Copyright is a form of intellectual property (as patents, trademarks and trade secrets are), applicable to any expressible form of an idea or information that is substantive and discrete. It is often shared, then percentage holders are commonly called rightsholders: legally, contractually and in associated 'rights' business functions.

Intellectual property

Intellectual property rights are the legally recognized exclusive rights to creations of the mind. Under intellectual property law, owners are granted certain exclusive rights to a variety of intangible assets, such as musical, literary, and artistic works; discoveries and inventions; and words, phrases, symbols, and designs. Common types of intellectual property rights include copyright, trademarks, patents, industrial design rights, trade dress, and in some jurisdictions trade secrets.

Patent

A patent is a set of exclusive rights granted by a sovereign state to an inventor or assignee for a limited period of time in exchange for detailed public disclosure of an invention. An invention is a solution to a specific technological problem and is a product or a process. Patents are a form of intellectual property.

Lanham Act

The Lanham Act (Pub.L. 79-489, 60 Stat. 427, enacted July 5, 1946, codified at 15 U.S.C. § 1051 et seq. (15 U.S.C. ch. 22)) is the primary federal trademark statute of law in the United States. The Act prohibits a number of activities, including trademark infringement, trademark dilution, and false advertising.

Arbitration

Arbitration, a form of alternative dispute resolution, is a technique for the resolution of disputes outside the courts. The parties to a dispute refer it to arbitration by one or more persons (the 'arbitrators', 'arbiters' or 'arbitral tribunal'), and agree to be bound by the arbitration decision (the 'award'). A third party reviews the evidence in the case and imposes a decision that is legally binding on both sides and enforceable in the courts.

Madrid system

The Madrid system is the primary international system for facilitating the registration of trademarks in multiple jurisdictions around the world. Its legal basis is the multilateral treaty Madrid Agreement Concerning the International Registration of Marks of 1891, as well as the Protocol Relating to the Madrid Agreement (1989).

The Madrid system provides a centrally administered system of obtaining a bundle of trademark registrations in separate jurisdictions.

Generic trademark

A generic trademark, also known as a genericised trademark or proprietary eponym, is a trademark or brand name that has become the generic name for, or synonymous with, a general class of product or service, against the usual intentions of the trademark's holder. Using a genericised trademark to refer to the general form of what that trademark represents is a form of metonymy.

A trademark is said to become genericised when it began as a distinctive product identifier but has changed in meaning to become generic.

Substantive law

Substantive law is the statutory, or written law, that defines rights and duties, such as crimes and punishments, civil rights and responsibilities in civil law. It is codified in legislated statutes or can be enacted through the initiative process.

Substantive law stands in contrast to procedural law, which is the 'machinery' for enforcing those rights and duties.

Corporation

A corporation is a separate legal entity that has been incorporated either directly through legislation or through a registration process established by law. Incorporated entities have legal rights and liabilities that are distinct from their employees and shareholders, and may conduct business as either a profit-seeking business or not-for-profit business. Early incorporated entities were established by charter (i.e. by an ad hoc act granted by a monarch or passed by a parliament or legislature).

Cybersquatting

Cybersquatting, according to the United States federal law known as the Anticybersquatting Consumer Protection Act, is registering, trafficking in, or using a domain name with bad faith intent to profit from the goodwill of a trademark belonging to someone else. The cybersquatter then offers to sell the domain to the person or company who owns a trademark contained within the name at an inflated price.

The term is derived from 'squatting', which is the act of occupying an abandoned or unoccupied space or building that the squatter does not own, rent, or otherwise have permission to use.

Trade

In professional sports, a trade is a sports league transaction involving an exchange of players' contracts or draft picks between sports clubs. Cash is another commodity that may be packaged together with contracts or draft picks to complete a trade.

9. Intellectual Property

CHAPTER HIGHLIGHTS & NOTES: KEY TERMS, PEOPLE, PLACES, CONCEPTS

Trade dress	Trade dress is a legal term of art that generally refers to characteristics of the visual appearance of a product or its packaging that signify the source of the product to consumers. Trade dress is a form of intellectual property.
Amendment	An amendment is a formal or official change made to a law, contract, constitution, or other legal document. It is based on the verb to amend, which means to change. Amendments can add, remove, or update parts of these agreements.
Certification	Certification refers to the confirmation of certain characteristics of an object, person, or organization. This confirmation is often, but not always, provided by some form of external review, education, assessment, or audit. Accreditation is a specific organization's process of certification.
Certification mark	A certification mark on a commercial product may indicate several things: On the part of the certifier, the label itself is a type of trademark whereby the listee, or manufacturer, uses the mark to indicate eligibility of the products for use in field installations in accordance with the requirements of the code, and/or the origin, material, mode of manufacture of products, mode of performance of services, quality, accuracy of other characteristics of products or services. Counterfeit consumer goods sometimes have bogus certification marks.
Collective mark	A collective trademark, collective trade mark, or collective mark is a trademark owned by an organization, used by its members them to identify themselves with a level of quality or accuracy, geographical origin, or other characteristics set by the organization. Collective trademarks are exceptions to the underlying principle of trademarks in that most trademarks serve as 'badges of origin'; they indicate the individual source of the goods or services. A collective trademark, however, can be used by a variety of traders, rather than just one individual concern, provided that the trader belongs to the association.
Service mark	A service mark or servicemark is a trademark used in the United States and several other countries to identify a service rather than a product. When a service mark is federally registered, the standard registration symbol ® or 'Reg U.S. Pat & TM Off' may be used (the same symbol is used to mark registered trademarks). Before it is registered, it is common practice (with some legal standing) to use the service mark symbol ? (a superscript SM).
Clayton Act	The Clayton Act of 1914 (Pub.L. 63-212, 38 Stat. 730, enacted October 15, 1914, codified at 15 U.S.C. §§ 12-27, 29 U.S.C. §§ 52-53), was a part of United States antitrust law with the goal of adding further substance to the U.S. antitrust law regime; the Clayton Act sought to prevent anticompetitive practices in their incipiency.

That regime started with the Sherman Antitrust Act of 1890, the first Federal law outlawing practices considered harmful to consumers (monopolies, cartels, and trusts). The Clayton Act specified particular prohibited conduct, the three-level enforcement scheme, the exemptions, and the remedial measures.

Fair use

Fair use is a limitation and exception to the exclusive right granted by copyright law to the author of a creative work. In United States copyright law, fair use is a doctrine that permits limited use of copyrighted material without acquiring permission from the rights holders. Examples of fair use include commentary, search engines, criticism, parody, news reporting, research, teaching, library archiving and scholarship.

Federal Circuit

The United States Court of Appeals for the Federal Circuit is a United States court of appeals headquartered in Washington, D.C.. The court was created by Congress with passage of the Federal Courts Improvement Act of 1982, which merged the United States Court of Customs and Patent Appeals and the appellate division of the United States Court of Claims, making the judges of the former courts into circuit judges. The Federal Circuit is particularly known for its decisions on patent law, as it is the only appellate-level court with the jurisdiction to hear patent case appeals.

Tortfeasor

A tort, in common law jurisdictions, is a civil wrong that unfairly causes someone else to suffer loss or harm resulting in legal liability for the person who commits the tortious act, called a tortfeasor. Although crimes may be torts, the cause of legal action is not necessarily a crime, as the harm may be due to negligence which does not amount to criminal negligence. The victim of the harm can recover their loss as damages in a lawsuit.

Economic espionage

Industrial espionage, economic espionage or corporate espionage is a form of espionage conducted for commercial purposes instead of purely national security. Economic espionage is conducted or orchestrated by governments and is international in scope, while industrial or corporate espionage is more often national and occurs between companies or corporations.

9. Intellectual Property

CHAPTER QUIZ: KEY TERMS, PEOPLE, PLACES, CONCEPTS

1. _________ refers to the confirmation of certain characteristics of an object, person, or organization. This confirmation is often, but not always, provided by some form of external review, education, assessment, or audit. Accreditation is a specific organization's process of _________.

   a. Small Business Liability Relief and Brownfields Revitalization Act
   b. Financial scandal in the Orthodox Church in America
   c. HP Autonomy
   d. Certification

2. _________ rights are the legally recognized exclusive rights to creations of the mind. Under _________ law, owners are granted certain exclusive rights to a variety of intangible assets, such as musical, literary, and artistic works; discoveries and inventions; and words, phrases, symbols, and designs. Common types of _________ rights include copyright, trademarks, patents, industrial design rights, trade dress, and in some jurisdictions trade secrets.

   a. Intellectual property
   b. Bilateral monopoly
   c. Chamberlinian monopolistic competition
   d. Competition Commission

3. The _________ (Pub.L. 79-489, 60 Stat. 427, enacted July 5, 1946, codified at 15 U.S.C. § 1051 et seq. (15 U.S.C. ch. 22)) is the primary federal trademark statute of law in the United States. The Act prohibits a number of activities, including trademark infringement, trademark dilution, and false advertising.

   a. Cynthia Cooper
   b. Lanham Act
   c. HP Autonomy
   d. James Henry Ting Wei

4. The United States Court of Appeals for the _________ is a United States court of appeals headquartered in Washington, D.C.. The court was created by Congress with passage of the Federal Courts Improvement Act of 1982, which merged the United States Court of Customs and Patent Appeals and the appellate division of the United States Court of Claims, making the judges of the former courts into circuit judges. The _________ is particularly known for its decisions on patent law, as it is the only appellate-level court with the jurisdiction to hear patent case appeals.

   a. Small Business Liability Relief and Brownfields Revitalization Act
   b. Financial scandal in the Orthodox Church in America
   c. HP Autonomy
   d. Federal Circuit

5. . _________ is a legal concept, enacted by most governments, that grants the creator of an original work exclusive rights to its use and distribution, usually for a limited time, with the intention of enabling the creator of intellectual wealth to receive compensation for their work and be able to financially support themselves.

_________ is a form of intellectual property (as patents, trademarks and trade secrets are), applicable to any expressible form of an idea or information that is substantive and discrete. It is often shared, then percentage holders are commonly called rightsholders: legally, contractually and in associated 'rights' business functions.

a. Copyright
b. Bilateral monopoly
c. Chamberlinian monopolistic competition
d. Competition Commission

ANSWER KEY
9. Intellectual Property

---

1. d
2. a
3. b
4. d
5. a

---

10. Contracts

CHAPTER OUTLINE: KEY TERMS, PEOPLE, PLACES, CONCEPTS

- Blackacre
- Contract
- Law merchant
- Lex mercatoria
- Administration
- Health Administration
- Common law
- Offer and acceptance
- Commission
- Trade
- Option
- Option contract
- Partnership
- Revocation
- Landlord
- Consideration
- Estoppel
- Capacity
- Void
- Voidable
- Voidable contract

10. Contracts

CHAPTER OUTLINE: KEY TERMS, PEOPLE, PLACES, CONCEPTS

- Unenforceable
- Plea
- Covenant not to compete
- Unconscionable contract
- Duress
- Misdemeanor
- Mistake
- Solicitation
- Undue influence
- Electronic signature
- Electronic Signatures in Global and National Commerce Act
- Uniform Electronic Transactions Act
- Fraud
- Parol evidence
- Environmental Protection
- Substantial performance
- Assignment
- Delegation
- Anticipatory breach
- Bankruptcy
- Portland Cement

10. Contracts

CHAPTER OUTLINE: KEY TERMS, PEOPLE, PLACES, CONCEPTS

	Novation
	Rescission
	Rehabilitation
	Rehabilitation Act
	Impracticability
	Liquidated damages
	Specific performance
	Quadro Tracker
	Arbitration
	Injunction
	Quantum meruit

CHAPTER HIGHLIGHTS & NOTES: KEY TERMS, PEOPLE, PLACES, CONCEPTS

Blackacre	Blackacre, Whiteacre, Greenacre, Brownacre, and variations are the placeholder names used for fictitious estates in land. The names are used by professors of law in common law jurisdictions, particularly in the area of real property and occasionally in contracts, to discuss the rights of various parties to a piece of land. A typical law school or bar exam question on real property might say: Adam, owner of a fee simple in Blackacre, conveyed the property 'to Bill for life, remainder to Charles, provided that if any person should consume alcohol on the property before the first born son of Charles turns twenty-one, then the property shall go to Dwight in fee simple.' Assume that neither Bill, Charles, or Dwight is an heir of Adam, and that Adam's only heir is his son, Edward.

10. Contracts

CHAPTER HIGHLIGHTS & NOTES: KEY TERMS, PEOPLE, PLACES, CONCEPTS

Contract

In common law legal systems, a contract is an agreement having a lawful object entered into voluntarily by two or more parties, each of whom intends to create one or more legal obligations between them. The elements of a contract are 'offer' and 'acceptance' by 'competent persons' having legal capacity who exchange 'consideration' to create 'mutuality of obligation.'

Proof of some or all of these elements may be done in writing, though contracts may be made entirely orally or by conduct. The remedy for breach of contract can be 'damages' in the form of compensation of money or specific performance enforced through an injunction.

Law merchant

Lex mercatoria, often referred to as 'the Law Merchant' in English, is the body of commercial law used by merchants throughout Europe during the medieval period. It evolved similar to English common law as a system of custom and best practice, which was enforced through a system of merchant courts along the main trade routes. It functioned as the international law of commerce.

Lex mercatoria

Lex mercatoria is the body of commercial law used by merchants throughout Europe during the medieval period. It evolved similar to English common law as a system of custom and best practice, which was enforced through a system of merchant courts along the main trade routes. It functioned as the international law of commerce.

Administration

As a legal concept, administration is a procedure under the insolvency laws of a number of common law jurisdictions. It functions as a rescue mechanism for insolvent entities and allows them to carry on running their business. The process - an alternative to liquidation - is often known as going into administration.

Health Administration

Health Administration or Healthcare Administration is the field relating to leadership, management, and administration of public health systems, health care systems, hospitals, and hospital networks. Health care administrators are considered health care professionals.

Common law

Common law is law developed by judges through decisions of courts and similar tribunals, as opposed to statutes adopted through the legislative process or regulations issued by the executive branch.

A 'common law system' is a legal system that gives great precedential weight to common law, on the principle that it is unfair to treat similar facts differently on different occasions. The body of precedent is called 'common law' and it binds future decisions.

Offer and acceptance

Offer and acceptance are elements required for the formation of a legally binding contract: the expression of an offer to contract on certain terms by one person to another person (the 'offeree'), and an indication by the offeree of its acceptance of those terms. The other elements traditionally required for a legally binding contract are (i) consideration and (ii) an intention to create legal relations.

Commission

The payment of commission as remuneration for services rendered or products sold is a common way to reward sales people. Payments often will be calculated on the basis of a percentage of the goods sold. This is a way for firms to solve the principal-agent problem, by attempting to realign employees' interests with those of the firm.

Trade

In professional sports, a trade is a sports league transaction involving an exchange of players' contracts or draft picks between sports clubs. Cash is another commodity that may be packaged together with contracts or draft picks to complete a trade. Typically, trades are completed between two clubs, but there are instances where trades are consummated between three or more clubs.

Option

In finance, an option is a contract which gives the buyer the right, but not the obligation, to buy or sell an underlying asset or instrument at a specified strike price on or before a specified date. The seller has the corresponding obligation to fulfill the transaction - that is to sell or buy - if the buyer (owner) 'exercises' the option. The buyer pays a premium to the seller for this right.

Option contract

An option contract, or simply option, is defined as 'a promise which meets the requirements for the formation of a contract and limits the promisor's power to revoke an offer.' Restatement of Contracts § 25 (1981).

An option contract is a type of contract that protects an offeree from an offeror's ability to revoke the contract.

Consideration for the option contract is still required as it is still a form of contract, cf.

Partnership

A partnership is an arrangement in which parties agree to cooperate to advance their mutual interests.

Since humans are social beings, partnerships between individuals, businesses, interest-based organizations, schools, governments, and varied combinations thereof, have always been and remain commonplace. In the most frequently associated instance of the term, a partnership is formed between one or more businesses in which partners (owners) co-labor to achieve and share profits and losses .

Revocation

Revocation is the act of recall or annulment. It is the reversal of an act, the recalling of a grant or privilege, or the making void of some deed previously existing.

A temporary revocation of a grant or privilege is called a suspension.

Landlord

A landlord is the owner of a house, apartment, condominium, land or real estate which is rented or leased to an individual or business, who is called a tenant . When a juristic person is in this position, the term landlord is used. Other terms include lessor and owner.

10. Contracts

Consideration	Consideration is the concept of legal value in connection with contracts. It is anything of value promised to another when making a contract. It can take the form of money, physical objects, services, promised actions, abstinence from a future action, and much more.
Estoppel	In law, estoppel is a set of doctrines in which a court prevents a litigant from taking an action the litigant normally would have the right to take, in order to prevent an inequitable result. For example, estoppel precludes 'a person from denying, or asserting anything to the contrary of, that which has, in contemplation of law, been established as the truth, either by the acts of judicial or legislative officers, or by his own deed, acts, or representations, either express or implied'.
Capacity	The capacity of both natural and legal persons determines whether they may make binding amendments to their rights, duties and obligations, such as getting married or merging, entering into contracts, making gifts, or writing a valid will. Capacity is an aspect of status and both are defined by a person's personal law:•for natural persons, the law of domicile or lex domicilii in common law jurisdictions, and either the law of nationality or lex patriae, or of habitual residence in civil law states;•for legal persons, the law of the place of incorporation, the lex incorporationis for companies while other forms of business entity derive their capacity either from the law of the place in which they were formed or the laws of the states in which they establish a presence for trading purposes depending on the nature of the entity and the transactions entered into. When the law limits or bars a person from engaging in specified activities, any agreements or contracts to do so are either voidable or void for incapacity. Sometimes such legal incapacity is referred to as incompetence.
Void	In law, void means of no legal effect. An action, document or transaction which is void is of no legal effect whatsoever: an absolute nullity -- the law treats it as if it had never existed or happened. The term void ab initio, which means 'to be treated as invalid from the outset,' comes from adding the Latin phrase ab initio (from the beginning) as a qualifier.
Voidable	In law, a transaction or action which is voidable is valid, but may be annulled by one of the parties to the transaction. Voidable is usually used in distinction to void ab initio (or void from the outset) and unenforceable. The act of invalidating the contract by the party exercising its rights to annul the voidable contract is usually referred to either as voiding the contract (in the United States and Canada) or avoiding the contract (in the United Kingdom, Australia and other common law countries).
Voidable contract	A voidable contract, unlike a void contract, is a valid contract. At most, one party to the contract is bound. The unbound party may repudiate the contract, at which time the contract is void.
Unenforceable	An unenforceable contract or transaction is one that is valid, but which the court will not enforce.

Unenforceable is usually used in contradistinction to void (or void ab initio) and voidable. If the parties perform the agreement, it will be valid, but the court will not compel them if they do not.

Plea

In legal terms, a plea is simply an answer to a claim made by someone in a criminal case under common law using the adversarial system. Colloquially, a plea has come to mean the assertion by a defendant at arraignment, or otherwise in response to a criminal charge, whether that person pleaded guilty, not guilty, no contest or (in the United States) Alford plea.

The concept of the plea is one of the major differences between criminal procedure under common law and procedure under the civil law system.

Covenant not to compete

A non-compete clause, or covenant not to compete is a term used in contract law under which one party (usually an employee) agrees not to enter into or start a similar profession or trade in competition against another party (usually the employer). As a contract provision, a CNC is bound by traditional contract requirements including the consideration doctrine. The use of such clauses is premised on the possibility that upon their termination or resignation, an employee might begin working for a competitor or starting a business, and gain competitive advantage by exploiting confidential information about their former employer's operations or trade secrets, or sensitive information such as customer/client lists, business practices, upcoming products, and marketing plans.

Unconscionable contract

Unconscionability is a doctrine in contract law that describes terms that are so extremely unjust, or overwhelmingly one-sided in favor of the party who has the superior bargaining power, that they are contrary to good conscience. Typically, an unconscionable contract is held to be unenforceable because no reasonable or informed person would otherwise agree to it. The perpetrator of the conduct is not allowed to benefit, because the consideration offered is lacking, or is so obviously inadequate, that to enforce the contract would be unfair to the party seeking to escape the contract.

Duress

In jurisprudence, duress or coercion refers to a situation whereby a person performs an act as a result of violence, threat or other pressure against the person. Black's Law Dictionary (6th ed). defines duress as 'any unlawful threat or coercion used... to induce another to act [or not act] in a manner [they] otherwise would not [or would]'.

Misdemeanor

A misdemeanor is any 'lesser' criminal act in some common law legal systems. Misdemeanors are generally punished less severely than felonies, but theoretically more so than administrative infractions (also known as minor, petty or summary offences) and regulatory offences. Many misdemeanors are punished with monetary fines.

Mistake

In contract law, a mistake is an erroneous belief, at contracting, that certain facts are true. It can be argued as a defence, and if raised successfully can lead to the agreement in question being found void ab initio or voidable, or alternatively an equitable remedy may be provided by the courts.

10. Contracts

CHAPTER HIGHLIGHTS & NOTES: KEY TERMS, PEOPLE, PLACES, CONCEPTS

Solicitation	'Solicitation,' the act of soliciting, means simply to ask for something. In criminal law, it most commonly refers to either the act of offering goods or services, or the act of attempting to purchase such goods or services. Legal status may be specific to the time and/or place where solicitation occurs.
Undue influence	In jurisprudence, undue influence is an equitable doctrine that involves one person taking advantage of a position of power over another person.
Electronic signature	An electronic signature, or e-signature, is any electronic means that indicates either that a person adopts the contents of an electronic message, or more broadly that the person who claims to have written a message is the one who wrote it . By comparison, a signature is a stylized script associated with a person. In commerce and the law, a signature on a document is an indication that the person adopts the intentions recorded in the document.
Electronic Signatures in Global and National Commerce Act	The Electronic Signatures in Global and National Commerce Act is a United States federal law passed by the U.S. Congress to facilitate the use of electronic records and electronic signatures in interstate and foreign commerce by ensuring the validity and legal effect of contracts entered into electronically. In 2010, both Houses of Congress passed a resolution at the request of industry leaders, recognizing June 30 as 'National ESIGN Day.' Although every state has at least one law pertaining to electronic signatures, it is the federal law that lays out the guidelines for interstate commerce. The general intent of the ESIGN Act is spelled out in the very first section(101.a), that a contract or signature "may not be denied legal effect, validity, or enforceability solely because it is in electronic form".
Uniform Electronic Transactions Act	The Uniform Electronic Transactions Act is one of the several United States Uniform Acts proposed by the National Conference of Commissioners on Uniform State Laws (NCCUSL). Since then 47 States, the District of Columbia, Puerto Rico, and the U.S. Virgin Islands have adopted it into their own laws. Its overarching purpose is to bring into line the differing State laws over such areas as retention of paper records (checks in particular), and the validity of electronic signatures, thereby supporting the validity of electronic contracts as a viable medium of agreement.
Fraud	Fraud is a deception deliberately practiced in order to secure unfair or unlawful gain (adjectival form fraudulent; to defraud is the verb). As a legal construct, fraud is both a civil wrong (i.e., a fraud victim may sue the fraud perpetrator to avoid the fraud and/or recover monetary compensation) and a criminal wrong (i.e., a fraud perpetrator may be prosecuted and imprisoned by governmental authorities). Defrauding people or organizations of money or valuables is the usual purpose of fraud, but it sometimes instead involves obtaining benefits without actually depriving anyone of money or valuables, such as obtaining a drivers license by way of false statements made in an application for the same.

Parol evidence	The parol evidence rule is a substantive common law rule in contract cases that prevents a party to a written contract from presenting extrinsic evidence that discloses an ambiguity and clarifies it or adds to the written terms of the contract that appears to be whole. The term of art parol means 'oral' and comes from Anglo-French, Anglo-Norman, or Legal French. The supporting rationale for this rule is that since the contracting parties have reduced their agreement to a single and final writing, extrinsic evidence of past agreements or terms should not be considered when interpreting that writing, as the parties had decided to ultimately leave them out of the contract.
Environmental Protection	Environmental protection is a practice of protecting the natural environment on individual, organizational or governmental levels, for the benefit of both the natural environment and humans. Due to the pressures of population and technology, the biophysical environment is being degraded, sometimes permanently. This has been recognized, and governments have begun placing restraints on activities that cause environmental degradation.
Substantial performance	At common law, substantial performance is an alternative principle to the perfect tender rule. It allows a court to imply a term that allows a partial or substantially similar performance to stand in for the performance specified in the contract. This principle is relevant when a contractor's performance is in some way deficient, through no willful act by the contractor, yet is so nearly equivalent that it would be unreasonable for the owner to deny the agreed upon payment.
Assignment	An assignment is a term used with similar meanings in the law of contracts and in the law of real estate. In both instances, it encompasses the transfer of rights held by one party--the assignor--to another party--the assignee. The details of the assignment determines some additional rights and liabilities (or duties).
Delegation	In contract law, delegation is the act of giving another person the responsibility of carrying out the performance agreed to in a contract. Three parties are concerned with this act - the party who had incurred the obligation to perform under the contract is called the delegator; the party who assumes the responsibility of performing this duty is called the delegatee; and the party to whom this performance is owed is called the obligee. The term is also a concept of Administrative Law.
Anticipatory breach	Anticipatory repudiation, also called an anticipatory breach, is a term in the law of contracts that describes a declaration by the promising party to a contract, that he or she does not intend to live up to his or her obligations under the contract.
Bankruptcy	Bankruptcy is a legal status of a person or other entity that cannot repay the debts it owes to creditors. In most jurisdictions, bankruptcy is imposed by a court order, often initiated by the debtor.

10. Contracts

CHAPTER HIGHLIGHTS & NOTES: KEY TERMS, PEOPLE, PLACES, CONCEPTS

Portland Cement	Portland cement is the most common type of cement in general use around the world, used as a basic ingredient of concrete, mortar, stucco, and most non-speciality grout. It developed from other types of hydraulic lime in England in the mid 19th century and usually originates from limestone. It is a fine powder produced by heating materials in a kiln to form what is called clinker, grinding the clinker, and adding small amounts of other materials.
Novation	In contract law and business law, novation is the act of either:•replacing an obligation to perform with a new obligation; or•adding an obligation to perform; or•replacing a party to an agreement with a new party. In contrast to an assignment, which is valid so long as the obligee is given notice, a novation is valid only with the consent of all parties to the original agreement: the obligee must consent to the replacement of the original obligor with the new obligor. A contract transferred by the novation process transfers all duties and obligations from the original obligor to the new obligor. For example, if there exists a contract where Dan will give a TV to Alex, and another contract where Alex will give a TV to Becky, then, it is possible to novate both contracts and replace them with a single contract wherein Dan agrees to give a TV to Becky.
Rescission	In contract law, rescission has been defined as the unmaking of a contract between parties. Rescission is the unwinding of a transaction. This is done to bring the parties, as far as possible, back to the position in which they were before they entered into a contract (the status quo ante).
Rehabilitation	Rehabilitation of sensory and cognitive function typically involves methods for retraining neural pathways or training new neural pathways to regain or improve neurocognitive functioning that has been diminished by disease or trauma. Three common neuropsychological problems treatable with rehabilitation are attention deficit/hyperactivity disorder (ADHD), concussion, and spinal cord injury. Rehabilitation research and practices are a fertile area for clinical neuropsychologists and others.
Rehabilitation Act	The Rehabilitation Act of 1973, (Pub.L. 93-112, 87 Stat. 355, enacted September 26, 1973), is a federal law, codified as 29 U.S.C. § 701. The principal sponsor of the bill was Rep. John Brademas [IN-3]. The Rehabilitation Act of 1973 replaces the Vocational Rehabilitation Act, to extend and revise the authorization of grants to States for vocational rehabilitation services, with special emphasis on services to those with the most severe disabilities, to expand special Federal responsibilities and research and training programs with respect to individuals with disabilities, to establish special responsibilities in the Secretary of Health, Education, and Welfare for coordination of all programs with respect to individuals with disabilities within the Department of Health, Education, and Welfare, and for other purposes.
Impracticability	The doctrine of impracticability in the common law of contracts excuses performance of a duty, where that duty has become unfeasibly difficult or expensive for the party who was to perform.

Impracticability is similar in some respects to the doctrine of impossibility because it is triggered by the occurrence of a condition which prevents one party from fulfilling the contract. The major difference between the two doctrines is that while impossibility excuses performance where the contractual duty cannot physically be performed, the doctrine of impracticability comes into play where performance is still physically possible, but would be very burdensome for the party whose performance is due.

Liquidated damages

Liquidated damages are damages whose amount the parties designate during the formation of a contract for the injured party to collect as compensation upon a specific breach (e.g., late performance).

When damages are not predetermined/assessed in advance, then the amount recoverable is said to be 'at large' (to be agreed or determined by a court or tribunal in the event of breach).

At common law, a liquidated damages clause will not be enforced if its purpose is to punish the wrongdoer/party in breach rather than to compensate the injured party (in which case it is referred to as a penal or penalty clause).

Specific performance

Specific performance is an order of a court which requires a party to perform a specific act, usually what is stated in a contract. It is an alternative to awarding damages, and is classed as an equitable remedy commonly used in the form of injunctive relief concerning confidential information or real property. While specific performance can be in the form of any type of forced action, it is usually used to complete a previously established transaction, thus being the most effective remedy in protecting the expectation interest of the innocent party to a contract.

Quadro Tracker

The Quadro Tracker, also known as the Positive Molecular Locator, was a 'detection device' sold by Quadro Corp. of Harleyville, South Carolina between 1993 and 1996. Around 1,000 were sold to police departments and school districts around the United States on the basis that it could detect hidden drugs, explosives, weapons and lost golf balls. In 1996, the FBI declared it to be a fake and obtained a permanent injunction barring the device from being manufactured or sold.

Arbitration

Arbitration, a form of alternative dispute resolution, is a technique for the resolution of disputes outside the courts. The parties to a dispute refer it to arbitration by one or more persons (the 'arbitrators', 'arbiters' or 'arbitral tribunal'), and agree to be bound by the arbitration decision (the 'award'). A third party reviews the evidence in the case and imposes a decision that is legally binding on both sides and enforceable in the courts.

Injunction

An injunction is an equitable remedy in the form of a court order that requires a party to do or refrain from doing specific acts. A party that fails to comply with an injunction faces criminal or civil penalties, including possible monetary sanctions and even imprisonment.

10. Contracts

CHAPTER HIGHLIGHTS & NOTES: KEY TERMS, PEOPLE, PLACES, CONCEPTS

Quantum meruit	Quantum meruit is a Latin phrase meaning 'what one has earned'. In the context of contract law, it means something along the lines of 'reasonable value of services'. In the United States, the elements of quantum meruit are determined by state common law.

CHAPTER QUIZ: KEY TERMS, PEOPLE, PLACES, CONCEPTS

1. In jurisprudence, _________ is an equitable doctrine that involves one person taking advantage of a position of power over another person.

   a. Undue influence
   b. Big boy letter
   c. Bonus clause
   d. Breach of contract

2. In contract law, _________ is the act of giving another person the responsibility of carrying out the performance agreed to in a contract. Three parties are concerned with this act - the party who had incurred the obligation to perform under the contract is called the delegator; the party who assumes the responsibility of performing this duty is called the delegatee; and the party to whom this performance is owed is called the obligee. The term is also a concept of Administrative Law.

   a. Delegation
   b. Big boy letter
   c. Bonus clause
   d. Breach of contract

3. _________ is the body of commercial law used by merchants throughout Europe during the medieval period. It evolved similar to English common law as a system of custom and best practice, which was enforced through a system of merchant courts along the main trade routes. It functioned as the international law of commerce.

   a. Commercial law
   b. Statutory liability
   c. Bulk sale
   d. Lex mercatoria

4. . In jurisprudence, _________ or coercion refers to a situation whereby a person performs an act as a result of violence, threat or other pressure against the person. Black's Law Dictionary (6th ed). defines _________ as 'any unlawful threat or coercion used... to induce another to act [or not act] in a manner [they] otherwise would not [or would]'.

   a. Beneficial interest

b. Big boy letter
c. Bonus clause
d. Duress

5. As a legal concept, _________ is a procedure under the insolvency laws of a number of common law jurisdictions. It functions as a rescue mechanism for insolvent entities and allows them to carry on running their business. The process - an alternative to liquidation - is often known as going into _________.

   a. Commercial law
   b. Lex mercatoria
   c. Administration
   d. Advertising regulation

ANSWER KEY
10. Contracts

---

1. a
2. a
3. d
4. d
5. c

---

11. Domestic and International Sales

CHAPTER OUTLINE: KEY TERMS, PEOPLE, PLACES, CONCEPTS

- Law merchant
- Lex mercatoria
- Common law
- Reinsurance
- Good faith
- Administration
- Health Administration
- Contract
- Firm offer
- Bargaining
- Sherman Act
- Fraud
- Parol evidence
- Trade
- Quadro Tracker
- President
- Output contract
- Requirements contract
- Commission
- Certification
- Perfect tender

11. Domestic and International Sales

CHAPTER OUTLINE: KEY TERMS, PEOPLE, PLACES, CONCEPTS

	Bankruptcy
	Disclaimer
	Warranty
	Rehabilitation
	Rehabilitation Act
	Plea
	Cover
	Corporation
	Consequential
	Constitution

CHAPTER HIGHLIGHTS & NOTES: KEY TERMS, PEOPLE, PLACES, CONCEPTS

Law merchant	Lex mercatoria, often referred to as 'the Law Merchant' in English, is the body of commercial law used by merchants throughout Europe during the medieval period. It evolved similar to English common law as a system of custom and best practice, which was enforced through a system of merchant courts along the main trade routes. It functioned as the international law of commerce.
Lex mercatoria	Lex mercatoria is the body of commercial law used by merchants throughout Europe during the medieval period. It evolved similar to English common law as a system of custom and best practice, which was enforced through a system of merchant courts along the main trade routes. It functioned as the international law of commerce.
Common law	Common law is law developed by judges through decisions of courts and similar tribunals, as opposed to statutes adopted through the legislative process or regulations issued by the executive branch.

A 'common law system' is a legal system that gives great precedential weight to common law, on the principle that it is unfair to treat similar facts differently on different occasions. The body of precedent is called 'common law' and it binds future decisions.

Reinsurance

Reinsurance is insurance that is purchased by an insurance company from one or more other insurance companies (the 'reinsurer') directly or through a broker as a means of risk management, sometimes in practice including tax mitigation and other reasons described below. The ceding company and the reinsurer enter into a reinsurance agreement which details the conditions upon which the reinsurer would pay a share of the claims incurred by the ceding company. The reinsurer is paid a 'reinsurance premium' by the ceding company, which issues insurance policies to its own policyholders.

Good faith

In philosophy, the concept of good faith denotes sincere, honest intention or belief, regardless of the outcome of an action; the opposed concepts are bad faith, mala fides and perfidy (pretense).

In law, bona fides denotes the mental and moral states of honesty and conviction regarding either the truth or the falsity of a proposition, or of a body of opinion; likewise regarding either the rectitude or the depravity of a line of conduct. As a legal concept bona fides is especially important in matters of equity .

Administration

As a legal concept, administration is a procedure under the insolvency laws of a number of common law jurisdictions. It functions as a rescue mechanism for insolvent entities and allows them to carry on running their business. The process - an alternative to liquidation - is often known as going into administration.

Health Administration

Health Administration or Healthcare Administration is the field relating to leadership, management, and administration of public health systems, health care systems, hospitals, and hospital networks. Health care administrators are considered health care professionals.

Contract

In common law legal systems, a contract is an agreement having a lawful object entered into voluntarily by two or more parties, each of whom intends to create one or more legal obligations between them. The elements of a contract are 'offer' and 'acceptance' by 'competent persons' having legal capacity who exchange 'consideration' to create 'mutuality of obligation.'

Proof of some or all of these elements may be done in writing, though contracts may be made entirely orally or by conduct. The remedy for breach of contract can be 'damages' in the form of compensation of money or specific performance enforced through an injunction.

Firm offer

A firm offer means an irrevocable offer made by a merchant. As a general rule, all offers are revocable at any time prior to acceptance, even those offers that purport to be irrevocable on their face.

11. Domestic and International Sales

CHAPTER HIGHLIGHTS & NOTES: KEY TERMS, PEOPLE, PLACES, CONCEPTS

Bargaining

Bargaining or haggling is a type of negotiation in which the buyer and seller of a good or service dispute the price which will be paid and the exact nature of the transaction that will take place, and eventually come to an agreement. Bargaining is an alternative pricing strategy to fixed prices. Optimally, if it costs the retailer nothing to engage and allow bargaining, he can divine the buyer's willingness to spend.

Sherman Act

The Sherman Antitrust Act (Sherman Act,26 Stat. 209, 15 U.S.C. §§ 1-7) is a landmark federal statute in the history of United States antitrust law (or 'competition law') passed by Congress in 1890. It prohibits certain business activities that federal government regulators deem to be anti-competitive, and requires the federal government to investigate and pursue trusts.

It has since, more broadly, been used to oppose the combination of entities that could potentially harm competition, such as monopolies or cartels.

According to its authors, it was not intended to impact market gains obtained by honest means, by benefiting the consumers more than the competitors.

Fraud

Fraud is a deception deliberately practiced in order to secure unfair or unlawful gain (adjectival form fraudulent; to defraud is the verb). As a legal construct, fraud is both a civil wrong (i.e., a fraud victim may sue the fraud perpetrator to avoid the fraud and/or recover monetary compensation) and a criminal wrong (i.e., a fraud perpetrator may be prosecuted and imprisoned by governmental authorities). Defrauding people or organizations of money or valuables is the usual purpose of fraud, but it sometimes instead involves obtaining benefits without actually depriving anyone of money or valuables, such as obtaining a drivers license by way of false statements made in an application for the same.

Parol evidence

The parol evidence rule is a substantive common law rule in contract cases that prevents a party to a written contract from presenting extrinsic evidence that discloses an ambiguity and clarifies it or adds to the written terms of the contract that appears to be whole. The term of art parol means 'oral' and comes from Anglo-French, Anglo-Norman, or Legal French.

The supporting rationale for this rule is that since the contracting parties have reduced their agreement to a single and final writing, extrinsic evidence of past agreements or terms should not be considered when interpreting that writing, as the parties had decided to ultimately leave them out of the contract.

Trade

In professional sports, a trade is a sports league transaction involving an exchange of players' contracts or draft picks between sports clubs. Cash is another commodity that may be packaged together with contracts or draft picks to complete a trade. Typically, trades are completed between two clubs, but there are instances where trades are consummated between three or more clubs.

Quadro Tracker

The Quadro Tracker, also known as the Positive Molecular Locator, was a 'detection device' sold by Quadro Corp. of Harleyville, South Carolina between 1993 and 1996. Around 1,000 were sold to police departments and school districts around the United States on the basis that it could detect hidden drugs, explosives, weapons and lost golf balls. In 1996, the FBI declared it to be a fake and obtained a permanent injunction barring the device from being manufactured or sold.

President

A President is a leader of an organization, company, community, club, trade union, university for this article. It is the legally recognized highest 'titled' corporate officer, ranking above the various Vice Presidents (e.g. Senior Vice President and Executive Vice President), however that post on its own is generally considered subordinate to the Chief Executive Officer. In a similar vein to the Chief Operating Officer, the title of corporate President as a separate position (as opposed to being combined with a 'C-Suite' designation, such as 'President and CEO' or 'President and COO') is also loosely defined.

Output contract

An output contract is an agreement in which a producer agrees to sell his or her entire production to the buyer, who in turn agrees to purchase the entire output. Example: an almond grower enters into an output contract with an almond packer: thus the producer has a 'home' for output of nuts, and the packer of nuts is happy to try the particular product. The converse of this situation is a requirements contract, under which a seller agrees to supply the buyer with as much of a good or service as the buyer wants, in exchange for the buyer's agreement not to buy that good or service elsewhere.

Requirements contract

A requirements contract is a contract in which one party agrees to supply as much of a good or service as is required by the other party, and in exchange the other party expressly or implicitly promises that it will obtain its goods or services exclusively from the first party. For example, a grocery store might enter into a contract with the farmer who grows oranges under which the farmer would supply the grocery store with as many oranges as the store could sell. The farmer could sue for breach of contract if the store were thereafter to purchase oranges for this purpose from any other party.

Commission

The payment of commission as remuneration for services rendered or products sold is a common way to reward sales people. Payments often will be calculated on the basis of a percentage of the goods sold. This is a way for firms to solve the principal-agent problem, by attempting to realign employees' interests with those of the firm.

Certification

Certification refers to the confirmation of certain characteristics of an object, person, or organization. This confirmation is often, but not always, provided by some form of external review, education, assessment, or audit. Accreditation is a specific organization's process of certification.

Perfect tender

The perfect tender rule refers to the legal right for a buyer of goods to insist upon 'perfect tender' by the seller.

11. Domestic and International Sales

CHAPTER HIGHLIGHTS & NOTES: KEY TERMS, PEOPLE, PLACES, CONCEPTS

In a contract for the sale of goods, if the goods fail to conform exactly to the description in the contract (whether as to quality, quantity or manner of delivery) the buyer may reject the goods. (UCC 2-601).

Bankruptcy

Bankruptcy is a legal status of a person or other entity that cannot repay the debts it owes to creditors. In most jurisdictions, bankruptcy is imposed by a court order, often initiated by the debtor.

Bankruptcy is not the only legal status that an insolvent person or other entity may have, and the term bankruptcy is therefore not a synonym for insolvency.

Disclaimer

A disclaimer is generally any statement intended to specify or delimit the scope of rights and obligations that may be exercised and enforced by parties in a legally recognized relationship. In contrast to other terms for legally operative language, the term disclaimer usually implies situations that involve some level of uncertainty, waiver, or risk.

A disclaimer may specify mutually agreed and privately arranged terms and conditions as part of a contract; or may specify warnings or expectations to the general public (or some other class of persons) in order to fulfill a duty of care owed to prevent unreasonable risk of harm or injury.

Warranty

In contract law, a warranty has various meanings but generally means a guarantee or promise which provides assurance by one party to the other party that specific facts or conditions are true or will happen. This factual guarantee may be enforced regardless of materiality which allows for a legal remedy if that promise is not true or followed.

Although a warranty is in its simplest form an element of a contract, some warranties run with a product so that a manufacturer makes the warranty to a consumer with which the manufacturer has no direct contractual relationship.

Rehabilitation

Rehabilitation of sensory and cognitive function typically involves methods for retraining neural pathways or training new neural pathways to regain or improve neurocognitive functioning that has been diminished by disease or trauma. Three common neuropsychological problems treatable with rehabilitation are attention deficit/hyperactivity disorder (ADHD), concussion, and spinal cord injury. Rehabilitation research and practices are a fertile area for clinical neuropsychologists and others.

Rehabilitation Act

The Rehabilitation Act of 1973, (Pub.L. 93-112, 87 Stat. 355, enacted September 26, 1973), is a federal law, codified as 29 U.S.C. § 701. The principal sponsor of the bill was Rep. John Brademas [IN-3].

Plea

In legal terms, a plea is simply an answer to a claim made by someone in a criminal case under common law using the adversarial system. Colloquially, a plea has come to mean the assertion by a defendant at arraignment, or otherwise in response to a criminal charge, whether that person pleaded guilty, not guilty, no contest or (in the United States) Alford plea.

The concept of the plea is one of the major differences between criminal procedure under common law and procedure under the civil law system.

Cover

Cover is a term used in the law of contracts to describe a remedy available to a merchant buyer who has received an anticipatory repudiation of a contract for the receipt of goods. Under the Uniform Commercial Code, the buyer is permitted (but not required) to find another source of the same type of goods. The buyer may then file a lawsuit against the breaching seller to recover the difference, if any, between the cost of the goods offered and the cost of the goods actually purchased.

Corporation

A corporation is a separate legal entity that has been incorporated either directly through legislation or through a registration process established by law. Incorporated entities have legal rights and liabilities that are distinct from their employees and shareholders, and may conduct business as either a profit-seeking business or not-for-profit business. Early incorporated entities were established by charter (i.e. by an ad hoc act granted by a monarch or passed by a parliament or legislature).

Consequential

The consequential mood is a verb form used in some Eskimo-Aleut languages to mark dependend adverbial clauses for reason ('because') or time ('when'). Due to the broader meaning of the term mood in the context of Eskimo grammar, the consequential can be considered outside of the proper scope of grammatical mood.

In Central Alaskan Yup'ik, the consequential expresses the meaning 'because':

In Central Siberian Yupik the two forms of the consequential mood are used only for the meanings 'when' and 'while', whereas 'because' is expressed by a particle added to the indicative.

Constitution

A constitution is the set of regulations which govern the conduct of non-political entities, whether incorporated or not. Such entities include corporations and voluntary associations.

11. Domestic and International Sales

CHAPTER QUIZ: KEY TERMS, PEOPLE, PLACES, CONCEPTS

1. Lex mercatoria, often referred to as 'the _________' in English, is the body of commercial law used by merchants throughout Europe during the medieval period. It evolved similar to English common law as a system of custom and best practice, which was enforced through a system of merchant courts along the main trade routes. It functioned as the international law of commerce.

   a. Law merchant
   b. Class Action Fairness Act
   c. Family Entertainment and Copyright Act
   d. Genetic Information Nondiscrimination Act

2. _________ or Healthcare Administration is the field relating to leadership, management, and administration of public health systems, health care systems, hospitals, and hospital networks. Health care administrators are considered health care professionals.

   a. Small Business Liability Relief and Brownfields Revitalization Act
   b. Lex mercatoria
   c. Health Administration
   d. Advertising regulation

3. _________ is the body of commercial law used by merchants throughout Europe during the medieval period. It evolved similar to English common law as a system of custom and best practice, which was enforced through a system of merchant courts along the main trade routes. It functioned as the international law of commerce.

   a. Lex mercatoria
   b. Statutory liability
   c. Bulk sale
   d. Business license

4. _________ is law developed by judges through decisions of courts and similar tribunals, as opposed to statutes adopted through the legislative process or regulations issued by the executive branch.

   A '_________ system' is a legal system that gives great precedential weight to _________, on the principle that it is unfair to treat similar facts differently on different occasions. The body of precedent is called '_________' and it binds future decisions.

   a. Small Business Liability Relief and Brownfields Revitalization Act
   b. Common law
   c. Bulk sale
   d. Business license

5. . _________ is insurance that is purchased by an insurance company from one or more other insurance companies (the 'reinsurer') directly or through a broker as a means of risk management, sometimes in practice including tax mitigation and other reasons described below. The ceding company and the reinsurer enter into a _________ agreement which details the conditions upon which the reinsurer would pay a share of the claims incurred by the ceding company.

The reinsurer is paid a '_________ premium' by the ceding company, which issues insurance policies to its own policyholders.

a. Bancassurance
b. Reinsurance
c. Business interruption insurance
d. Business overhead expense disability insurance

ANSWER KEY
11. Domestic and International Sales

---

1. a
2. c
3. a
4. b
5. b

---

12. Negotiable Instruments, Credit, and Bankruptcy

CHAPTER OUTLINE: KEY TERMS, PEOPLE, PLACES, CONCEPTS

- Pollution
- Portland Cement
- Negotiable instrument
- Promissory note
- Discrimination
- Holder
- Diversity
- Madrid system
- Point
- Mortgage note
- Amendment
- Commission
- First Amendment
- Siemens
- Trade
- Corporation
- Deposit insurance
- Insurance
- Disclaimer
- Discounting
- Estate

12. Negotiable Instruments, Credit, and Bankruptcy

CHAPTER OUTLINE: KEY TERMS, PEOPLE, PLACES, CONCEPTS

- President
- Real estate
- Warranty
- Bankruptcy
- Bankruptcy court
- OPEC
- Partnership
- Arbitration
- Creditor
- Unsecured creditor
- Superfund
- Exoneration
- Secured transaction
- Security interest
- Subrogation
- Lien
- Repossession
- Trust
- Deficiency judgment
- Garnishment
- Principal

12. Negotiable Instruments, Credit, and Bankruptcy

CHAPTER OUTLINE: KEY TERMS, PEOPLE, PLACES, CONCEPTS

______	Tort
______	Ponzi scheme
______	Reinsurance
______	Mechanic's lien
______	Writ
______	CARD Act
______	Credit counseling
______	Liquidation
______	Secured creditor

CHAPTER HIGHLIGHTS & NOTES: KEY TERMS, PEOPLE, PLACES, CONCEPTS

Pollution	Pollution is the introduction of contaminants into the natural environment that cause adverse change. Pollution can take the form of chemical substances or energy, such as noise, heat or light. Pollutants, the components of pollution, can be either foreign substances/energies or naturally occurring contaminants.
Portland Cement	Portland cement is the most common type of cement in general use around the world, used as a basic ingredient of concrete, mortar, stucco, and most non-speciality grout. It developed from other types of hydraulic lime in England in the mid 19th century and usually originates from limestone. It is a fine powder produced by heating materials in a kiln to form what is called clinker, grinding the clinker, and adding small amounts of other materials.
Negotiable instrument	A negotiable instrument is a document guaranteeing the payment of a specific amount of money, either on demand, or at a set time, with the payer named on the document. More specifically, it is a document contemplated by or consisting of a contract, which promises the payment of money without condition, which may be paid either on demand or at a future date.

12. Negotiable Instruments, Credit, and Bankruptcy

Promissory note

A promissory note is a legal instrument, in which one party (the maker or issuer) promises in writing to pay a determinate sum of money to the other (the payee), either at a fixed or determinable future time or on demand of the payee, under specific terms. If the promissory note is unconditional and readily salable, it is called a negotiable instrument.

Referred to as a note payable in accounting (as distinguished from accounts payable), or commonly as just a 'note', it is internationally defined by the Convention providing a uniform law for bills of exchange and promissory notes, although regional variations exist.

Discrimination

Discrimination is action that denies social participation or human rights to categories of people based on prejudice. This includes treatment of an individual or group based on their actual or perceived membership in a certain group or social category, 'in a way that is worse than the way people are usually treated'. It involves the group's initial reaction or interaction, influencing the individual's actual behavior towards the group or the group leader, restricting members of one group from opportunities or privileges that are available to another group, leading to the exclusion of the individual or entities based on logical or irrational decision making.

Holder

Holder is a term used iof any person that has in his custody a promissory note, bill of exchange or cheque. It should be entitled in his own named.

Diversity

The 'business case for diversity' stem from the progression of the models of diversity within the workplace since the 1960s. The original model for diversity was situated around affirmative action drawing strength from the law and a need to comply with equal opportunity employment objectives. This compliance-based model gave rise to the idea that tokenism was the reason an individual was hired into a company when they differed from the dominant group.

Madrid system

The Madrid system is the primary international system for facilitating the registration of trademarks in multiple jurisdictions around the world. Its legal basis is the multilateral treaty Madrid Agreement Concerning the International Registration of Marks of 1891, as well as the Protocol Relating to the Madrid Agreement (1989).

The Madrid system provides a centrally administered system of obtaining a bundle of trademark registrations in separate jurisdictions.

Point

Points, sometimes also called 'discount points', are a form of pre-paid interest. One point equals one percent of the loan amount. By charging a borrower points, a lender effectively increases the yield on the loan above the amount of the stated interest rate.

Mortgage note

In the United States, a mortgage note is a promissory note secured by a specified mortgage loan; it is a written promise to repay a specified sum of money plus interest at a specified rate and length of time to fulfill the promise.

While the mortgage deed or contract itself hypothecates or imposes a lien on the title to real property as security for a loan, the mortgage note states the amount of debt and the rate of interest, and obligates the borrower, who signs the note, personally responsible for repayment. In foreclosure proceedings in certain jurisdictions, borrowers may require the foreclosing party to produce the note as evidence that they are the true owners of the debt.

Amendment

An amendment is a formal or official change made to a law, contract, constitution, or other legal document. It is based on the verb to amend, which means to change. Amendments can add, remove, or update parts of these agreements.

Commission

The payment of commission as remuneration for services rendered or products sold is a common way to reward sales people. Payments often will be calculated on the basis of a percentage of the goods sold. This is a way for firms to solve the principal-agent problem, by attempting to realign employees' interests with those of the firm.

First Amendment

The First Amendment to the United States Constitution prohibits the making of any law respecting an establishment of religion, impeding the free exercise of religion, abridging the freedom of speech, infringing on the freedom of the press, interfering with the right to peaceably assemble or prohibiting the petitioning for a governmental redress of grievances. It was adopted on December 15, 1791, as one of the ten amendments that constitute the Bill of Rights.

The Bill of Rights was originally proposed as a measure to assuage Anti-Federalist opposition to Constitutional ratification.

Siemens

Siemens AG is a German multinational engineering and electronics conglomerate company headquartered in Berlin and Munich. It is Europe's largest engineering company and maker of medical diagnostics equipment and its medical health-care division, which generates about 12 percent of the company's total sales, is its second-most profitable unit behind the industrial automation division.

Siemens' principal activities are in the fields of industry, energy, transportation and healthcare.

Trade

In professional sports, a trade is a sports league transaction involving an exchange of players' contracts or draft picks between sports clubs. Cash is another commodity that may be packaged together with contracts or draft picks to complete a trade. Typically, trades are completed between two clubs, but there are instances where trades are consummated between three or more clubs.

Corporation

A corporation is a separate legal entity that has been incorporated either directly through legislation or through a registration process established by law. Incorporated entities have legal rights and liabilities that are distinct from their employees and shareholders, and may conduct business as either a profit-seeking business or not-for-profit business. Early incorporated entities were established by charter (i.e.

Deposit insurance

Explicit deposit insurance is a measure implemented in many countries to protect bank depositors, in full or in part, from losses caused by a bank's inability to pay its debts when due. Deposit insurance systems are one component of a financial system safety net that promotes financial stability.

Insurance

Insurance is the equitable transfer of the risk of a loss, from one entity to another in exchange for payment. It is a form of risk management primarily used to hedge against the risk of a contingent, uncertain loss.

According to study texts of The Chartered Insurance Institute, there are the following categories of risk:•Financial risks which means that the risk must have financial measurement.•Pure risks which means that the risk must be real and not related to gambling•Particular risks which means that these risks are not widespread in their effect, for example such as earthquake risk for the region prone to it.

It is commonly accepted that only financial, pure and particular risks are insurable.

Disclaimer

A disclaimer is generally any statement intended to specify or delimit the scope of rights and obligations that may be exercised and enforced by parties in a legally recognized relationship. In contrast to other terms for legally operative language, the term disclaimer usually implies situations that involve some level of uncertainty, waiver, or risk.

A disclaimer may specify mutually agreed and privately arranged terms and conditions as part of a contract; or may specify warnings or expectations to the general public (or some other class of persons) in order to fulfill a duty of care owed to prevent unreasonable risk of harm or injury.

Discounting

Discounting is a financial mechanism in which a debtor obtains the right to delay payments to a creditor, for a defined period of time, in exchange for a charge or fee. Essentially, the party that owes money in the present purchases the right to delay the payment until some future date. The discount, or charge, is the difference (expressed as a difference in the same units (absolute) or in percentage terms (relative), or as a ratio) between the original amount owed in the present and the amount that has to be paid in the future to settle the debt.

Estate

An estate comprises the houses and outbuildings and supporting farmland and woods that surround the gardens and grounds of a very large property, such as a country house or mansion. It is the modern term for a manor, but lacks the latter's now abolished jurisdictional authority. It is an 'estate' because the profits from its produce and rents are sufficient to support the household in the house at its center, formerly known as the manor house.

President

A President is a leader of an organization, company, community, club, trade union, university for this article. It is the legally recognized highest 'titled' corporate officer, ranking above the various Vice Presidents (e.g.

Senior Vice President and Executive Vice President), however that post on its own is generally considered subordinate to the Chief Executive Officer. In a similar vein to the Chief Operating Officer, the title of corporate President as a separate position (as opposed to being combined with a 'C-Suite' designation, such as 'President and CEO' or 'President and COO') is also loosely defined.

Real estate

Real estate is “property consisting of land and the buildings on it, along with its natural resources such as crops, minerals, or water; immovable property of this nature; an interest vested in this; an item of real property; (more generally) buildings or housing in general. Also: the business of real estate; the profession of buying, selling, or renting land, buildings or housing.”

It is a legal term used in jurisdictions such as the United States, United Kingdom, Canada, Nigeria, Australia, and New Zealand.

Warranty

In contract law, a warranty has various meanings but generally means a guarantee or promise which provides assurance by one party to the other party that specific facts or conditions are true or will happen. This factual guarantee may be enforced regardless of materiality which allows for a legal remedy if that promise is not true or followed.

Although a warranty is in its simplest form an element of a contract, some warranties run with a product so that a manufacturer makes the warranty to a consumer with which the manufacturer has no direct contractual relationship.

Bankruptcy

Bankruptcy is a legal status of a person or other entity that cannot repay the debts it owes to creditors. In most jurisdictions, bankruptcy is imposed by a court order, often initiated by the debtor.

Bankruptcy is not the only legal status that an insolvent person or other entity may have, and the term bankruptcy is therefore not a synonym for insolvency.

Bankruptcy court

United States bankruptcy courts are courts created under Article I of the United States Constitution. They function as units of the district courts and have subject-matter jurisdiction over bankruptcy cases. The federal district courts have original and exclusive jurisdiction over all cases arising under the bankruptcy code and bankruptcy cases cannot be filed in state court.

OPEC

OPEC is an international organization and economic cartel whose mission is to coordinate the policies of the oil-producing countries. The goal is to secure a steady income to the member states and to collude in influencing world oil prices through economic means.

OPEC is an intergovernmental organization that was created at the Baghdad Conference on 10-14 September 1960, by Iraq, Kuwait, Iran, Saudi Arabia and Venezuela.

12. Negotiable Instruments, Credit, and Bankruptcy

CHAPTER HIGHLIGHTS & NOTES: KEY TERMS, PEOPLE, PLACES, CONCEPTS

Partnership

A partnership is an arrangement in which parties agree to cooperate to advance their mutual interests.

Since humans are social beings, partnerships between individuals, businesses, interest-based organizations, schools, governments, and varied combinations thereof, have always been and remain commonplace. In the most frequently associated instance of the term, a partnership is formed between one or more businesses in which partners (owners) co-labor to achieve and share profits and losses .

Arbitration

Arbitration, a form of alternative dispute resolution, is a technique for the resolution of disputes outside the courts. The parties to a dispute refer it to arbitration by one or more persons (the 'arbitrators', 'arbiters' or 'arbitral tribunal'), and agree to be bound by the arbitration decision (the 'award'). A third party reviews the evidence in the case and imposes a decision that is legally binding on both sides and enforceable in the courts.

Creditor

A creditor is a party that has a claim on the services of a second party. It is a person or institution to whom money is owed. The first party, in general, has provided some property or service to the second party under the assumption (usually enforced by contract) that the second party will return an equivalent property and service.

Unsecured creditor

An unsecured creditor is a creditor other than a preferential creditor that does not have the benefit of any security interests in the assets of the debtor.

In the event of the bankruptcy of the debtor, the unsecured creditors usually obtain a pari passu distribution out of the assets of the insolvent company on a liquidation in accordance with the size of their debt after the secured creditors have enforced their security and the preferential creditors have exhausted their claims.

Although in a liquidation the unsecured creditors will usually realize the smallest proportion of their claims, in some legal systems, unsecured creditors who are also indebted to the insolvent debtor can set off the debts, actually putting the unsecured creditor with a matured liability to the debtor in a pre-preferential position.

Superfund

Superfund or Comprehensive Environmental Response, Compensation, and Liability Act of 1980 is a United States federal law designed to clean up sites contaminated with hazardous substances as well as broadly defined 'pollutants or contaminants'. Superfund also gives authority to federal natural resource agencies, states and Native American tribes to recover natural resource damages caused by releases of hazardous substances, and it created the Agency for Toxic Substances and Disease Registry .•A section 104..

Exoneration

Exoneration occurs when a person who has been convicted of a crime is later proved to have been innocent of that crime.

Attempts to exonerate convicts are particularly controversial in death penalty cases, especially where new evidence is put forth after the execution has taken place.

The term 'exoneration' also is used in criminal law to indicate a surety bail bond has been satisfied, completed, and exonerated.

Secured transaction

Generally, a secured transaction is a loan or a credit transaction in which the lender acquires a security interest in collateral owned by the borrower and is entitled to foreclose on or repossess the collateral in the event of the borrower's default. The terms of the relationship are governed by a contract, or security agreement. A common example would be a consumer who purchases a car on credit.

Security interest

A security interest is a property interest created by agreement or by operation of law over assets to secure the performance of an obligation, usually the payment of a debt. It gives the beneficiary of the security interest certain preferential rights in the disposition of secured assets. Such rights vary according to the type of security interest, but in most cases, a holder of the security interest is entitled to seize, and usually sell, the property to discharge the debt that the security interest secures.

Subrogation

Subrogation is the legal doctrine whereby one person takes over the rights or remedies of a creditor against his/her debtor. Rights of subrogation can arise two different ways: either automatically as a matter of law, or by agreement as part of a contract. Subrogation by contract most commonly arises in contracts of insurance.

Lien

In law, a lien is a form of security interest granted over an item of property to secure the payment of a debt or performance of some other obligation. The owner of the property, who grants the lien, is referred to as the lieneeand the person who has the benefit of the lien is referred to as the lienor or lien holder.

The etymological root is Anglo-French lien, loyen 'bond', 'restraint', from Latin ligamen, from ligare 'to bind'.

Repossession

Repossession is generally used to refer to a financial institution taking back an object that was either used as collateral or rented or leased in a transaction. Repossession is a 'self-help' type of action in which the party having right of ownership of the property in question takes the property back from the party having right of possession without invoking court proceedings. The property is then sold on by either the financial institution or 3rd party sellers.

Trust

A 'trust,' or 'corporate trust' is a large business. Originally, it was Standard Oil, which was already the largest corporation in the world

12. Negotiable Instruments, Credit, and Bankruptcy

CHAPTER HIGHLIGHTS & NOTES: KEY TERMS, PEOPLE, PLACES, CONCEPTS

Deficiency judgment	A deficiency judgment is an unsecured money judgment against a borrower whose mortgage foreclosure sale did not produce sufficient funds to pay the underlying promissory note, or loan, in full. The availability of a deficiency judgment depends on whether the lender has a recourse or nonrecourse loan, which is largely a matter of state law. In some jurisdictions, the original loan(s) obtained to purchase property is/are non-recourse, but subsequent refinancing of a first mortgage and/or acquisition of a 2nd (3rd., etc).
Garnishment	Garnishment is an American legal order for collecting a monetary judgment on behalf of a plaintiff from a defendant. The money can come directly from the defendant (the garnishee) or - at a court's discretion - from a third party. Jurisdiction law may allow for collection - without a judgment or other court order - in the case of collecting for taxes.
Principal	In commercial law, a principal is a person, legal or natural, who authorizes an agent to act to create one or more legal relationships with a third party. This branch of law is called agency and relies on the common law proposition qui facit per alium, facit per se (Latin 'he who acts through another, acts personally'). It is a parallel concept to vicarious liability and strict liability (in which one person is held liable for the acts or omissions of another) in criminal law or torts.
Tort	A tort, in common law jurisdictions, is a civil wrong that unfairly causes someone else to suffer loss or harm resulting in legal liability for the person who commits the tortious act, called a tortfeasor. Although crimes may be torts, the cause of legal action is not necessarily a crime, as the harm may be due to negligence which does not amount to criminal negligence. The victim of the harm can recover their loss as damages in a lawsuit.
Ponzi scheme	A Ponzi scheme is a fraudulent investment operation where the operator, an individual or organization, pays returns to its investors from new capital paid to the operators by new investors, rather than from profit earned by the operator. Operators of Ponzi schemes usually entice new investors by offering higher returns than other investments, in the form of short-term returns that are either abnormally high or unusually consistent. The perpetuation of the high returns requires an ever-increasing flow of money from new investors to sustain the scheme.
Reinsurance	Reinsurance is insurance that is purchased by an insurance company from one or more other insurance companies (the 'reinsurer') directly or through a broker as a means of risk management, sometimes in practice including tax mitigation and other reasons described below. The ceding company and the reinsurer enter into a reinsurance agreement which details the conditions upon which the reinsurer would pay a share of the claims incurred by the ceding company. The reinsurer is paid a 'reinsurance premium' by the ceding company, which issues insurance policies to its own policyholders.

Mechanic's lien	A mechanic's lien is a security interest in the title to property for the benefit of those who have supplied labor or materials that improve the property. The lien exists for both real property and personal property. In the realm of real property, it is called by various names, including, generically, construction lien.
Writ	In common law, a writ is a formal written order issued by a body with administrative or judicial jurisdiction; in modern usage, this body is generally a court. Warrants, prerogative writs and subpoenas are common types of writs but there are many others.
CARD Act	The Credit Card Accountability Responsibility and Disclosure Act of 2009 or Credit CARD Act of 2009 is a federal statute passed by the United States Congress and signed by President Barack Obama on May 22, 2009. It is comprehensive credit card reform legislation that aims '...to establish fair and transparent practices relating to the extension of credit under an open end consumer credit plan, and for other purposes.' The bill was passed with bipartisan support by both the House of Representatives and the Senate.
Credit counseling	Credit counseling is a process that involves offering education to consumers about how to avoid incurring debts that cannot be repaid through establishing an effective Debt Management Plan and Budget. Credit counseling is usually less typified by functions of credit education or the psychology of spending habits, rather credit counseling establishes a planned method of debt relief, typically through a Debt Management Plan. Credit counseling often involves negotiating with creditors to establish a debt management plan (DMP) for a consumer.
Liquidation	In law, liquidation is the process by which a company is brought to an end, and the assets and property of the company are redistributed. Liquidation is also sometimes referred to as winding-up or dissolution, although dissolution technically refers to the last stage of liquidation. The process of liquidation also arises when customs, an authority or agency in a country responsible for collecting and safeguarding customs duties, determines the final computation or ascertainment of the duties or drawback accruing on an entry.
Secured creditor	A secured creditor is a creditor with the benefit of a security interest over some or all of the assets of the debtor. In the event of the bankruptcy of the debtor, the secured creditor can enforce security against the assets of the debtor and avoid competing for a distribution on liquidation with the unsecured creditors. In most legal systems, secured creditors also have the option of releasing their security and proving in the liquidation, although, in practice, they would rarely do so.

12. Negotiable Instruments, Credit, and Bankruptcy

CHAPTER QUIZ: KEY TERMS, PEOPLE, PLACES, CONCEPTS

1. A _________ is a separate legal entity that has been incorporated either directly through legislation or through a registration process established by law. Incorporated entities have legal rights and liabilities that are distinct from their employees and shareholders, and may conduct business as either a profit-seeking business or not-for-profit business. Early incorporated entities were established by charter (i.e. by an ad hoc act granted by a monarch or passed by a parliament or legislature).

   a. Bulk sale
   b. Business license
   c. Business method patent
   d. Corporation

2. In law, a _________ is a form of security interest granted over an item of property to secure the payment of a debt or performance of some other obligation. The owner of the property, who grants the _________, is referred to as the lieneeand the person who has the benefit of the _________ is referred to as the lienor or _________ holder.

   The etymological root is Anglo-French _________, loyen 'bond', 'restraint', from Latin ligamen, from ligare 'to bind'.

   a. Bulk sale
   b. Lien
   c. Business method patent
   d. Business valuation

3. The 'business case for _________' stem from the progression of the models of _________ within the workplace since the 1960s. The original model for _________ was situated around affirmative action drawing strength from the law and a need to comply with equal opportunity employment objectives. This compliance-based model gave rise to the idea that tokenism was the reason an individual was hired into a company when they differed from the dominant group.

   a. Being Globally Responsible Conference
   b. Black Company
   c. Bribery Act 2010
   d. Diversity

4. . A _________ is a legal instrument, in which one party (the maker or issuer) promises in writing to pay a determinate sum of money to the other (the payee), either at a fixed or determinable future time or on demand of the payee, under specific terms. If the _________ is unconditional and readily salable, it is called a negotiable instrument.

   Referred to as a note payable in accounting (as distinguished from accounts payable), or commonly as just a 'note', it is internationally defined by the Convention providing a uniform law for bills of exchange and _________s, although regional variations exist.

   a. 3D floor plan
   b. 999-year lease
   c. Promissory note

5. _________ is a legal status of a person or other entity that cannot repay the debts it owes to creditors. In most jurisdictions, _________ is imposed by a court order, often initiated by the debtor.

   _________ is not the only legal status that an insolvent person or other entity may have, and the term _________ is therefore not a synonym for insolvency.

   a. Bankruptcy
   b. Financial scandal in the Orthodox Church in America
   c. HP Autonomy
   d. James Henry Ting Wei

ANSWER KEY
12. Negotiable Instruments, Credit, and Bankruptcy

---

1. d
2. b
3. d
4. c
5. a

---

13. Business Organizations

CHAPTER OUTLINE: KEY TERMS, PEOPLE, PLACES, CONCEPTS

- ____ Business name
- ____ General partnership
- ____ Partnership
- ____ Proprietorship
- ____ Sole
- ____ Revised Uniform Partnership Act
- ____ Uniform Partnership Act
- ____ Duty
- ____ Commission
- ____ Limited partnership
- ____ Revised Uniform Limited Partnership Act
- ____ Articles of Incorporation
- ____ Certificate of incorporation
- ____ Charter
- ____ Corporation
- ____ Quorum
- ____ Shareholder
- ____ Board of directors
- ____ Business judgment
- ____ Business judgment rule
- ____ President

13. Business Organizations

CHAPTER OUTLINE: KEY TERMS, PEOPLE, PLACES, CONCEPTS

- Madrid system
- Double taxation
- Procedural law
- Professional corporation
- Insurance
- Pollution
- Income
- OPEC
- Reinsurance
- Operating agreement
- Limited liability
- Trade
- Trade dress
- Fraud

Business name	A trade name, trading name, or business name, is a name that a business uses for trading commercial products or services. A business may also use its registered, legal name for contracts and other formal purposes. In English writing, trade names are generally treated as proper nouns.
General partnership	In the commercial and legal parlance of most countries, a general partnership, refers to an association of persons or an unincorporated company with the following major features: It is a partnership in which partners share equally in both responsibility and liability.
Partnership	A partnership is an arrangement in which parties agree to cooperate to advance their mutual interests. Since humans are social beings, partnerships between individuals, businesses, interest-based organizations, schools, governments, and varied combinations thereof, have always been and remain commonplace. In the most frequently associated instance of the term, a partnership is formed between one or more businesses in which partners (owners) co-labor to achieve and share profits and losses .
Proprietorship	A sole proprietorship, also known as the sole trader or simply a proprietorship, is a type of business entity that is owned and run by one individual and in which there is no legal distinction between the owner and the business. The owner receives all profits and has unlimited responsibility for all losses and debts. Every asset of the business is owned by the proprietor and all debts of the business are the proprietor's.
Sole	Sole is a group of flatfish belonging to several families. Generally speaking, they are members of the family Soleidae, but, outside Europe, the name sole is also applied to various other similar flatfish, especially other members of the sole suborder Soleoidei as well as members of the flounder family. In European cookery, there are several species which may be considered true soles, but the common or Dover sole Solea solea, often simply called the sole, is the most esteemed and most widely available.
Revised Uniform Partnership Act	The Uniform Partnership Act, which includes revisions that are sometimes called the Revised Uniform Partnership Act is a uniform act (similar to a model statute), proposed by the National Conference of Commissioners on Uniform State Laws ('NCCUSL') for the governance of business partnerships by U.S. States. Several versions of UPA have been promulgated by the NCCUSL, the earliest having been put forth in 1914, and the most recent in 1997.
Uniform Partnership Act	The Uniform Partnership Act, which includes revisions that are sometimes called the Revised Uniform Partnership Act is a uniform act (similar to a model statute), proposed by the National Conference of Commissioners on Uniform State Laws ('NCCUSL') for the governance of business partnerships by U.S. States.

Several versions of Uniform Partnership Act have been promulgated by the NCCUSL, the earliest having been put forth in 1914, and the most recent in 1997.

Duty

Duty is a term that conveys a sense of moral commitment or obligation to someone or something. The moral commitment should result in action; it is not a matter of passive feeling or mere recognition. When someone recognizes a duty, that person theoretically commits themself to its fulfillment without considering their own self-interest.

Commission

The payment of commission as remuneration for services rendered or products sold is a common way to reward sales people. Payments often will be calculated on the basis of a percentage of the goods sold. This is a way for firms to solve the principal-agent problem, by attempting to realign employees' interests with those of the firm.

Limited partnership

A limited partnership is a form of partnership similar to a general partnership, except that in addition to one or more general partners, there are one or more limited partners (LPs). It is a partnership in which only one partner is required to be a general partner.

The GPs are, in all major respects, in the same legal position as partners in a conventional firm, i.e. they have management control, share the right to use partnership property, share the profits of the firm in predefined proportions, and have joint and several liability for the debts of the partnership.

Revised Uniform Limited Partnership Act

The Uniform Limited Partnership Act, which includes its 1976 revision called the Revised Uniform Limited Partnership Act is a uniform act (similar to a model statute), proposed by the National Conference of Commissioners on Uniform State Laws ('NCCUSL') for the governance of business partnerships by U.S. States. The NCCUSL promulgated the original ULPA in 1916 and the most recent revision in 2001.

Articles of Incorporation

The 'Articles of Incorporation' are the primary rules governing the management of a corporation in the United States and Canada, and are filed with a state or other regulatory agency.

An equivalent term for LLCs in the United States is the Articles of Organization. For terms with similar meaning in other countries, see articles of association.

Certificate of incorporation

A certificate of incorporation is a legal document relating to the formation of a company or corporation. It is a license to form a corporation issued by state government. Its precise meaning depends upon the legal system in which it is used.

Charter

A charter is the grant of authority or rights, stating that the granter formally recognizes the prerogative of the recipient to exercise the rights specified. It is implicit that the granter retains superiority (or sovereignty), and that the recipient admits a limited (or inferior) status within the relationship, and it is within that sense that charters were historically granted, and that sense is retained in modern usage of the term.

Corporation	A corporation is a separate legal entity that has been incorporated either directly through legislation or through a registration process established by law. Incorporated entities have legal rights and liabilities that are distinct from their employees and shareholders, and may conduct business as either a profit-seeking business or not-for-profit business. Early incorporated entities were established by charter (i.e. by an ad hoc act granted by a monarch or passed by a parliament or legislature).
Quorum	A quorum is the minimum number of members of a deliberative assembly necessary to conduct the business of that group. According to Robert's Rules of Order Newly Revised, the 'requirement for a quorum is protection against totally unrepresentative action in the name of the body by an unduly small number of persons.' The term quorum is from a Middle English wording of the commission formerly issued to justices of the peace, derived from Latin quorum, 'of whom', genitive plural of qui, 'who'. As a result, quora as plural of quorum is not a valid Latin formation.
Shareholder	A shareholder or stockholder is an individual or institution that legally owns a share of stock in a public or private corporation. Shareholders are the owners of a limited company. They buy shares which represent part ownership of a company.
Board of directors	A board of directors is a body of elected or appointed members who jointly oversee the activities of a company or organization. Other names include board of governors, board of managers, board of regents, board of trustees, and board of visitors. It is often simply referred to as 'the board'.
Business judgment	The business judgment rule is a United States case law-derived doctrine in corporations law where courts defer to the business judgment of corporate executives. This doctrine is rooted in the principle that the 'directors of a corporation . . . are clothed with the presumption, which the law accords to them, of being motivated in their conduct by a bona fide regard for the interests of the corporation whose affairs the stockholders have committed to their charge'.
Business judgment rule	The business judgment rule is a United States case law-derived doctrine in corporations law where courts defer to the business judgment of corporate executives. This doctrine is rooted in the principle that the 'directors of a corporation .
President	A President is a leader of an organization, company, community, club, trade union, university for this article. It is the legally recognized highest 'titled' corporate officer, ranking above the various Vice Presidents (e.g. Senior Vice President and Executive Vice President), however that post on its own is generally considered subordinate to the Chief Executive Officer. In a similar vein to the Chief Operating Officer, the title of corporate President as a separate position (as opposed to being combined with a 'C-Suite' designation, such as 'President and CEO' or 'President and COO') is also loosely defined.

Madrid system	The Madrid system is the primary international system for facilitating the registration of trademarks in multiple jurisdictions around the world. Its legal basis is the multilateral treaty Madrid Agreement Concerning the International Registration of Marks of 1891, as well as the Protocol Relating to the Madrid Agreement (1989). The Madrid system provides a centrally administered system of obtaining a bundle of trademark registrations in separate jurisdictions.
Double taxation	Double taxation is the levying of tax by two or more jurisdictions on the same declared income, asset (in the case of capital taxes), or financial transaction (in the case of sales taxes). This double liability is often mitigated by tax treaties between countries. The term 'double taxation' is additionally used, particularly in the USA, to refer to the fact that corporate profits are taxed and the shareholders of the corporation are (usually) subject to personal taxation when they receive dividends or distributions of those profits.
Procedural law	Procedural law or adjective law comprises the rules by which a court hears and determines what happens in civil lawsuit, criminal or administrative proceedings. The rules are designed to ensure a fair and consistent application of due process (in the U.S). or fundamental justice (in other common law countries) to all cases that come before a court.
Professional corporation	Professional corporations are those corporate entities for which many corporation statutes make special provision, regulating the use of the corporate form by licensed professionals such as attorneys, architects, engineers, public accountants and physicians. Legal regulations applying to professional corporations typically differ in important ways from those applying to other corporations. Professional corporations, which may have a single director or multiple directors, do not usually afford that person or persons the same degree of limitation of liability as ordinary business corporations (cf.
Insurance	Insurance is the equitable transfer of the risk of a loss, from one entity to another in exchange for payment. It is a form of risk management primarily used to hedge against the risk of a contingent, uncertain loss. According to study texts of The Chartered Insurance Institute, there are the following categories of risk:•Financial risks which means that the risk must have financial measurement.•Pure risks which means that the risk must be real and not related to gambling•Particular risks which means that these risks are not widespread in their effect, for example such as earthquake risk for the region prone to it. It is commonly accepted that only financial, pure and particular risks are insurable.

Pollution	Pollution is the introduction of contaminants into the natural environment that cause adverse change. Pollution can take the form of chemical substances or energy, such as noise, heat or light. Pollutants, the components of pollution, can be either foreign substances/energies or naturally occurring contaminants.
Income	Income is the consumption and savings opportunity gained by an entity within a specified timeframe, which is generally expressed in monetary terms. However, for households and individuals, 'income is the sum of all the wages, salaries, profits, interests payments, rents and other forms of earnings received... in a given period of time.' In the field of public economics, the term may refer to the accumulation of both monetary and non-monetary consumption ability, with the former (monetary) being used as a proxy for total income.
OPEC	OPEC is an international organization and economic cartel whose mission is to coordinate the policies of the oil-producing countries. The goal is to secure a steady income to the member states and to collude in influencing world oil prices through economic means. OPEC is an intergovernmental organization that was created at the Baghdad Conference on 10-14 September 1960, by Iraq, Kuwait, Iran, Saudi Arabia and Venezuela.
Reinsurance	Reinsurance is insurance that is purchased by an insurance company from one or more other insurance companies (the 'reinsurer') directly or through a broker as a means of risk management, sometimes in practice including tax mitigation and other reasons described below. The ceding company and the reinsurer enter into a reinsurance agreement which details the conditions upon which the reinsurer would pay a share of the claims incurred by the ceding company. The reinsurer is paid a 'reinsurance premium' by the ceding company, which issues insurance policies to its own policyholders.
Operating agreement	An operating agreement is an agreement among limited liability company Members governing the LLC's business, and Member's financial and managerial rights and duties. Many states in the United States require an LLC to have an Operating Agreement. LLCs operating without an Operating Agreement are governed by the State's default rules contained in the relevant statute and developed through state court decisions.
Limited liability	Limited liability is where a person's financial liability is limited to a fixed sum, most commonly the value of a person's investment in a company or partnership. If a company with limited liability is sued, then the plaintiffs are suing the company, not its owners or investors. A shareholder in a limited company is not personally liable for any of the debts of the company, other than for the value of their investment in that company.
Trade	In professional sports, a trade is a sports league transaction involving an exchange of players' contracts or draft picks between sports clubs.

13. Business Organizations

CHAPTER HIGHLIGHTS & NOTES: KEY TERMS, PEOPLE, PLACES, CONCEPTS

	Cash is another commodity that may be packaged together with contracts or draft picks to complete a trade. Typically, trades are completed between two clubs, but there are instances where trades are consummated between three or more clubs.
Trade dress	Trade dress is a legal term of art that generally refers to characteristics of the visual appearance of a product or its packaging that signify the source of the product to consumers. Trade dress is a form of intellectual property.
Fraud	Fraud is a deception deliberately practiced in order to secure unfair or unlawful gain (adjectival form fraudulent; to defraud is the verb). As a legal construct, fraud is both a civil wrong (i.e., a fraud victim may sue the fraud perpetrator to avoid the fraud and/or recover monetary compensation) and a criminal wrong (i.e., a fraud perpetrator may be prosecuted and imprisoned by governmental authorities). Defrauding people or organizations of money or valuables is the usual purpose of fraud, but it sometimes instead involves obtaining benefits without actually depriving anyone of money or valuables, such as obtaining a drivers license by way of false statements made in an application for the same.

CHAPTER QUIZ: KEY TERMS, PEOPLE, PLACES, CONCEPTS

1. A _________ or stockholder is an individual or institution that legally owns a share of stock in a public or private corporation. _________s are the owners of a limited company. They buy shares which represent part ownership of a company.

   a. Small Business Liability Relief and Brownfields Revitalization Act
   b. Business license
   c. Business method patent
   d. Shareholder

2. The payment of _________ as remuneration for services rendered or products sold is a common way to reward sales people. Payments often will be calculated on the basis of a percentage of the goods sold. This is a way for firms to solve the principal-agent problem, by attempting to realign employees' interests with those of the firm.

   a. Commission
   b. Big boy letter
   c. Bonus clause
   d. Breach of contract

3. . The Uniform Partnership Act, which includes revisions that are sometimes called the _________ is a uniform act (similar to a model statute), proposed by the National Conference of Commissioners on Uniform State Laws ('NCCUSL') for the governance of business partnerships by U.S. States.

Several versions of UPA have been promulgated by the NCCUSL, the earliest having been put forth in 1914, and the most recent in 1997.

a. Small Business Liability Relief and Brownfields Revitalization Act
b. Business license
c. Business method patent
d. Revised Uniform Partnership Act

4. A trade name, trading name, or _________, is a name that a business uses for trading commercial products or services. A business may also use its registered, legal name for contracts and other formal purposes. In English writing, trade names are generally treated as proper nouns.

   a. Business name
   b. Class Action Fairness Act
   c. Family Entertainment and Copyright Act
   d. Genetic Information Nondiscrimination Act

5. In the commercial and legal parlance of most countries, a _________, refers to an association of persons or an unincorporated company with the following major features:

   It is a partnership in which partners share equally in both responsibility and liability.

   a. General partnership
   b. Limited partner
   c. Partnership agreement
   d. Revised Uniform Partnership Act

ANSWER KEY
13. Business Organizations

---

1. d
2. a
3. d
4. a
5. a

---

14. Agency and the Employment Relationship

CHAPTER OUTLINE: KEY TERMS, PEOPLE, PLACES, CONCEPTS

- Blackacre
- Lanham Act
- President
- Special agent
- Commission
- Ratification
- Estoppel
- Principal
- Apparent authority
- Implied authority
- Duty
- Duty of loyalty
- Reasonable care
- Contract
- Disclaimer
- Warranty
- Undisclosed principal
- Income
- Corporation
- Independent contractor
- Environmental Protection

CHAPTER OUTLINE: KEY TERMS, PEOPLE, PLACES, CONCEPTS

	Bechtel
	Communications Decency Act
	Patent
	Patent troll
	Tort
	Troll
	Constitution
	Resource
	Respondeat superior
	Pollution
	Negligent hiring

CHAPTER HIGHLIGHTS & NOTES: KEY TERMS, PEOPLE, PLACES, CONCEPTS

Blackacre

Blackacre, Whiteacre, Greenacre, Brownacre, and variations are the placeholder names used for fictitious estates in land.

The names are used by professors of law in common law jurisdictions, particularly in the area of real property and occasionally in contracts, to discuss the rights of various parties to a piece of land. A typical law school or bar exam question on real property might say:

Adam, owner of a fee simple in Blackacre, conveyed the property 'to Bill for life, remainder to Charles, provided that if any person should consume alcohol on the property before the first born son of Charles turns twenty-one, then the property shall go to Dwight in fee simple.' Assume that neither Bill, Charles, or Dwight is an heir of Adam, and that Adam's only heir is his son, Edward.

Lanham Act

The Lanham Act (Pub.L. 79-489, 60 Stat. 427, enacted July 5, 1946, codified at 15 U.S.C.

§ 1051 et seq. (15 U.S.C. ch. 22)) is the primary federal trademark statute of law in the United States. The Act prohibits a number of activities, including trademark infringement, trademark dilution, and false advertising.

President

A President is a leader of an organization, company, community, club, trade union, university for this article. It is the legally recognized highest 'titled' corporate officer, ranking above the various Vice Presidents (e.g. Senior Vice President and Executive Vice President), however that post on its own is generally considered subordinate to the Chief Executive Officer. In a similar vein to the Chief Operating Officer, the title of corporate President as a separate position (as opposed to being combined with a 'C-Suite' designation, such as 'President and CEO' or 'President and COO') is also loosely defined.

Special agent

In the United States, Special Agent is usually the title for a detective or investigator for a state, county, municipal, federal or tribal government who conducts criminal investigations and has arrest authority. An Agent is a federal law enforcement officer with arrest authority but who does not conduct major criminal investigations or who may conduct investigations but does not have arrest authority, Special Agents being distinctly able to do both.

Commission

The payment of commission as remuneration for services rendered or products sold is a common way to reward sales people. Payments often will be calculated on the basis of a percentage of the goods sold. This is a way for firms to solve the principal-agent problem, by attempting to realign employees' interests with those of the firm.

Ratification

Ratification is a principal's approval of an act of its agent where the agent lacked authority to legally bind the principal. The term applies to private contract law, international treaties, and constitutions in federations such as the United States and Canada.

Estoppel

In law, estoppel is a set of doctrines in which a court prevents a litigant from taking an action the litigant normally would have the right to take, in order to prevent an inequitable result. For example, estoppel precludes 'a person from denying, or asserting anything to the contrary of, that which has, in contemplation of law, been established as the truth, either by the acts of judicial or legislative officers, or by his own deed, acts, or representations, either express or implied'.

Principal

In commercial law, a principal is a person, legal or natural, who authorizes an agent to act to create one or more legal relationships with a third party. This branch of law is called agency and relies on the common law proposition qui facit per alium, facit per se (Latin 'he who acts through another, acts personally').

It is a parallel concept to vicarious liability and strict liability (in which one person is held liable for the acts or omissions of another) in criminal law or torts.

Apparent authority	In the United States, the United Kingdom and South Africa, apparent authority relates to the doctrines of the law of agency. It is relevant particularly in corporate law and constitutional law. Apparent authority refers to a situation where a reasonable person would understand that an agent had authority to act.
Implied authority	Not written responsibilities is a legal term. In contract law, it is the implied ability of an individual to make a legally binding contract on behalf of an organization, by way of uniform or interaction with the public on behalf of that organization. When a person is wearing a uniform or nametag bearing the logo or trademark of a business or organization; or if that person is functioning in an obviously authorized capacity on behalf of a business or organization, that person carries an Implied Authority of Contract.
Duty	Duty is a term that conveys a sense of moral commitment or obligation to someone or something. The moral commitment should result in action; it is not a matter of passive feeling or mere recognition. When someone recognizes a duty, that person theoretically commits themself to its fulfillment without considering their own self-interest.
Duty of loyalty	Duty of Loyalty is a term used in corporation law to describe a fiduciaries' 'conflicts of interest and requires fiduciaries to put the corporation's interests ahead of their own.' 'Corporate fiduciaries breach their duty of loyalty when they divert corporate assets, opportunities, or information for personal gain.' It is generally acceptable if a director makes a decision for the corporation that profits both him and the corporation. The duty of loyalty is breached when the director puts his or her interest in front of that of the corporation.
Reasonable care	In tort law, a duty of care is a legal obligation, which is imposed on an individual requiring adherence to a standard of reasonable care while performing any acts that could foreseeably harm others. It is the first element that must be established to proceed with an action in negligence. The claimant must be able to show a duty of care imposed by law which the defendant has breached.
Contract	In common law legal systems, a contract is an agreement having a lawful object entered into voluntarily by two or more parties, each of whom intends to create one or more legal obligations between them. The elements of a contract are 'offer' and 'acceptance' by 'competent persons' having legal capacity who exchange 'consideration' to create 'mutuality of obligation.' Proof of some or all of these elements may be done in writing, though contracts may be made entirely orally or by conduct. The remedy for breach of contract can be 'damages' in the form of compensation of money or specific performance enforced through an injunction.
Disclaimer	A disclaimer is generally any statement intended to specify or delimit the scope of rights and obligations that may be exercised and enforced by parties in a legally recognized relationship.

In contrast to other terms for legally operative language, the term disclaimer usually implies situations that involve some level of uncertainty, waiver, or risk.

A disclaimer may specify mutually agreed and privately arranged terms and conditions as part of a contract; or may specify warnings or expectations to the general public (or some other class of persons) in order to fulfill a duty of care owed to prevent unreasonable risk of harm or injury.

Warranty

In contract law, a warranty has various meanings but generally means a guarantee or promise which provides assurance by one party to the other party that specific facts or conditions are true or will happen. This factual guarantee may be enforced regardless of materiality which allows for a legal remedy if that promise is not true or followed.

Although a warranty is in its simplest form an element of a contract, some warranties run with a product so that a manufacturer makes the warranty to a consumer with which the manufacturer has no direct contractual relationship.

Undisclosed principal

In agency law, an undisclosed principal is a person who uses an agent for negotiations with a third party who has no knowledge of the identity of the agent's principal. Often in such situations, the agent pretends to be acting for himself or herself. As a result, the third party does not know to look to the real principal in a dispute.

Income

Income is the consumption and savings opportunity gained by an entity within a specified timeframe, which is generally expressed in monetary terms. However, for households and individuals, 'income is the sum of all the wages, salaries, profits, interests payments, rents and other forms of earnings received... in a given period of time.'

In the field of public economics, the term may refer to the accumulation of both monetary and non-monetary consumption ability, with the former (monetary) being used as a proxy for total income.

Corporation

A corporation is a separate legal entity that has been incorporated either directly through legislation or through a registration process established by law. Incorporated entities have legal rights and liabilities that are distinct from their employees and shareholders, and may conduct business as either a profit-seeking business or not-for-profit business. Early incorporated entities were established by charter (i.e. by an ad hoc act granted by a monarch or passed by a parliament or legislature).

Independent contractor

An independent contractor is a natural person, business, or corporation that provides goods or services to another entity under terms specified in a contract or within a verbal agreement. Unlike an employee, an independent contractor does not work regularly for an employer but works as and when required, during which time he or she may be subject to law of agency. Independent contractors are usually paid on a freelance basis.

Environmental Protection	Environmental protection is a practice of protecting the natural environment on individual, organizational or governmental levels, for the benefit of both the natural environment and humans. Due to the pressures of population and technology, the biophysical environment is being degraded, sometimes permanently. This has been recognized, and governments have begun placing restraints on activities that cause environmental degradation.
Bechtel	Bechtel Corporation (Bechtel Group) is the largest construction and engineering company in the United States, ranking as the 4th-largest privately owned company in the United States. Its headquarters are in the South of Market, San Francisco. As of 2012, Bechtel had $37.9 billion in revenue and employed 53,000 workers on projects in nearly 50 countries.
Communications Decency Act	The Communications Decency Act of 1996, also known by some legislators as the 'Great Cyberporn Panic of 1995', was the first notable attempt by the United States Congress to regulate pornographic material on the Internet. In 1997, in the landmark cyberlaw case of Reno v. ACLU, the United States Supreme Court struck the anti-indecency provisions of the Act. The Act was Title V of the Telecommunications Act of 1996. It was introduced to the Senate Committee of Commerce, Science, and Transportation by Senators James Exon (D-NE) and Slade Gorton (R-WA) in 1995. The amendment that became the Communications Decency Act was added to the Telecommunications Act in the Senate by an 84-16 vote on June 14, 1995.
Patent	A patent is a set of exclusive rights granted by a sovereign state to an inventor or assignee for a limited period of time in exchange for detailed public disclosure of an invention. An invention is a solution to a specific technological problem and is a product or a process. Patents are a form of intellectual property.
Patent troll	A patent troll, also called a patent assertion entity, is a person or company who enforces patent rights against accused infringers in an attempt to collect licensing fees, but does not manufacture products or supply services based upon the patents in question, thus engaging in economic rent-seeking. Related, less pejorative terms include patent holding company, the type of light bulb Edison wanted to develop. Edison bought the patent for US$5,000 ($122,190 in present-day terms) to eliminate the possibility of a later challenge by Woodward and Evans.•Opposition proceeding.
Tort	A tort, in common law jurisdictions, is a civil wrong that unfairly causes someone else to suffer loss or harm resulting in legal liability for the person who commits the tortious act, called a tortfeasor. Although crimes may be torts, the cause of legal action is not necessarily a crime, as the harm may be due to negligence which does not amount to criminal negligence. The victim of the harm can recover their loss as damages in a lawsuit.

14. Agency and the Employment Relationship

CHAPTER HIGHLIGHTS & NOTES: KEY TERMS, PEOPLE, PLACES, CONCEPTS

Troll

In Internet slang, a troll is a person who sows discord on the Internet by starting arguments or upsetting people, by posting inflammatory, extraneous, or off-topic messages in an online community (such as a newsgroup, forum, chat room, or blog) with the deliberate intent of provoking readers into an emotional response or of otherwise disrupting normal on-topic discussion.

This sense of the word troll and its associated verb trolling are associated with Internet discourse, but have been used more widely. Media attention in recent years has equated trolling with online harassment.

Constitution

A constitution is the set of regulations which govern the conduct of non-political entities, whether incorporated or not. Such entities include corporations and voluntary associations.

Resource

A resource is a source or supply from which benefit is produced. Typically resources are materials, energy, services, staff, knowledge, or other assets that are transformed to produce benefit and in the process may be consumed or made unavailable. Benefits of resource utilization may include increased wealth, meeting needs or wants, proper functioning of a system, or enhanced well being.

Respondeat superior

Respondeat superior is a legal doctrine which states that, in many circumstances, an employer is responsible for the actions of employees performed within the course of their employment. This rule is also called the 'Master-Servant Rule', recognized in both common law and civil law jurisdictions.

In a broader scope, respondeat superior is based upon the concept of vicarious liability.

Pollution

Pollution is the introduction of contaminants into the natural environment that cause adverse change. Pollution can take the form of chemical substances or energy, such as noise, heat or light. Pollutants, the components of pollution, can be either foreign substances/energies or naturally occurring contaminants.

Negligent hiring

Negligence in employment encompasses several causes of action in tort law that arise where an employer is held liable for the tortious acts of an employee because that employer was negligent in providing the employee with the ability to engage in a particular act. Four basic causes of action may arise from such a scenario: negligent hiring, negligent retention, negligent supervision and negligent training. While negligence in employment may overlap with negligent entrustment and vicarious liability, the concepts are distinct grounds of liability.

1. _________ is a principal's approval of an act of its agent where the agent lacked authority to legally bind the principal. The term applies to private contract law, international treaties, and constitutions in federations such as the United States and Canada.

   a. Statute of repose
   b. statute
   c. Statutory Law
   d. Ratification

2. In agency law, an _________ is a person who uses an agent for negotiations with a third party who has no knowledge of the identity of the agent's principal. Often in such situations, the agent pretends to be acting for himself or herself. As a result, the third party does not know to look to the real principal in a dispute.

   a. Undisclosed principal
   b. Nominee trust
   c. Partially disclosed principal
   d. Payment for order flow

3. _________ is a term that conveys a sense of moral commitment or obligation to someone or something. The moral commitment should result in action; it is not a matter of passive feeling or mere recognition. When someone recognizes a _________, that person theoretically commits themself to its fulfillment without considering their own self -interest.

   a. Beneficial interest
   b. Big boy letter
   c. Bonus clause
   d. Duty

4. The payment of _________ as remuneration for services rendered or products sold is a common way to reward sales people. Payments often will be calculated on the basis of a percentage of the goods sold. This is a way for firms to solve the principal-agent problem, by attempting to realign employees' interests with those of the firm.

   a. Beneficial interest
   b. Big boy letter
   c. Commission
   d. Breach of contract

5. . In the United States, _________ is usually the title for a detective or investigator for a state, county, municipal, federal or tribal government who conducts criminal investigations and has arrest authority. An Agent is a federal law enforcement officer with arrest authority but who does not conduct major criminal investigations or who may conduct investigations but does not have arrest authority, _________s being distinctly able to do both.

   a. Small Business Liability Relief and Brownfields Revitalization Act
   b. Chartered Secretaries Australia
   c. Chartered Secretaries New Zealand

ANSWER KEY
14. Agency and the Employment Relationship

---

1. d
2. a
3. d
4. c
5. d

---

15. The Regulatory Process

CHAPTER OUTLINE: KEY TERMS, PEOPLE, PLACES, CONCEPTS

- Income
- Delegation
- Administrative law
- Procedural law
- Lanham Act
- Corporation
- Substantive law
- Resource
- Administration
- Judicial review
- Jurisdiction
- Cost-benefit
- Risk
- Commission
- President

15. The Regulatory Process

CHAPTER HIGHLIGHTS & NOTES: KEY TERMS, PEOPLE, PLACES, CONCEPTS

Income

Income is the consumption and savings opportunity gained by an entity within a specified timeframe, which is generally expressed in monetary terms. However, for households and individuals, 'income is the sum of all the wages, salaries, profits, interests payments, rents and other forms of earnings received... in a given period of time.'

In the field of public economics, the term may refer to the accumulation of both monetary and non-monetary consumption ability, with the former (monetary) being used as a proxy for total income.

Delegation

In contract law, delegation is the act of giving another person the responsibility of carrying out the performance agreed to in a contract. Three parties are concerned with this act - the party who had incurred the obligation to perform under the contract is called the delegator; the party who assumes the responsibility of performing this duty is called the delegatee; and the party to whom this performance is owed is called the obligee. The term is also a concept of Administrative Law.

Administrative law

Administrative law is the body of law that governs the activities of administrative agencies of government. Government agency action can include rulemaking, adjudication, or the enforcement of a specific regulatory agenda. Administrative law is considered a branch of public law.

Procedural law

Procedural law or adjective law comprises the rules by which a court hears and determines what happens in civil lawsuit, criminal or administrative proceedings. The rules are designed to ensure a fair and consistent application of due process (in the U.S). or fundamental justice (in other common law countries) to all cases that come before a court.

Lanham Act

The Lanham Act (Pub.L. 79-489, 60 Stat. 427, enacted July 5, 1946, codified at 15 U.S.C. § 1051 et seq. (15 U.S.C. ch. 22)) is the primary federal trademark statute of law in the United States. The Act prohibits a number of activities, including trademark infringement, trademark dilution, and false advertising.

Corporation

A corporation is a separate legal entity that has been incorporated either directly through legislation or through a registration process established by law. Incorporated entities have legal rights and liabilities that are distinct from their employees and shareholders, and may conduct business as either a profit-seeking business or not-for-profit business. Early incorporated entities were established by charter (i.e. by an ad hoc act granted by a monarch or passed by a parliament or legislature).

Substantive law

Substantive law is the statutory, or written law, that defines rights and duties, such as crimes and punishments, civil rights and responsibilities in civil law. It is codified in legislated statutes or can be enacted through the initiative process.

Substantive law stands in contrast to procedural law, which is the 'machinery' for enforcing those rights and duties.

Resource	A resource is a source or supply from which benefit is produced. Typically resources are materials, energy, services, staff, knowledge, or other assets that are transformed to produce benefit and in the process may be consumed or made unavailable. Benefits of resource utilization may include increased wealth, meeting needs or wants, proper functioning of a system, or enhanced well being.
Administration	As a legal concept, administration is a procedure under the insolvency laws of a number of common law jurisdictions. It functions as a rescue mechanism for insolvent entities and allows them to carry on running their business. The process - an alternative to liquidation - is often known as going into administration.
Judicial review	Judicial Review is the doctrine under which legislative and/or executive actions are subject to review by the judiciary. A specific court with judicial review power may annul the acts of the state when it finds them incompatible with a higher authority (such as the terms of a written constitution). Judicial review is an example of check and balances in a modern governmental system (where the judiciary checks the other branches of government).
Jurisdiction	Jurisdiction is the practical authority granted to a formally constituted legal body or to a political leader to deal with and make pronouncements on legal matters and, by implication, to administer justice within a defined area of responsibility. The term is also used to denote the geographical area or subject-matter to which such authority applies. Areas of jurisdiction apply to local, state, and federal levels.
Cost-benefit	Cost-benefit analysis, sometimes called benefit-cost analysis (BCA), is a systematic approach to estimating the strengths and weaknesses of alternatives that satisfy transactions, activities or functional requirements for a business. It is a technique that is used to determine options that provide the best approach for the adoption and practice in terms of benefits in labour, time and cost savings etc. (David, Ngulube and Dube, 2013).
Risk	Risk is the potential of losing something of value, weighed against the potential to gain something of value. Values (such as physical health, social status, emotional well being or financial wealth) can be gained or lost when taking risk resulting from a given action, activity and/or inaction, foreseen or unforeseen. Risk can also be defined as the intentional interaction with uncertainty.
Commission	The payment of commission as remuneration for services rendered or products sold is a common way to reward sales people. Payments often will be calculated on the basis of a percentage of the goods sold. This is a way for firms to solve the principal-agent problem, by attempting to realign employees' interests with those of the firm.
President	A President is a leader of an organization, company, community, club, trade union, university for this article. It is the legally recognized highest 'titled' corporate officer, ranking above the various Vice Presidents (e.g. Senior Vice President and Executive Vice President), however that post on its own is generally considered subordinate to the Chief Executive Officer.

15. The Regulatory Process

CHAPTER QUIZ: KEY TERMS, PEOPLE, PLACES, CONCEPTS

1. _________ is the doctrine under which legislative and/or executive actions are subject to review by the judiciary. A specific court with _________ power may annul the acts of the state when it finds them incompatible with a higher authority (such as the terms of a written constitution). _________ is an example of check and balances in a modern governmental system (where the judiciary checks the other branches of government).

   a. certiorari
   b. Small Business Liability Relief and Brownfields Revitalization Act
   c. Judicial review
   d. Advertising regulation

2. _________ is the consumption and savings opportunity gained by an entity within a specified timeframe, which is generally expressed in monetary terms. However, for households and individuals, '_________ is the sum of all the wages, salaries, profits, interests payments, rents and other forms of earnings received... in a given period of time.'

   In the field of public economics, the term may refer to the accumulation of both monetary and non-monetary consumption ability, with the former (monetary) being used as a proxy for total _________.

   a. Electronic Signatures in Global and National Commerce Act
   b. Amish
   c. Ethical culture
   d. Income

3. The _________ (Pub.L. 79-489, 60 Stat. 427, enacted July 5, 1946, codified at 15 U.S.C. § 1051 et seq. (15 U.S.C. ch. 22)) is the primary federal trademark statute of law in the United States. The Act prohibits a number of activities, including trademark infringement, trademark dilution, and false advertising.

   a. Cynthia Cooper
   b. Lanham Act
   c. HP Autonomy
   d. James Henry Ting Wei

4. _________ is the body of law that governs the activities of administrative agencies of government. Government agency action can include rulemaking, adjudication, or the enforcement of a specific regulatory agenda. _________ is considered a branch of public law.

   a. Obligee
   b. Electronic Signatures in Global and National Commerce Act
   c. Amish
   d. Administrative law

5. . A _________ is a leader of an organization, company, community, club, trade union, university for this article. It is the legally recognized highest 'titled' corporate officer, ranking above the various Vice _________s (e.g. Senior Vice _________ and Executive Vice _________), however that post on its own is generally considered subordinate to the Chief Executive Officer.

In a similar vein to the Chief Operating Officer, the title of corporate _________ as a separate position (as opposed to being combined with a 'C-Suite' designation, such as '_________ and CEO' or '_________ and COO') is also loosely defined.

a. Boardroom coup
b. Chartered Secretaries Australia
c. President
d. Chief administrative officer

ANSWER KEY
15. The Regulatory Process

---

1. c
2. d
3. b
4. d
5. c

---

16. Employment and Labor Regulations

CHAPTER OUTLINE: KEY TERMS, PEOPLE, PLACES, CONCEPTS

- Income
- Public law
- Tortfeasor
- Commission
- Ponzi scheme
- Administration
- Amendment
- Hazard
- Hazard Communication Standard
- Workers' compensation
- Corporation
- Independent contractor
- Reinsurance
- Worker Adjustment and Retraining Notification Act
- Principal
- Employee Retirement Income Security Act
- Vesting
- Labor relations
- National Labor Relations Act
- National Labor Relations Board
- Treaty

16. Employment and Labor Regulations

CHAPTER OUTLINE: KEY TERMS, PEOPLE, PLACES, CONCEPTS

Contract

Yellow-dog contract

Landrum-Griffin Act

Unfair labor practice

Rehabilitation

Rehabilitation Act

Complaint

Bargaining

Labor law

Lanham Act

Teacher

Plaintiff

Bankruptcy

Bankruptcy court

Collective bargaining

Right-to-work law

Local union

Madrid system

Arbitration

Arbitration clause

Grievance

CHAPTER OUTLINE: KEY TERMS, PEOPLE, PLACES, CONCEPTS

	President
	Lockout

CHAPTER HIGHLIGHTS & NOTES: KEY TERMS, PEOPLE, PLACES, CONCEPTS

Income

Income is the consumption and savings opportunity gained by an entity within a specified timeframe, which is generally expressed in monetary terms. However, for households and individuals, 'income is the sum of all the wages, salaries, profits, interests payments, rents and other forms of earnings received... in a given period of time.'

In the field of public economics, the term may refer to the accumulation of both monetary and non-monetary consumption ability, with the former (monetary) being used as a proxy for total income.

Public law

Public law is that part of law which governs relationships between individuals and the government, and those relationships between individuals which are of direct concern to the society. Public law comprises constitutional law, administrative law, tax law and criminal law, as well as all procedural law. In public law, mandatory rules (not optional) prevail.

Tortfeasor

A tort, in common law jurisdictions, is a civil wrong that unfairly causes someone else to suffer loss or harm resulting in legal liability for the person who commits the tortious act, called a tortfeasor. Although crimes may be torts, the cause of legal action is not necessarily a crime, as the harm may be due to negligence which does not amount to criminal negligence. The victim of the harm can recover their loss as damages in a lawsuit.

Commission

The payment of commission as remuneration for services rendered or products sold is a common way to reward sales people. Payments often will be calculated on the basis of a percentage of the goods sold. This is a way for firms to solve the principal-agent problem, by attempting to realign employees' interests with those of the firm.

Ponzi scheme

A Ponzi scheme is a fraudulent investment operation where the operator, an individual or organization, pays returns to its investors from new capital paid to the operators by new investors, rather than from profit earned by the operator. Operators of Ponzi schemes usually entice new investors by offering higher returns than other investments, in the form of short-term returns that are either abnormally high or unusually consistent. The perpetuation of the high returns requires an ever-increasing flow of money from new investors to sustain the scheme.

16. Employment and Labor Regulations

CHAPTER HIGHLIGHTS & NOTES: KEY TERMS, PEOPLE, PLACES, CONCEPTS

Administration	As a legal concept, administration is a procedure under the insolvency laws of a number of common law jurisdictions. It functions as a rescue mechanism for insolvent entities and allows them to carry on running their business. The process - an alternative to liquidation - is often known as going into administration.
Amendment	An amendment is a formal or official change made to a law, contract, constitution, or other legal document. It is based on the verb to amend, which means to change. Amendments can add, remove, or update parts of these agreements.
Hazard	A hazard is any biological, chemical, mechanical, environmental or physical agent that is reasonably likely to cause harm or damage to humans, other organisms, or the environment in the absence of its control. This can include, but is not limited to: asbestos, electricity, microbial pathogens, motor vehicles, nuclear power plants, pesticides, vaccines, and X-rays. Identification of hazards is the first step in performing a risk assessment and in some cases risk assessment may not even be necessary.
Hazard Communication Standard	The Hazard Communication Standard requires employers to disclose toxic and hazardous substances in workplaces. This is related to the Worker Protection Standard. Specifically, this requires unrestricted employee access to the Material Safety Data Sheet or equivalent, and appropriate training needed to understand health and safety risks.
Workers' compensation	Workers' compensation is a form of insurance providing wage replacement and medical benefits to employees injured in the course of employment in exchange for mandatory relinquishment of the employee's right to sue his or her employer for the tort of negligence. The tradeoff between assured, limited coverage and lack of recourse outside the worker compensation system is known as 'the compensation bargain'. While plans differ among jurisdictions, provision can be made for weekly payments in place of wages (functioning in this case as a form of disability insurance), compensation for economic loss (past and future), reimbursement or payment of medical and like expenses (functioning in this case as a form of health insurance), and benefits payable to the dependents of workers killed during employment (functioning in this case as a form of life insurance).
Corporation	A corporation is a separate legal entity that has been incorporated either directly through legislation or through a registration process established by law. Incorporated entities have legal rights and liabilities that are distinct from their employees and shareholders, and may conduct business as either a profit-seeking business or not-for-profit business. Early incorporated entities were established by charter (i.e. by an ad hoc act granted by a monarch or passed by a parliament or legislature).

Independent contractor	An independent contractor is a natural person, business, or corporation that provides goods or services to another entity under terms specified in a contract or within a verbal agreement. Unlike an employee, an independent contractor does not work regularly for an employer but works as and when required, during which time he or she may be subject to law of agency. Independent contractors are usually paid on a freelance basis.
Reinsurance	Reinsurance is insurance that is purchased by an insurance company from one or more other insurance companies (the 'reinsurer') directly or through a broker as a means of risk management, sometimes in practice including tax mitigation and other reasons described below. The ceding company and the reinsurer enter into a reinsurance agreement which details the conditions upon which the reinsurer would pay a share of the claims incurred by the ceding company. The reinsurer is paid a 'reinsurance premium' by the ceding company, which issues insurance policies to its own policyholders.
Worker Adjustment and Retraining Notification Act	The Worker Adjustment and Retraining Notification Act is a United States labor law which protects employees, their families, and communities by requiring most employers with 100 or more employees to provide 60 calendar-day advance notification of plant closings and mass layoffs of employees. In 2001, there were about 2,000 mass layoffs and plant closures which were subject to WARN advance notice requirements and which affected about 660,000 employees. Employees entitled to notice under the WARN Act include managers and supervisors, hourly wage, and salaried workers.
Principal	In commercial law, a principal is a person, legal or natural, who authorizes an agent to act to create one or more legal relationships with a third party. This branch of law is called agency and relies on the common law proposition qui facit per alium, facit per se (Latin 'he who acts through another, acts personally'). It is a parallel concept to vicarious liability and strict liability (in which one person is held liable for the acts or omissions of another) in criminal law or torts.
Employee Retirement Income Security Act	The Employee Retirement Income Security Act of 1974 (Pub.L. 93-406, 88 Stat. 829, enacted September 2, 1974, codified in part at 29 U.S.C. ch. 18) is a federal law that establishes minimum standards for pension plans in private industry and provides for extensive rules on the federal income tax effects of transactions associated with employee benefit plans. Employee Retirement Income Security Act was enacted to protect the interests of employee benefit plan participants and their beneficiaries by:•Requiring the disclosure of financial and other information concerning the plan to beneficiaries;•Establishing standards of conduct for plan fiduciaries;•Providing for appropriate remedies and access to the federal courts.

Employee Retirement Income Security Act is sometimes used to refer to the full body of laws regulating employee benefit plans, which are found mainly in the Internal Revenue Code and Employee Retirement Income Security Act itself.

Responsibility for the interpretation and enforcement of Employee Retirement Income Security Act is divided among the Department of Labor, the Department of the Treasury (particularly the Internal Revenue Service), and the Pension Benefit Guaranty Corporation.

Vesting

In law, vesting is to give an immediately secured right of present or future deployment. One has a vested right to an asset that cannot be taken away by any third party, even though one may not yet possess the asset. When the right, interest, or title to the present or future possession of a legal estate can be transferred to any other party, it is termed a vested interest.

Labor relations

Labor relations is the study and practice of managing unionized employment situations. In academia, labor relations is frequently a subarea within industrial relations, though scholars from many disciplines--including economics, sociology, history, law, and political science--also study labor unions and labor movements. In practice, labor relations is frequently a subarea within human resource management.

National Labor Relations Act

The National Labor Relations Act of 1935 29 U.S.C. § 151-169 (also known as the Wagner Act after NY Senator Robert F. Wagner) is a foundational statute of US labor law which guarantees basic rights of private sector employees to organize into trade unions, engage in collective bargaining for better terms and conditions at work, and take collective action including strike if necessary. The act also created the National Labor Relations Board, which conducts elections that can require employers to engage in collective bargaining with labor unions (also known as trade unions). The Act does not apply to workers who are covered by the Railway Labor Act, agricultural employees, domestic employees, supervisors, federal, state or local government workers, independent contractors and some close relatives of individual employers.

National Labor Relations Board

The National Labor Relations Board is an independent agency of the United States government charged with conducting elections for labor union representation and with investigating and remedying unfair labor practices. Unfair labor practices may involve union-related situations or instances of protected concerted activity. The National Labor Relations Board is governed by a five -person board and a General Counsel, all of whom are appointed by the President with the consent of the Senate.

Treaty

A treaty is an agreement under international law entered into by actors in international law, namely sovereign states and international organizations. A treaty may also be known as an (international) agreement, protocol, covenant, convention, pact, or exchange of letters, among other terms.

Contract

In common law legal systems, a contract is an agreement having a lawful object entered into voluntarily by two or more parties, each of whom intends to create one or more legal obligations between them. The elements of a contract are 'offer' and 'acceptance' by 'competent persons' having legal capacity who exchange 'consideration' to create 'mutuality of obligation.'

Proof of some or all of these elements may be done in writing, though contracts may be made entirely orally or by conduct. The remedy for breach of contract can be 'damages' in the form of compensation of money or specific performance enforced through an injunction.

Yellow-dog contract

A yellow-dog contract is an agreement between an employer and an employee in which the employee agrees, as a condition of employment, not to be a member of a labor union. In the United States, such contracts were, until the 1930s, widely used by employers to prevent the formation of unions, most often by permitting employers to take legal action against union organizers. In 1932, yellow-dog contracts were outlawed in the United States under the Norris-LaGuardia Act.

Landrum-Griffin Act

The Labor Management Reporting and Disclosure Act of 1959 (also 'LMRDA' or the 'Landrum-Griffin Act'), is a United States labor law that regulates labor unions' internal affairs and their officials' relationships with employers.

Unfair labor practice

In United States labor law, the term unfair labor practice refers to certain actions taken by employers or unions that violate the National Labor Relations Act and other legislation. Such acts are investigated by the National Labor Relations Board (NLRB).

Rehabilitation

Rehabilitation of sensory and cognitive function typically involves methods for retraining neural pathways or training new neural pathways to regain or improve neurocognitive functioning that has been diminished by disease or trauma. Three common neuropsychological problems treatable with rehabilitation are attention deficit/hyperactivity disorder (ADHD), concussion, and spinal cord injury. Rehabilitation research and practices are a fertile area for clinical neuropsychologists and others.

Rehabilitation Act

The Rehabilitation Act of 1973, (Pub.L. 93-112, 87 Stat. 355, enacted September 26, 1973), is a federal law, codified as 29 U.S.C. § 701. The principal sponsor of the bill was Rep. John Brademas [IN-3]. The Rehabilitation Act of 1973 replaces the Vocational Rehabilitation Act, to extend and revise the authorization of grants to States for vocational rehabilitation services, with special emphasis on services to those with the most severe disabilities, to expand special Federal responsibilities and research and training programs with respect to individuals with disabilities, to establish special responsibilities in the Secretary of Health, Education, and Welfare for coordination of all programs with respect to individuals with disabilities within the Department of Health, Education, and Welfare, and for other purposes.

16. Employment and Labor Regulations

CHAPTER HIGHLIGHTS & NOTES: KEY TERMS, PEOPLE, PLACES, CONCEPTS

Complaint

In legal terminology, a complaint is any formal legal document that sets out the facts and legal reasons that the filing party or parties (the plaintiff(s)) believes are sufficient to support a claim against the party or parties against whom the claim is brought (the defendant(s)) that entitles the plaintiff(s) to a remedy (either money damages or injunctive relief)]). For example, the Federal Rules of Civil Procedure (FRCP) that govern civil litigation in United States courts provide that a civil action is commenced with the filing or service of a pleading called a complaint. Civil court rules in states that have incorporated the Federal Rules of Civil Procedure use the same term for the same pleading.

Bargaining

Bargaining or haggling is a type of negotiation in which the buyer and seller of a good or service dispute the price which will be paid and the exact nature of the transaction that will take place, and eventually come to an agreement. Bargaining is an alternative pricing strategy to fixed prices. Optimally, if it costs the retailer nothing to engage and allow bargaining, he can divine the buyer's willingness to spend.

Labor law

Labour law (also labor law or employment law) mediates the relationship between workers, employers, trade unions and the government. Collective labour law relates to the tripartite relationship between employee, employer and union. Individual labour law concerns employees' rights at work and through the contract for work.

Lanham Act

The Lanham Act (Pub.L. 79-489, 60 Stat. 427, enacted July 5, 1946, codified at 15 U.S.C. § 1051 et seq. (15 U.S.C. ch. 22)) is the primary federal trademark statute of law in the United States. The Act prohibits a number of activities, including trademark infringement, trademark dilution, and false advertising.

Teacher

A teacher is a person who provides education for students.

Plaintiff

A plaintiff, also known as a claimant or complainant, is the term used in some jurisdictions for the party who initiates a lawsuit (also known as an action) before a court. By doing so, the plaintiff seeks a legal remedy, and if successful, the court will issue judgment in favor of the plaintiff and make the appropriate court order (e.g., an order for damages).

In some jurisdictions the commencement of a lawsuit is done by filing a summons, claim form and/or a complaint.

Bankruptcy

Bankruptcy is a legal status of a person or other entity that cannot repay the debts it owes to creditors. In most jurisdictions, bankruptcy is imposed by a court order, often initiated by the debtor.

Bankruptcy is not the only legal status that an insolvent person or other entity may have, and the term bankruptcy is therefore not a synonym for insolvency.

Bankruptcy court

United States bankruptcy courts are courts created under Article I of the United States Constitution.

They function as units of the district courts and have subject-matter jurisdiction over bankruptcy cases. The federal district courts have original and exclusive jurisdiction over all cases arising under the bankruptcy code and bankruptcy cases cannot be filed in state court.

Collective bargaining

Collective bargaining is a process of negotiations between employers and a group of employees aimed at reaching agreements to regulate working conditions. The interests of the employees are commonly presented by representatives of a trade union to which the employees belong. The collective agreements reached by these negotiations usually set out wage scales, working hours, training, health and safety, overtime, grievance mechanisms, and rights to participate in workplace or company affairs.

Right-to-work law

A 'right-to-work' law is a statute in the United States that prohibits union security agreements, or agreements between labor unions and employers, that govern the extent to which an established union can require employees' membership, payment of union dues, or fees as a condition of employment, either before or after hiring. Right-to-work laws do not aim to provide general guarantee of employment to people seeking work, but rather are a government regulation of the contractual agreements between employers and labor unions that prevents them from excluding non-union workers, or requiring employees to pay a fee to unions that have negotiated the labor contract all the employees work under.

Right-to-work provisions (either by law or by constitutional provision) exist in 24 U.S. states, mostly in the southern and western United States, but also including, as of 2012, the midwestern states of Michigan and Indiana.

Local union

A local union, often shortened to local, in North America, or a union branch in the United Kingdom and other countries, is a locally-based trade union organisation which forms part of a larger (usually national) union.

Local branches are organised to represent the union's members from a particular geographic area, company, or business sector. Local unions have their own governing bodies which represent the interests of the national union while at the same time responding to the desires of their constituents, and organise regular meetings for members.

Madrid system

The Madrid system is the primary international system for facilitating the registration of trademarks in multiple jurisdictions around the world. Its legal basis is the multilateral treaty Madrid Agreement Concerning the International Registration of Marks of 1891, as well as the Protocol Relating to the Madrid Agreement (1989).

The Madrid system provides a centrally administered system of obtaining a bundle of trademark registrations in separate jurisdictions.

16. Employment and Labor Regulations

CHAPTER HIGHLIGHTS & NOTES: KEY TERMS, PEOPLE, PLACES, CONCEPTS

Arbitration	Arbitration, a form of alternative dispute resolution, is a technique for the resolution of disputes outside the courts. The parties to a dispute refer it to arbitration by one or more persons (the 'arbitrators', 'arbiters' or 'arbitral tribunal'), and agree to be bound by the arbitration decision (the 'award'). A third party reviews the evidence in the case and imposes a decision that is legally binding on both sides and enforceable in the courts.
Arbitration clause	An arbitration clause is a clause in a contract that requires the parties to resolve their disputes through an arbitration process. Although such a clause may or may not specify that arbitration occur within a specific jurisdiction, it always binds the parties to a type of resolution outside of the courts, and is therefore considered a kind of forum selection clause. In the United States, the federal government has expressed a policy of support of arbitration clauses, because they reduce the burden on court systems to resolve disputes.
Grievance	In a trade union, a grievance is a complaint filed by an employee which may be resolved by procedures provided for in a collective agreement or by mechanisms established by an employer. Such a grievance may arise from a violation of the collective bargaining agreement or violations of the law, such as workplace safety regulations. All employees have the contractual right to raise a grievance, and there is a statutory Acas Code of Practice for handling grievances.
President	A President is a leader of an organization, company, community, club, trade union, university for this article. It is the legally recognized highest 'titled' corporate officer, ranking above the various Vice Presidents (e.g. Senior Vice President and Executive Vice President), however that post on its own is generally considered subordinate to the Chief Executive Officer. In a similar vein to the Chief Operating Officer, the title of corporate President as a separate position (as opposed to being combined with a 'C-Suite' designation, such as 'President and CEO' or 'President and COO') is also loosely defined.
Lockout	A lockout is a temporary work stoppage or denial of employment initiated by the management of a company during a labor dispute. This is different from a strike, in which employees refuse to work. It is usually implemented by simply refusing to admit employees onto company premises, and may include actions such as changing locks and hiring security guards for the premises.

1. _________ is the consumption and savings opportunity gained by an entity within a specified timeframe, which is generally expressed in monetary terms. However, for households and individuals, '_________ is the sum of all the wages, salaries, profits, interests payments, rents and other forms of earnings received... in a given period of time.'

   In the field of public economics, the term may refer to the accumulation of both monetary and non-monetary consumption ability, with the former (monetary) being used as a proxy for total _________.

   a. Electronic Signatures in Global and National Commerce Act
   b. Amish
   c. Income
   d. American Federation of Labor

2. A _________ is an agreement under international law entered into by actors in international law, namely sovereign states and international organizations. A _________ may also be known as an (international) agreement, protocol, covenant, convention, pact, or exchange of letters, among other terms. Regardless of terminology, all of these forms of agreements are, under international law, equally considered _________(ies) and the rules are the same.

   a. Cynthia Cooper
   b. Financial scandal in the Orthodox Church in America
   c. HP Autonomy
   d. Treaty

3. _________ is that part of law which governs relationships between individuals and the government, and those relationships between individuals which are of direct concern to the society. _________ comprises constitutional law, administrative law, tax law and criminal law, as well as all procedural law. In _________, mandatory rules (not optional) prevail.

   a. Small Business Liability Relief and Brownfields Revitalization Act
   b. Class Action Fairness Act
   c. Family Entertainment and Copyright Act
   d. Public law

4. A _________, often shortened to local, in North America, or a union branch in the United Kingdom and other countries, is a locally-based trade union organisation which forms part of a larger (usually national) union.

   Local branches are organised to represent the union's members from a particular geographic area, company, or business sector. _________s have their own governing bodies which represent the interests of the national union while at the same time responding to the desires of their constituents, and organise regular meetings for members.

   a. Commonwealth Trade Union Group
   b. Local union
   c. Coordinating Committee of International Staff Unions and Associations of the United Nations System
   d. Directly Affiliated Local Union

5. As a legal concept, _________ is a procedure under the insolvency laws of a number of common law jurisdictions. It functions as a rescue mechanism for insolvent entities and allows them to carry on running their business. The process - an alternative to liquidation - is often known as going into _________.

   a. Commercial law
   b. Lex mercatoria
   c. Statutory liability
   d. Administration

ANSWER KEY
16. Employment and Labor Regulations

---

1. c
2. d
3. d
4. b
5. d

---

17. Employment Discrimination

CHAPTER OUTLINE: KEY TERMS, PEOPLE, PLACES, CONCEPTS

Commission

Discrimination

Labor relations

Rehabilitation

Rehabilitation Act

Religious discrimination

Reverse discrimination

Undue hardship

Amendment

Harassment

Pregnancy discrimination

Sexual harassment

Electronic signature

Lanham Act

Constitution

Disparate treatment

President

Prima facie

Pretext

Corporation

Disparate impact

17. Employment Discrimination

CHAPTER OUTLINE: KEY TERMS, PEOPLE, PLACES, CONCEPTS

______________	Bona fide
______________	Seniority
______________	Skill
______________	Affirmative action
______________	Workforce
______________	Disability discrimination
______________	Employment discrimination
______________	Local union
______________	EDGAR

CHAPTER HIGHLIGHTS & NOTES: KEY TERMS, PEOPLE, PLACES, CONCEPTS

Commission	The payment of commission as remuneration for services rendered or products sold is a common way to reward sales people. Payments often will be calculated on the basis of a percentage of the goods sold. This is a way for firms to solve the principal-agent problem, by attempting to realign employees' interests with those of the firm.
Discrimination	Discrimination is action that denies social participation or human rights to categories of people based on prejudice. This includes treatment of an individual or group based on their actual or perceived membership in a certain group or social category, 'in a way that is worse than the way people are usually treated'. It involves the group's initial reaction or interaction, influencing the individual's actual behavior towards the group or the group leader, restricting members of one group from opportunities or privileges that are available to another group, leading to the exclusion of the individual or entities based on logical or irrational decision making.
Labor relations	Labor relations is the study and practice of managing unionized employment situations. In academia, labor relations is frequently a subarea within industrial relations, though scholars from many disciplines--including economics, sociology, history, law, and political science--also study labor unions and labor movements.

Rehabilitation	Rehabilitation of sensory and cognitive function typically involves methods for retraining neural pathways or training new neural pathways to regain or improve neurocognitive functioning that has been diminished by disease or trauma. Three common neuropsychological problems treatable with rehabilitation are attention deficit/hyperactivity disorder (ADHD), concussion, and spinal cord injury. Rehabilitation research and practices are a fertile area for clinical neuropsychologists and others.
Rehabilitation Act	The Rehabilitation Act of 1973, (Pub.L. 93-112, 87 Stat. 355, enacted September 26, 1973), is a federal law, codified as 29 U.S.C. § 701. The principal sponsor of the bill was Rep. John Brademas [IN-3]. The Rehabilitation Act of 1973 replaces the Vocational Rehabilitation Act, to extend and revise the authorization of grants to States for vocational rehabilitation services, with special emphasis on services to those with the most severe disabilities, to expand special Federal responsibilities and research and training programs with respect to individuals with disabilities, to establish special responsibilities in the Secretary of Health, Education, and Welfare for coordination of all programs with respect to individuals with disabilities within the Department of Health, Education, and Welfare, and for other purposes.
Religious discrimination	Religious discrimination is valuing or treating a person or group differently because of what they do or do not believe. Specifically, it is when adherents of different religions (or denominations) are treated unequally, either before the law or in institutional settings such as employment or housing. Religious discrimination is related to religious persecution, the most extreme forms of which would include instances in which people have been executed for beliefs perceived to be heretic.
Reverse discrimination	Reverse discrimination is discrimination against members of a dominant or majority group or in favor of members of a minority or historically disadvantaged group. Groups may be defined in terms of race, gender, ethnicity, or other factors. This discrimination may seek to redress social inequalities where minority groups have been denied access to the same privileges of the majority group.
Undue hardship	An undue hardship is an accommodating action that places significant difficulty or expense on the employer. Employers are required to provide a reasonable accommodation to qualified individuals with disabilities, but when an accommodation becomes too taxing on the organization it is classified as an undue hardship and is no longer required. These hardships include the nature and cost of the accommodation in relation to the size, resources, nature, and structure of the employer's operation.
Amendment	An amendment is a formal or official change made to a law, contract, constitution, or other legal document. It is based on the verb to amend, which means to change. Amendments can add, remove, or update parts of these agreements.
Harassment	Harassment covers a wide range of behaviours of an offensive nature. It is commonly understood as behaviour intended to disturb or upset, and it is characteristically repetitive.

17. Employment Discrimination

CHAPTER HIGHLIGHTS & NOTES: KEY TERMS, PEOPLE, PLACES, CONCEPTS

Pregnancy discrimination	Pregnancy discrimination occurs when expectant people are fired, not hired, or otherwise discriminated against due to their pregnancy or intention to become pregnant. Common forms of pregnancy discrimination include not being hired due to visible pregnancy or likelihood of becoming pregnant, being fired after informing an employer of one's pregnancy, being fired after maternity leave, and receiving a pay dock due to pregnancy.
Sexual harassment	Sexual harassment is bullying or coercion of a sexual nature, or the unwelcome or inappropriate promise of rewards in exchange for sexual favors. In most modern legal contexts, sexual harassment is illegal. As defined by the US EEOC, 'It is unlawful to harass a person (an applicant or employee) because of that person's sex.' Harassment can include 'sexual harassment' or unwelcome sexual advances, requests for sexual favors, and other verbal or physical harassment of a sexual nature.
Electronic signature	An electronic signature, or e-signature, is any electronic means that indicates either that a person adopts the contents of an electronic message, or more broadly that the person who claims to have written a message is the one who wrote it . By comparison, a signature is a stylized script associated with a person. In commerce and the law, a signature on a document is an indication that the person adopts the intentions recorded in the document.
Lanham Act	The Lanham Act (Pub.L. 79-489, 60 Stat. 427, enacted July 5, 1946, codified at 15 U.S.C. § 1051 et seq. (15 U.S.C. ch. 22)) is the primary federal trademark statute of law in the United States. The Act prohibits a number of activities, including trademark infringement, trademark dilution, and false advertising.
Constitution	A constitution is the set of regulations which govern the conduct of non-political entities, whether incorporated or not. Such entities include corporations and voluntary associations.
Disparate treatment	Disparate treatment is one of the theories of discrimination under Title VII of the United States Civil Rights Act; the other theory is disparate impact. Title VII prohibits employers from treating applicants or employees differently because of their membership in a protected class. A disparate treatment violation is made out when an individual of a protected group is shown to have been singled out and treated less favorably than others similarly situated on the basis of an impermissible criterion under Title VII. The issue is whether the employer's actions were motivated by discriminatory intent.
President	A President is a leader of an organization, company, community, club, trade union, university for this article. It is the legally recognized highest 'titled' corporate officer, ranking above the various Vice Presidents (e.g. Senior Vice President and Executive Vice President), however that post on its own is generally considered subordinate to the Chief Executive Officer.

Prima facie	Prima facie is a Latin expression meaning on its first encounter or at first sight. The literal translation would be 'at first face' or 'at first appearance', from the feminine form of primus ('first') and facies ('face'), both in the ablative case. In modern, colloquial and conversational English, a common translation would be, 'on the face of it'.
Pretext	A pretext is an excuse to do something or say something that is not accurate. Pretexts may be based on a half-truth or developed in the context of a misleading fabrication. Pretexts have been used to conceal the true purpose or rationale behind actions and words.
Corporation	A corporation is a separate legal entity that has been incorporated either directly through legislation or through a registration process established by law. Incorporated entities have legal rights and liabilities that are distinct from their employees and shareholders, and may conduct business as either a profit-seeking business or not-for-profit business. Early incorporated entities were established by charter (i.e. by an ad hoc act granted by a monarch or passed by a parliament or legislature).
Disparate impact	In United States employment law, the doctrine of disparate impact holds that employment practices may be considered discriminatory and illegal if they have a disproportionate 'adverse impact' on persons along the lines of a protected trait. Although the protected traits vary by statute, most federal civil rights laws include race, color, religion, national origin, and gender as protected traits, and some laws include disability status and other traits as well. Under the doctrine, a violation of Title VII of the 1964 Civil Rights Act may be proven by showing that an employment practice or policy has a disproportionately adverse effect on members of the protected class as compared with non-members of the protected class.
Bona fide	Good faith is fair and open dealing in human interactions. This is often thought to require sincere, honest intentions or belief, regardless of the outcome of an action. Some Latin phrases lose their literal meaning over centuries, this is not the case with bona fides, it is still widely used and interchangeable with its generally accepted modern day translation of good faith.
Seniority	In finance, seniority refers to the order of repayment in the event of a sale or bankruptcy of the issuer. Seniority can refer to either debt or preferred stock. Senior debt must be repaid before subordinated (or junior) debt is repaid.
Skill	Skill is a measure of the amount of worker's expertise, specialization, wages, and supervisory capacity. Skilled workers are generally more trained, higher paid, and have more responsibilities than unskilled workers. Skilled workers have long had historical import as masons, carpenters, blacksmiths, bakers, brewers, coopers, printers and other occupations that are economically productive.

17. Employment Discrimination

CHAPTER HIGHLIGHTS & NOTES: KEY TERMS, PEOPLE, PLACES, CONCEPTS

Affirmative action

Affirmative action or positive discrimination is the policy of providing special opportunities for, and favoring members of, a disadvantaged group who suffer from discrimination.

The nature of positive discrimination policies varies from region to region. Some countries, such as India, use a quota system, whereby a certain percentage of jobs or school vacancies must be set aside for members of a certain group.

Workforce

The workforce is the labour pool in employment. It is generally used to describe those working for a single company or industry, but can also apply to a geographic region like a city, state, country, etc. The term generally excludes the employers or management, and can imply those involved in manual labour.

Disability discrimination

Ableism is a form of discrimination or social prejudice against people with disabilities. It may also be referred to as disability discrimination, ablecentrism, physicalism, handicapism, and disability oppression. It includes apotemnophobia and dysmorphophobia.

Employment discrimination

The employment discrimination is a form of discrimination based on race, sex, religion, national origin, physical disability, and age by employers. Earnings differentials or occupational differentiation is not in and of itself evidence of employment discrimination. Discrimination can be intended and involve disparate treatment of a group or be unintended, yet create disparate impact for a group.

Local union

A local union, often shortened to local, in North America, or a union branch in the United Kingdom and other countries, is a locally-based trade union organisation which forms part of a larger (usually national) union.

Local branches are organised to represent the union's members from a particular geographic area, company, or business sector. Local unions have their own governing bodies which represent the interests of the national union while at the same time responding to the desires of their constituents, and organise regular meetings for members.

EDGAR

EDGAR, the Electronic Data Gathering, Analysis, and Retrieval system, performs automated collection, validation, indexing, acceptance, and forwarding of submissions by companies and others who are required by law to file forms with the U.S. Securities and Exchange Commission (the 'SEC'). The database is freely available to the public via the Internet (Web or FTP).

1. The _________ (Pub.L. 79-489, 60 Stat. 427, enacted July 5, 1946, codified at 15 U.S.C. § 1051 et seq. (15 U.S.C. ch. 22)) is the primary federal trademark statute of law in the United States. The Act prohibits a number of activities, including trademark infringement, trademark dilution, and false advertising.

   a. Cynthia Cooper
   b. Lanham Act
   c. HP Autonomy
   d. James Henry Ting Wei

2. In finance, _________ refers to the order of repayment in the event of a sale or bankruptcy of the issuer. _________ can refer to either debt or preferred stock. Senior debt must be repaid before subordinated (or junior) debt is repaid.

   a. 722 redemption
   b. Seniority
   c. Bankruptcy and Insolvency Act
   d. Bankruptcy prediction

3. A _________ is a separate legal entity that has been incorporated either directly through legislation or through a registration process established by law. Incorporated entities have legal rights and liabilities that are distinct from their employees and shareholders, and may conduct business as either a profit-seeking business or not-for-profit business. Early incorporated entities were established by charter (i.e. by an ad hoc act granted by a monarch or passed by a parliament or legislature).

   a. Bulk sale
   b. Corporation
   c. Business method patent
   d. Business valuation

4. _________ occurs when expectant people are fired, not hired, or otherwise discriminated against due to their pregnancy or intention to become pregnant. Common forms of _________ include not being hired due to visible pregnancy or likelihood of becoming pregnant, being fired after informing an employer of one's pregnancy, being fired after maternity leave, and receiving a pay dock due to pregnancy.

   a. Berman hearing
   b. Companionship Exemption
   c. Pregnancy discrimination
   d. De Havilland Law

5. . A _________ is an excuse to do something or say something that is not accurate. _________s may be based on a half-truth or developed in the context of a misleading fabrication. _________s have been used to conceal the true purpose or rationale behind actions and words.

   a. Pretext
   b. Clickjacking
   c. Cyber spying

ANSWER KEY
17. Employment Discrimination

---

1. b
2. b
3. b
4. c
5. a

---

18. Environmental Law

CHAPTER OUTLINE: KEY TERMS, PEOPLE, PLACES, CONCEPTS

- Pollution
- Private law
- Tortfeasor
- Trespass
- Water law
- Commission
- President
- Environmental Protection
- Pollutant
- Clean Water Act
- Bankruptcy
- Plaintiff
- Point
- Product liability
- Economic Development
- Resource
- Resource Conservation and Recovery Act
- Madrid system
- Superfund
- Ponzi scheme
- Income

18. Environmental Law

CHAPTER OUTLINE: KEY TERMS, PEOPLE, PLACES, CONCEPTS

	Diversity
	Treaty
	EDGAR
	Environmental law

CHAPTER HIGHLIGHTS & NOTES: KEY TERMS, PEOPLE, PLACES, CONCEPTS

Pollution	Pollution is the introduction of contaminants into the natural environment that cause adverse change. Pollution can take the form of chemical substances or energy, such as noise, heat or light. Pollutants, the components of pollution, can be either foreign substances/energies or naturally occurring contaminants.
Private law	Private law is that part of a civil law legal system which is part of the jus commune that involves relationships between individuals, such as the law of contracts or torts, and the law of obligations (as it is called in civil legal systems). It is to be distinguished from public law, which deals with relationships between both natural and artificial persons (i.e., organizations) and the state, including regulatory statutes, penal law and other law that affects the public order. In general terms, private law involves interactions between private citizens, whereas public law involves interrelations between the state and the general population.
Tortfeasor	A tort, in common law jurisdictions, is a civil wrong that unfairly causes someone else to suffer loss or harm resulting in legal liability for the person who commits the tortious act, called a tortfeasor. Although crimes may be torts, the cause of legal action is not necessarily a crime, as the harm may be due to negligence which does not amount to criminal negligence. The victim of the harm can recover their loss as damages in a lawsuit.
Trespass	Trespass is an area of tort law broadly divided into three groups: trespass to the person, trespass to chattels and trespass to land. Trespass to the person historically involved six separate trespasses: threats, assault, battery, wounding, mayhem, and maiming.

Through the evolution of the common law in various jurisdictions, and the codification of common law torts, most jurisdictions now broadly recognize three trespasses to the person: assault, which is 'any act of such a nature as to excite an apprehension of battery'; battery, 'any intentional and unpermitted contact with the plaintiff's person or anything attached to it and practically identified with it'; and false imprisonment, the 'unlaw[ful] obstruct[ion] or depriv[ation] of freedom from restraint of movement'.

Water law

Water law is the field of law dealing with the ownership, control, and use of water as a resource. It is most closely related to property law, but has also become influenced by environmental law. Because water is vital to living things and to a variety of economic activities, laws attempting to govern it have far-reaching effects.

Commission

The payment of commission as remuneration for services rendered or products sold is a common way to reward sales people. Payments often will be calculated on the basis of a percentage of the goods sold. This is a way for firms to solve the principal-agent problem, by attempting to realign employees' interests with those of the firm.

President

A President is a leader of an organization, company, community, club, trade union, university for this article. It is the legally recognized highest 'titled' corporate officer, ranking above the various Vice Presidents (e.g. Senior Vice President and Executive Vice President), however that post on its own is generally considered subordinate to the Chief Executive Officer. In a similar vein to the Chief Operating Officer, the title of corporate President as a separate position (as opposed to being combined with a 'C-Suite' designation, such as 'President and CEO' or 'President and COO') is also loosely defined.

Environmental Protection

Environmental protection is a practice of protecting the natural environment on individual, organizational or governmental levels, for the benefit of both the natural environment and humans. Due to the pressures of population and technology, the biophysical environment is being degraded, sometimes permanently. This has been recognized, and governments have begun placing restraints on activities that cause environmental degradation.

Pollutant

A pollutant is a substance or energy introduced into the environment that has undesired effects, or adversely affects the usefulness of a resource. A pollutant may cause long- or short-term damage by changing the growth rate of plant or animal species, or by interfering with human amenities, comfort, health, or property values. Some pollutants are biodegradable and therefore will not persist in the environment in the long term.

Clean Water Act

The Clean Water Act is a law enacted by the Legislative Assembly of Ontario, Canada. The purpose of this Act is to protect existing and future sources of drinking water.

18. Environmental Law

CHAPTER HIGHLIGHTS & NOTES: KEY TERMS, PEOPLE, PLACES, CONCEPTS

Bankruptcy	Bankruptcy is a legal status of a person or other entity that cannot repay the debts it owes to creditors. In most jurisdictions, bankruptcy is imposed by a court order, often initiated by the debtor. Bankruptcy is not the only legal status that an insolvent person or other entity may have, and the term bankruptcy is therefore not a synonym for insolvency.
Plaintiff	A plaintiff, also known as a claimant or complainant, is the term used in some jurisdictions for the party who initiates a lawsuit (also known as an action) before a court. By doing so, the plaintiff seeks a legal remedy, and if successful, the court will issue judgment in favor of the plaintiff and make the appropriate court order (e.g., an order for damages). In some jurisdictions the commencement of a lawsuit is done by filing a summons, claim form and/or a complaint.
Point	Points, sometimes also called 'discount points', are a form of pre-paid interest. One point equals one percent of the loan amount. By charging a borrower points, a lender effectively increases the yield on the loan above the amount of the stated interest rate.
Product liability	Product liability is the area of law in which manufacturers, distributors, suppliers, retailers, and others who make products available to the public are held responsible for the injuries those products cause. Although the word 'product' has broad connotations, product liability as an area of law is traditionally limited to products in the form of tangible personal property.
Economic Development	Economic development is the process and policies by which a nation improves the economic, political, and social well-being of its people. The term has been used frequently by economists, politicians, and others in the 20th century. The concept, however, has been in existence in the West for centuries.
Resource	A resource is a source or supply from which benefit is produced. Typically resources are materials, energy, services, staff, knowledge, or other assets that are transformed to produce benefit and in the process may be consumed or made unavailable. Benefits of resource utilization may include increased wealth, meeting needs or wants, proper functioning of a system, or enhanced well being.
Resource Conservation and Recovery Act	The Resource Conservation and Recovery Act, enacted in 1976, is the principal federal law in the United States governing the disposal of solid waste and hazardous waste.
Madrid system	The Madrid system is the primary international system for facilitating the registration of trademarks in multiple jurisdictions around the world. Its legal basis is the multilateral treaty Madrid Agreement Concerning the International Registration of Marks of 1891, as well as the Protocol Relating to the Madrid Agreement (1989).

Superfund

Superfund or Comprehensive Environmental Response, Compensation, and Liability Act of 1980 is a United States federal law designed to clean up sites contaminated with hazardous substances as well as broadly defined 'pollutants or contaminants'. Superfund also gives authority to federal natural resource agencies, states and Native American tribes to recover natural resource damages caused by releases of hazardous substances, and it created the Agency for Toxic Substances and Disease Registry .•A section 104..

Ponzi scheme

A Ponzi scheme is a fraudulent investment operation where the operator, an individual or organization, pays returns to its investors from new capital paid to the operators by new investors, rather than from profit earned by the operator. Operators of Ponzi schemes usually entice new investors by offering higher returns than other investments, in the form of short-term returns that are either abnormally high or unusually consistent. The perpetuation of the high returns requires an ever-increasing flow of money from new investors to sustain the scheme.

Income

Income is the consumption and savings opportunity gained by an entity within a specified timeframe, which is generally expressed in monetary terms. However, for households and individuals, 'income is the sum of all the wages, salaries, profits, interests payments, rents and other forms of earnings received... in a given period of time.'

In the field of public economics, the term may refer to the accumulation of both monetary and non-monetary consumption ability, with the former (monetary) being used as a proxy for total income.

Diversity

The 'business case for diversity' stem from the progression of the models of diversity within the workplace since the 1960s. The original model for diversity was situated around affirmative action drawing strength from the law and a need to comply with equal opportunity employment objectives. This compliance-based model gave rise to the idea that tokenism was the reason an individual was hired into a company when they differed from the dominant group.

Treaty

A treaty is an agreement under international law entered into by actors in international law, namely sovereign states and international organizations. A treaty may also be known as an (international) agreement, protocol, covenant, convention, pact, or exchange of letters, among other terms. Regardless of terminology, all of these forms of agreements are, under international law, equally considered treaties and the rules are the same.

EDGAR

EDGAR, the Electronic Data Gathering, Analysis, and Retrieval system, performs automated collection, validation, indexing, acceptance, and forwarding of submissions by companies and others who are required by law to file forms with the U.S. Securities and Exchange Commission (the 'SEC'). The database is freely available to the public via the Internet (Web or FTP).

18. Environmental Law

CHAPTER HIGHLIGHTS & NOTES: KEY TERMS, PEOPLE, PLACES, CONCEPTS

Environmental law	Environmental law is a collective term describing international treaties, statutes, regulations, and common law or national legislation (where applicable) that operates to regulate the interaction of humanity and the natural environment, toward the purpose of reducing the impacts of human activity. The topic may be divided into two major subjects: pollution control and remediation, and resource conservation, individual exhaustion. The limitations and expenses that such laws may impose on commerce, and the often unquantifiable (non-monetized) benefit of environmental protection, have generated and continue to generate significant controversy.

CHAPTER QUIZ: KEY TERMS, PEOPLE, PLACES, CONCEPTS

1. _________ is a collective term describing international treaties, statutes, regulations, and common law or national legislation (where applicable) that operates to regulate the interaction of humanity and the natural environment, toward the purpose of reducing the impacts of human activity.

   The topic may be divided into two major subjects: pollution control and remediation, and resource conservation, individual exhaustion. The limitations and expenses that such laws may impose on commerce, and the often unquantifiable (non-monetized) benefit of environmental protection, have generated and continue to generate significant controversy.

   a. Cynthia Cooper
   b. Financial scandal in the Orthodox Church in America
   c. Environmental law
   d. James Henry Ting Wei

2. _________ is the process and policies by which a nation improves the economic, political, and social well-being of its people. The term has been used frequently by economists, politicians, and others in the 20th century. The concept, however, has been in existence in the West for centuries.

   a. Electronic Signatures in Global and National Commerce Act
   b. Economic Development
   c. HP Autonomy
   d. James Henry Ting Wei

3. . _________s, sometimes also called 'discount _________s', are a form of pre-paid interest. One _________ equals one percent of the loan amount. By charging a borrower _________s, a lender effectively increases the yield on the loan above the amount of the stated interest rate.

   a. Balloon payment mortgage

b. Bank walkaway
c. Point
d. Cash out refinancing

4. _________ or Comprehensive Environmental Response, Compensation, and Liability Act of 1980 is a United States federal law designed to clean up sites contaminated with hazardous substances as well as broadly defined 'pollutants or contaminants'. _________ also gives authority to federal natural resource agencies, states and Native American tribes to recover natural resource damages caused by releases of hazardous substances, and it created the Agency for Toxic Substances and Disease Registry .•A section 104..

a. Small Business Liability Relief and Brownfields Revitalization Act
b. Brand piracy
c. Superfund
d. Chartered mark

5. A _________ is a source or supply from which benefit is produced. Typically _________s are materials, energy, services, staff, knowledge, or other assets that are transformed to produce benefit and in the process may be consumed or made unavailable. Benefits of _________ utilization may include increased wealth, meeting needs or wants, proper functioning of a system, or enhanced well being.

a. Crude
b. Gordon-Schaefer Model
c. Resource
d. Material flow accounting

ANSWER KEY
18. Environmental Law

---

1. c
2. b
3. c
4. c
5. c

---

19. Consumer Protection

CHAPTER OUTLINE: KEY TERMS, PEOPLE, PLACES, CONCEPTS

- Consumer protection
- Amendment
- Reinsurance
- Wyeth v. Levine
- Consent decree
- Commission
- Trade
- Fraud
- Lanham Act
- Advertising regulation
- Contract
- Trade regulation
- Alliance
- Cape
- Madrid system
- Arbitration
- Finance charge
- Lease
- CARD Act
- Sherman Act
- Equal Credit Opportunity Act

19. Consumer Protection

CHAPTER OUTLINE: KEY TERMS, PEOPLE, PLACES, CONCEPTS

	Red flag
	Debt collection
	Garnishment
	Tortfeasor
	Consumer Financial Protection Bureau
	Mistake

CHAPTER HIGHLIGHTS & NOTES: KEY TERMS, PEOPLE, PLACES, CONCEPTS

Consumer protection	Consumer protection is a group of laws and organizations designed to ensure the rights of consumers as well as fair trade, competition and accurate information in the marketplace. The laws are designed to prevent businesses that engage in fraud or specified unfair practices from gaining an advantage over competitors. They may also provide additional protection for those most vulnerable in society.
Amendment	An amendment is a formal or official change made to a law, contract, constitution, or other legal document. It is based on the verb to amend, which means to change. Amendments can add, remove, or update parts of these agreements.
Reinsurance	Reinsurance is insurance that is purchased by an insurance company from one or more other insurance companies (the 'reinsurer') directly or through a broker as a means of risk management, sometimes in practice including tax mitigation and other reasons described below. The ceding company and the reinsurer enter into a reinsurance agreement which details the conditions upon which the reinsurer would pay a share of the claims incurred by the ceding company. The reinsurer is paid a 'reinsurance premium' by the ceding company, which issues insurance policies to its own policyholders.
Wyeth v. Levine	Wyeth v. Levine, 555 U.S. 555 (2009), is a United States Supreme Court case holding that Federal regulatory approval of a medication does not shield the manufacturer from liability under state law.
Consent decree	A consent decree is an agreement or settlement to resolve a dispute between two parties without admission of guilt.

The plaintiff and the defendant ask the court to enter into their agreement, and the court maintains supervision over the implementation of the decree in monetary exchanges or restructured interactions between parties. It is similar to and sometimes referred to as an antitrust decree, stipulated judgement, settlement agreements or consent judgment.

Commission

The payment of commission as remuneration for services rendered or products sold is a common way to reward sales people. Payments often will be calculated on the basis of a percentage of the goods sold. This is a way for firms to solve the principal-agent problem, by attempting to realign employees' interests with those of the firm.

Trade

In professional sports, a trade is a sports league transaction involving an exchange of players' contracts or draft picks between sports clubs. Cash is another commodity that may be packaged together with contracts or draft picks to complete a trade. Typically, trades are completed between two clubs, but there are instances where trades are consummated between three or more clubs.

Fraud

Fraud is a deception deliberately practiced in order to secure unfair or unlawful gain (adjectival form fraudulent; to defraud is the verb). As a legal construct, fraud is both a civil wrong (i.e., a fraud victim may sue the fraud perpetrator to avoid the fraud and/or recover monetary compensation) and a criminal wrong (i.e., a fraud perpetrator may be prosecuted and imprisoned by governmental authorities). Defrauding people or organizations of money or valuables is the usual purpose of fraud, but it sometimes instead involves obtaining benefits without actually depriving anyone of money or valuables, such as obtaining a drivers license by way of false statements made in an application for the same.

Lanham Act

The Lanham Act (Pub.L. 79-489, 60 Stat. 427, enacted July 5, 1946, codified at 15 U.S.C. § 1051 et seq. (15 U.S.C. ch. 22)) is the primary federal trademark statute of law in the United States. The Act prohibits a number of activities, including trademark infringement, trademark dilution, and false advertising.

Advertising regulation

Advertising regulation refers to the laws and rules defining the ways in which products can be advertised in a particular region. Rules can define a wide number of different aspects, such as placement, timing, and content. In the United States, false advertising and health-related ads are regulated the most.

Contract

In common law legal systems, a contract is an agreement having a lawful object entered into voluntarily by two or more parties, each of whom intends to create one or more legal obligations between them. The elements of a contract are 'offer' and 'acceptance' by 'competent persons' having legal capacity who exchange 'consideration' to create 'mutuality of obligation.'

Proof of some or all of these elements may be done in writing, though contracts may be made entirely orally or by conduct.

Trade regulation	Trade regulation is a field of law, often bracketed with antitrust (as in the phrase "antitrust and trade regulation law"), including government regulation of unfair methods of competition and unfair or deceptive business acts or practices. Antitrust law is often considered a subset of trade regulation law. Franchise and distribution law, consumer protection law, and advertising law are sometimes considered parts of trade regulation law.
Alliance	An alliance is a pact, coalition or friendship between two or more parties, made in order to advance common goals and to secure common interests. It is a Political agreement between countries to support each other in disputes with other countries. See also military alliance, treaty, contract, coalition (disambiguation) and business alliance.
Cape	In old British law, a cape was a judicial writ concerning a plea of lands and tenements; so called, as most writs are, from the word which carried the chief intention of the writ. The writ was divided into cape magnum, or the grand cape, and cape parvum, or the petit cape. While they were alike in their effect, as to taking hold of immovable things, they differed in the following circumstances: first, in that the cape magnum lay before, and the cape parvum after; second, cape magnum summoned the defendant to answer to the default, in addition to answering to the plaintiff, while cape parvum only summoned the defendant to answer to the default.
Madrid system	The Madrid system is the primary international system for facilitating the registration of trademarks in multiple jurisdictions around the world. Its legal basis is the multilateral treaty Madrid Agreement Concerning the International Registration of Marks of 1891, as well as the Protocol Relating to the Madrid Agreement (1989). The Madrid system provides a centrally administered system of obtaining a bundle of trademark registrations in separate jurisdictions.
Arbitration	Arbitration, a form of alternative dispute resolution, is a technique for the resolution of disputes outside the courts. The parties to a dispute refer it to arbitration by one or more persons (the 'arbitrators', 'arbiters' or 'arbitral tribunal'), and agree to be bound by the arbitration decision (the 'award'). A third party reviews the evidence in the case and imposes a decision that is legally binding on both sides and enforceable in the courts.
Finance charge	In United States law, a finance charge is any fee representing the cost of credit, or the cost of borrowing. It is interest accrued on, and fees charged for, some forms of credit. It includes not only interest but other charges as well, such as financial transaction fees.
Lease	A lease is a contractual arrangement calling for the lessee to pay the lessor (owner) for use of an asset.

The narrower term rental agreement can be used to describe a lease in which the asset is tangible property. Language used is that the user rents the land or goods let or rented out by the owner.

CARD Act

The Credit Card Accountability Responsibility and Disclosure Act of 2009 or Credit CARD Act of 2009 is a federal statute passed by the United States Congress and signed by President Barack Obama on May 22, 2009. It is comprehensive credit card reform legislation that aims '...to establish fair and transparent practices relating to the extension of credit under an open end consumer credit plan, and for other purposes.' The bill was passed with bipartisan support by both the House of Representatives and the Senate.

Sherman Act

The Sherman Antitrust Act (Sherman Act,26 Stat. 209, 15 U.S.C. §§ 1-7) is a landmark federal statute in the history of United States antitrust law (or 'competition law') passed by Congress in 1890. It prohibits certain business activities that federal government regulators deem to be anti-competitive, and requires the federal government to investigate and pursue trusts.

It has since, more broadly, been used to oppose the combination of entities that could potentially harm competition, such as monopolies or cartels.

According to its authors, it was not intended to impact market gains obtained by honest means, by benefiting the consumers more than the competitors.

Equal Credit Opportunity Act

The Equal Credit Opportunity Act is a United States law (codified at 15 U.S.C. § 1691 et seq)., enacted in 1974, that makes it unlawful for any creditor to discriminate against any applicant, with respect to any aspect of a credit transaction, on the basis of race, color, religion, national origin, sex, marital status, or age (provided the applicant has the capacity to contract); to the fact that all or part of the applicant's income derives from a public assistance program; or to the fact that the applicant has in good faith exercised any right under the Consumer Credit Protection Act. The law applies to any person who, in the ordinary course of business, regularly participates in a credit decision, including banks, retailers, bankcard companies, finance companies, and credit unions.

Failure to comply with the Equal Credit Opportunity Act's Regulation B can subject a financial institution to civil liability for actual and punitive damages in individual or class actions.

Red flag

In politics, a red flag is a symbol of Socialism, or Communism, or sometimes left-wing politics in general. It has been associated with left-wing politics since the French Revolution. Socialists adopted the symbol during the Revolutions of 1848 and it became a symbol of communism as a result of its use by the Paris Commune of 1871. The flags of several communist states, including China, Vietnam and the Soviet Union, are explicitly based on the original red flag.

Debt collection

A collection agency, also known as a debt collector, is a business or other entity that specializes in debt collection, i.e. pursues payments of debts owed by individuals or businesses.

Most collection agencies operate as agents of creditors and collect debts for a fee or percentage of the total amount owed.

There are many types of collection agencies.

Garnishment

Garnishment is an American legal order for collecting a monetary judgment on behalf of a plaintiff from a defendant. The money can come directly from the defendant (the garnishee) or - at a court's discretion - from a third party. Jurisdiction law may allow for collection - without a judgment or other court order - in the case of collecting for taxes.

Tortfeasor

A tort, in common law jurisdictions, is a civil wrong that unfairly causes someone else to suffer loss or harm resulting in legal liability for the person who commits the tortious act, called a tortfeasor. Although crimes may be torts, the cause of legal action is not necessarily a crime, as the harm may be due to negligence which does not amount to criminal negligence. The victim of the harm can recover their loss as damages in a lawsuit.

Consumer Financial Protection Bureau

The Consumer Financial Protection Bureau is an independent agency of the United States government responsible for consumer protection in the financial sector. Its jurisdiction includes banks, credit unions, securities firms, payday lenders, mortgage-servicing operations, foreclosure relief services, debt collectors and other financial companies operating in the United States.

The Consumer Financial Protection Bureau's creation was authorized by the Dodd-Frank Wall Street Reform and Consumer Protection Act, whose passage in 2010 was a legislative response to the financial crisis of 2007-08 and the subsequent Great Recession.

Mistake

In contract law, a mistake is an erroneous belief, at contracting, that certain facts are true. It can be argued as a defence, and if raised successfully can lead to the agreement in question being found void ab initio or voidable, or alternatively an equitable remedy may be provided by the courts. Common law has identified three different types of mistake in contract: the 'unilateral mistake', the 'mutual mistake' and the 'common mistake'.

19. Consumer Protection

CHAPTER QUIZ: KEY TERMS, PEOPLE, PLACES, CONCEPTS

1. _________ is a group of laws and organizations designed to ensure the rights of consumers as well as fair trade, competition and accurate information in the marketplace. The laws are designed to prevent businesses that engage in fraud or specified unfair practices from gaining an advantage over competitors. They may also provide additional protection for those most vulnerable in society.

   a. Consumer protection
   b. Financial scandal in the Orthodox Church in America
   c. HP Autonomy
   d. James Henry Ting Wei

2. The _________ is an independent agency of the United States government responsible for consumer protection in the financial sector. Its jurisdiction includes banks, credit unions, securities firms, payday lenders, mortgage-servicing operations, foreclosure relief services, debt collectors and other financial companies operating in the United States.

   The _________'s creation was authorized by the Dodd-Frank Wall Street Reform and Consumer Protection Act, whose passage in 2010 was a legislative response to the financial crisis of 2007-08 and the subsequent Great Recession.

   a. Commodity Futures Trading Commission
   b. Cynthia Cooper
   c. Financial scandal in the Orthodox Church in America
   d. Consumer Financial Protection Bureau

3. The payment of _________ as remuneration for services rendered or products sold is a common way to reward sales people. Payments often will be calculated on the basis of a percentage of the goods sold. This is a way for firms to solve the principal-agent problem, by attempting to realign employees' interests with those of the firm.

   a. Commission
   b. Big boy letter
   c. Bonus clause
   d. Breach of contract

4. An _________ is a formal or official change made to a law, contract, constitution, or other legal document. It is based on the verb to amend, which means to change. _________s can add, remove, or update parts of these agreements.

   a. Amendment
   b. Financial scandal in the Orthodox Church in America
   c. HP Autonomy
   d. James Henry Ting Wei

5. . In professional sports, a _________ is a sports league transaction involving an exchange of players' contracts or draft picks between sports clubs. Cash is another commodity that may be packaged together with contracts or draft picks to complete a _________. Typically, _________s are completed between two clubs, but there are instances where _________s are consummated between three or more clubs.

a. Restricted free agent
b. Cynthia Cooper
c. Trade
d. HP Autonomy

ANSWER KEY
19. Consumer Protection

---

1. a
2. d
3. a
4. a
5. c

---

20. Antitrust Law

CHAPTER OUTLINE: KEY TERMS, PEOPLE, PLACES, CONCEPTS

- Clayton Act
- Sherman Act
- Antitrust
- Labor relations
- National Labor Relations Act
- Rehabilitation
- Rehabilitation Act
- Monopolization
- Rule of reason
- Tort
- Merger
- Market power
- Procedural law
- Ponzi scheme
- Trade
- OPEC
- Cartel
- President
- Price fixing
- Arbitration
- Copyright

20. Antitrust Law

CHAPTER OUTLINE: KEY TERMS, PEOPLE, PLACES, CONCEPTS

	Joint venture
	Corporation
	Commission
	Vertical restraints
	Intellectual property
	Tying
	Discrimination
	Predatory pricing
	Price discrimination
	Bidding
	Reinsurance

CHAPTER HIGHLIGHTS & NOTES: KEY TERMS, PEOPLE, PLACES, CONCEPTS

Clayton Act	The Clayton Act of 1914 (Pub.L. 63-212, 38 Stat. 730, enacted October 15, 1914, codified at 15 U.S.C. §§ 12-27, 29 U.S.C. §§ 52-53), was a part of United States antitrust law with the goal of adding further substance to the U.S. antitrust law regime; the Clayton Act sought to prevent anticompetitive practices in their incipiency. That regime started with the Sherman Antitrust Act of 1890, the first Federal law outlawing practices considered harmful to consumers (monopolies, cartels, and trusts). The Clayton Act specified particular prohibited conduct, the three-level enforcement scheme, the exemptions, and the remedial measures.
Sherman Act	The Sherman Antitrust Act (Sherman Act,26 Stat. 209, 15 U.S.C. §§ 1-7) is a landmark federal statute in the history of United States antitrust law (or 'competition law') passed by Congress in 1890. It prohibits certain business activities that federal government regulators deem to be anti-competitive, and requires the federal government to investigate and pursue trusts.

It has since, more broadly, been used to oppose the combination of entities that could potentially harm competition, such as monopolies or cartels.

According to its authors, it was not intended to impact market gains obtained by honest means, by benefiting the consumers more than the competitors.

Antitrust

Competition law is law that promotes or seeks to maintain market competition by regulating anti-competitive conduct by companies. Competition law is implemented through Public and Private Enforcement

Competition law is known as antitrust law in the United States and anti-monopoly law in China and Russia. In previous years it has been known as trade practices law in the United Kingdom and Australia.

Labor relations

Labor relations is the study and practice of managing unionized employment situations. In academia, labor relations is frequently a subarea within industrial relations, though scholars from many disciplines--including economics, sociology, history, law, and political science--also study labor unions and labor movements. In practice, labor relations is frequently a subarea within human resource management.

National Labor Relations Act

The National Labor Relations Act of 1935 29 U.S.C. § 151-169 (also known as the Wagner Act after NY Senator Robert F. Wagner) is a foundational statute of US labor law which guarantees basic rights of private sector employees to organize into trade unions, engage in collective bargaining for better terms and conditions at work, and take collective action including strike if necessary. The act also created the National Labor Relations Board, which conducts elections that can require employers to engage in collective bargaining with labor unions (also known as trade unions). The Act does not apply to workers who are covered by the Railway Labor Act, agricultural employees, domestic employees, supervisors, federal, state or local government workers, independent contractors and some close relatives of individual employers.

Rehabilitation

Rehabilitation of sensory and cognitive function typically involves methods for retraining neural pathways or training new neural pathways to regain or improve neurocognitive functioning that has been diminished by disease or trauma. Three common neuropsychological problems treatable with rehabilitation are attention deficit/hyperactivity disorder (ADHD), concussion, and spinal cord injury. Rehabilitation research and practices are a fertile area for clinical neuropsychologists and others.

Rehabilitation Act

The Rehabilitation Act of 1973, (Pub.L. 93-112, 87 Stat. 355, enacted September 26, 1973), is a federal law, codified as 29 U.S.C. § 701. The principal sponsor of the bill was Rep. John Brademas [IN-3].

20. Antitrust Law

CHAPTER HIGHLIGHTS & NOTES: KEY TERMS, PEOPLE, PLACES, CONCEPTS

Monopolization	In US antitrust law, monopolization is an offense and the main categories of prohibited behavior include exclusive dealing, price discrimination, refusing to supply an essential facility, product tying and predatory pricing. Monopolization is an offense under Section 2 of the American Sherman Antitrust Act 1890 The Sherman Act 1890 §2 states that any person 'who shall monopolize .
Rule of reason	The Rule of Reason is a doctrine developed by the United States Supreme Court in its interpretation of the Sherman Antitrust Act. The rule, stated and applied in the case of Standard Oil Co. of New Jersey v. United States, 221 U.S. 1 (1911), is that only combinations and contracts unreasonably restraining trade are subject to actions under the anti-trust laws. Possession of monopoly power is not in itself illegal.
Tort	A tort, in common law jurisdictions, is a civil wrong that unfairly causes someone else to suffer loss or harm resulting in legal liability for the person who commits the tortious act, called a tortfeasor. Although crimes may be torts, the cause of legal action is not necessarily a crime, as the harm may be due to negligence which does not amount to criminal negligence. The victim of the harm can recover their loss as damages in a lawsuit.
Merger	Mergers and acquisitions are both aspects of strategic management, corporate finance and management dealing with the buying, selling, dividing and combining of different companies and similar entities that can help an enterprise grow rapidly in its sector or location of origin, or a new field or new location, without creating a subsidiary, other child entity or using a joint venture. Mergers and acquisitions activity can be defined as a type of restructuring in that they result in some entity reorganization with the aim to provide growth or positive value. Consolidation of an industry or sector occurs when widespread M&A activity concentrates the resources of many small companies into a few larger ones, such as occurred with the automotive industry between 1910 and 1940.
Market power	In economics and particularly in industrial organization, market power is the ability of a firm to profitably raise the market price of a good or service over marginal cost. In perfectly competitive markets, market participants have no market power. A firm with total market power can raise prices without losing any customers to competitors.
Procedural law	Procedural law or adjective law comprises the rules by which a court hears and determines what happens in civil lawsuit, criminal or administrative proceedings. The rules are designed to ensure a fair and consistent application of due process (in the U.S). or fundamental justice (in other common law countries) to all cases that come before a court.
Ponzi scheme	A Ponzi scheme is a fraudulent investment operation where the operator, an individual or organization, pays returns to its investors from new capital paid to the operators by new investors, rather than from profit earned by the operator. Operators of Ponzi schemes usually entice new investors by offering higher returns than other investments, in the form of short-term returns that are either abnormally high or unusually consistent.

Trade

In professional sports, a trade is a sports league transaction involving an exchange of players' contracts or draft picks between sports clubs. Cash is another commodity that may be packaged together with contracts or draft picks to complete a trade. Typically, trades are completed between two clubs, but there are instances where trades are consummated between three or more clubs.

OPEC

OPEC is an international organization and economic cartel whose mission is to coordinate the policies of the oil-producing countries. The goal is to secure a steady income to the member states and to collude in influencing world oil prices through economic means.

OPEC is an intergovernmental organization that was created at the Baghdad Conference on 10-14 September 1960, by Iraq, Kuwait, Iran, Saudi Arabia and Venezuela.

Cartel

A cartel is a formal, explicit agreement among competing firms. It is a formal organization of producers and manufacturers that agree to fix prices, marketing, and production. Cartels usually occur in an oligopolistic industry, where the number of sellers is small (usually because barriers to entry, most notably startup costs, are high) and the products being traded are usually commodities.

President

A President is a leader of an organization, company, community, club, trade union, university for this article. It is the legally recognized highest 'titled' corporate officer, ranking above the various Vice Presidents (e.g. Senior Vice President and Executive Vice President), however that post on its own is generally considered subordinate to the Chief Executive Officer. In a similar vein to the Chief Operating Officer, the title of corporate President as a separate position (as opposed to being combined with a 'C-Suite' designation, such as 'President and CEO' or 'President and COO') is also loosely defined.

Price fixing

Price fixing is an agreement between participants on the same side in a market to buy or sell a product, service, or commodity only at a fixed price, or maintain the market conditions such that the price is maintained at a given level by controlling supply and demand.

The intent of price fixing may be to push the price of a product as high as possible, leading to profits for all sellers but may also have the goal to fix, peg, discount, or stabilize prices. The defining characteristic of price fixing is any agreement regarding price, whether expressed or implied.

Arbitration

Arbitration, a form of alternative dispute resolution, is a technique for the resolution of disputes outside the courts. The parties to a dispute refer it to arbitration by one or more persons (the 'arbitrators', 'arbiters' or 'arbitral tribunal'), and agree to be bound by the arbitration decision (the 'award'). A third party reviews the evidence in the case and imposes a decision that is legally binding on both sides and enforceable in the courts.

20. Antitrust Law

CHAPTER HIGHLIGHTS & NOTES: KEY TERMS, PEOPLE, PLACES, CONCEPTS

Copyright

Copyright is a legal concept, enacted by most governments, that grants the creator of an original work exclusive rights to its use and distribution, usually for a limited time, with the intention of enabling the creator of intellectual wealth to receive compensation for their work and be able to financially support themselves.

Copyright is a form of intellectual property (as patents, trademarks and trade secrets are), applicable to any expressible form of an idea or information that is substantive and discrete. It is often shared, then percentage holders are commonly called rightsholders: legally, contractually and in associated 'rights' business functions.

Joint venture

A joint venture is a business agreement in which the parties agree to develop, for a finite time, a new entity and new assets by contributing equity. They exercise control over the enterprise and consequently share revenues, expenses and assets. There are other types of companies such as JV limited by guarantee, joint ventures limited by guarantee with partners holding shares.

Corporation

A corporation is a separate legal entity that has been incorporated either directly through legislation or through a registration process established by law. Incorporated entities have legal rights and liabilities that are distinct from their employees and shareholders, and may conduct business as either a profit-seeking business or not-for-profit business. Early incorporated entities were established by charter (i.e. by an ad hoc act granted by a monarch or passed by a parliament or legislature).

Commission

The payment of commission as remuneration for services rendered or products sold is a common way to reward sales people. Payments often will be calculated on the basis of a percentage of the goods sold. This is a way for firms to solve the principal-agent problem, by attempting to realign employees' interests with those of the firm.

Vertical restraints

Vertical restraints are competition restrictions in agreements between firms or individuals at different levels of the production and distribution process. Vertical restraints are to be distinguished from so-called "horizontal restraints", which are found in agreements between horizontal competitors. Vertical restraints can take numerous forms, ranging from a requirement that dealers accept returns of a manufacturer's product, to resale price maintenance agreements setting the minimum or maximum price that dealers can charge for the manufacturer's product.

Intellectual property

Intellectual property rights are the legally recognized exclusive rights to creations of the mind. Under intellectual property law, owners are granted certain exclusive rights to a variety of intangible assets, such as musical, literary, and artistic works; discoveries and inventions; and words, phrases, symbols, and designs. Common types of intellectual property rights include copyright, trademarks, patents, industrial design rights, trade dress, and in some jurisdictions trade secrets.

Tying

Tying is the practice of selling one product or service as a mandatory addition to the purchase of a different product or service.

In legal terms, a tying sale makes the sale of one good (the tying good) to the de facto customer (or de jure customer) conditional on the purchase of a second distinctive good (the tied good). Tying is often illegal when the products are not naturally related.

Discrimination

Discrimination is action that denies social participation or human rights to categories of people based on prejudice. This includes treatment of an individual or group based on their actual or perceived membership in a certain group or social category, 'in a way that is worse than the way people are usually treated'. It involves the group's initial reaction or interaction, influencing the individual's actual behavior towards the group or the group leader, restricting members of one group from opportunities or privileges that are available to another group, leading to the exclusion of the individual or entities based on logical or irrational decision making.

Predatory pricing

Predatory pricing is a pricing strategy where a product or service is set at a very low price, intending to drive competitors out of the market, or create barriers to entry for potential new competitors. If competitors or potential competitors cannot sustain equal or lower prices without losing money, they go out of business or choose not to enter the business. The predatory merchant then has fewer competitors or is even a de facto monopoly.

Price discrimination

Price discrimination or price differentiation is a pricing strategy where identical or largely similar goods or services are transacted at different prices by the same provider in different markets or territories. Price differentiation is distinguished from product differentiation by the more substantial difference in production cost for the differently priced products involved in the latter strategy. Price differentiation essentially relies on the variation in the customers' willingness to pay.

Bidding

Bidding is an offer of setting a price one is willing to pay for something or a demand that something be done. A price offer is called a bid. The term may be used in context of auctions, stock exchange, card games, or real estate.

Reinsurance

Reinsurance is insurance that is purchased by an insurance company from one or more other insurance companies (the 'reinsurer') directly or through a broker as a means of risk management, sometimes in practice including tax mitigation and other reasons described below. The ceding company and the reinsurer enter into a reinsurance agreement which details the conditions upon which the reinsurer would pay a share of the claims incurred by the ceding company. The reinsurer is paid a 'reinsurance premium' by the ceding company, which issues insurance policies to its own policyholders.

20. Antitrust Law

CHAPTER QUIZ: KEY TERMS, PEOPLE, PLACES, CONCEPTS

1. _________ is an international organization and economic cartel whose mission is to coordinate the policies of the oil-producing countries. The goal is to secure a steady income to the member states and to collude in influencing world oil prices through economic means.

   _________ is an intergovernmental organization that was created at the Baghdad Conference on 10-14 September 1960, by Iraq, Kuwait, Iran, Saudi Arabia and Venezuela.

   a. Carbon bubble
   b. Carbon-based fuel
   c. Clean coal
   d. OPEC

2. The payment of _________ as remuneration for services rendered or products sold is a common way to reward sales people. Payments often will be calculated on the basis of a percentage of the goods sold. This is a way for firms to solve the principal-agent problem, by attempting to realign employees' interests with those of the firm.

   a. Beneficial interest
   b. Big boy letter
   c. Bonus clause
   d. Commission

3. _________ is an agreement between participants on the same side in a market to buy or sell a product, service, or commodity only at a fixed price, or maintain the market conditions such that the price is maintained at a given level by controlling supply and demand.

   The intent of _________ may be to push the price of a product as high as possible, leading to profits for all sellers but may also have the goal to fix, peg, discount, or stabilize prices. The defining characteristic of _________ is any agreement regarding price, whether expressed or implied.

   a. 2008 Liechtenstein tax affair
   b. Bait-and-switch
   c. Price fixing
   d. Cheque fraud

4. . A _________, in common law jurisdictions, is a civil wrong that unfairly causes someone else to suffer loss or harm resulting in legal liability for the person who commits the tortious act, called a tortfeasor. Although crimes may be _________s, the cause of legal action is not necessarily a crime, as the harm may be due to negligence which does not amount to criminal negligence. The victim of the harm can recover their loss as damages in a lawsuit.

   a. Malicious prosecution
   b. superseding cause
   c. Nuisance

5. The _________ of 1914 (Pub.L. 63-212, 38 Stat. 730, enacted October 15, 1914, codified at 15 U.S.C. §§ 12-27, 29 U.S.C. §§ 52-53), was a part of United States antitrust law with the goal of adding further substance to the U.S. antitrust law regime; the _________ sought to prevent anticompetitive practices in their incipiency. That regime started with the Sherman Antitrust Act of 1890, the first Federal law outlawing practices considered harmful to consumers (monopolies, cartels, and trusts). The _________ specified particular prohibited conduct, the three-level enforcement scheme, the exemptions, and the remedial measures.

   a. Sherman Act
   b. Sherman Antitrust
   c. Clayton Antitrust Act
   d. Clayton Act

ANSWER KEY
20. Antitrust Law

1. d
2. d
3. c
4. d
5. d

You can take the complete Online Interactive Chapter Practice Test

for 20. Antitrust Law

on all key terms, persons, places, and concepts.

No Additional Costs

http://www.Cram101.com

Register, send an email request to Travis.Reese@Cram101.com to get your user Id and password.

Include your customer order number, and ISBN number from your studyguide Retailer.

21. Securities Regulation

CHAPTER OUTLINE: KEY TERMS, PEOPLE, PLACES, CONCEPTS

- Blue sky law
- EDGAR
- Environmental Protection
- Disclaimer
- Warranty
- Regulation S-K
- Registration statement
- Quadro Tracker
- Regulation D
- Accredited investor
- Private law
- Arbitration
- Mediation
- Issuer
- Public law
- Commission
- Trade
- Tender offer
- Fraud
- Securities fraud
- Insider

21. Securities Regulation

CHAPTER OUTLINE: KEY TERMS, PEOPLE, PLACES, CONCEPTS

	Insider trading
	Chiarella v. United States
	Amendment
	Landlord
	Lien
	Mutual fund
	Ponzi scheme
	Financial Industry Regulatory Authority
	Administration
	Health Administration

CHAPTER HIGHLIGHTS & NOTES: KEY TERMS, PEOPLE, PLACES, CONCEPTS

Blue sky law	A blue sky law is a state law in the United States that regulates the offering and sale of securities to protect the public from fraud. Though the specific provisions of these laws vary among states, they all require the registration of all securities offerings and sales, as well as of stockbrokers and brokerage firms. Each state's blue sky law is administered by its appropriate regulatory agency, and most also provide private causes of action for private investors who have been injured by securities fraud.
EDGAR	EDGAR, the Electronic Data Gathering, Analysis, and Retrieval system, performs automated collection, validation, indexing, acceptance, and forwarding of submissions by companies and others who are required by law to file forms with the U.S. Securities and Exchange Commission (the 'SEC'). The database is freely available to the public via the Internet (Web or FTP).
Environmental Protection	Environmental protection is a practice of protecting the natural environment on individual, organizational or governmental levels, for the benefit of both the natural environment and humans.

Due to the pressures of population and technology, the biophysical environment is being degraded, sometimes permanently. This has been recognized, and governments have begun placing restraints on activities that cause environmental degradation.

Disclaimer

A disclaimer is generally any statement intended to specify or delimit the scope of rights and obligations that may be exercised and enforced by parties in a legally recognized relationship. In contrast to other terms for legally operative language, the term disclaimer usually implies situations that involve some level of uncertainty, waiver, or risk.

A disclaimer may specify mutually agreed and privately arranged terms and conditions as part of a contract; or may specify warnings or expectations to the general public (or some other class of persons) in order to fulfill a duty of care owed to prevent unreasonable risk of harm or injury.

Warranty

In contract law, a warranty has various meanings but generally means a guarantee or promise which provides assurance by one party to the other party that specific facts or conditions are true or will happen. This factual guarantee may be enforced regardless of materiality which allows for a legal remedy if that promise is not true or followed.

Although a warranty is in its simplest form an element of a contract, some warranties run with a product so that a manufacturer makes the warranty to a consumer with which the manufacturer has no direct contractual relationship.

Regulation S-K

Regulation S-K is a prescribed regulation under the US Securities Act of 1933 that lays out reporting requirements for various SEC filings used by public companies. Companies are also often called issuers (issuing or contemplating issuing shares), filers (entities that must file reports with the SEC) or registrants (entities that must register (usually shares) with the SEC).

Registration statement

In the United States, a registration statement is a set of documents, including a prospectus, which a company must file with the U.S. Securities and Exchange Commission before it proceeds with a public offering.

Quadro Tracker

The Quadro Tracker, also known as the Positive Molecular Locator, was a 'detection device' sold by Quadro Corp. of Harleyville, South Carolina between 1993 and 1996. Around 1,000 were sold to police departments and school districts around the United States on the basis that it could detect hidden drugs, explosives, weapons and lost golf balls. In 1996, the FBI declared it to be a fake and obtained a permanent injunction barring the device from being manufactured or sold.

Regulation D

In the United States under the Securities Act of 1933, any offer to sell securities must either be registered with the United States Securities and Exchange Commission or meet certain qualifications to exempt them from such registration. Regulation D contains the rules providing exemptions from the registration requirements, allowing some companies to offer and sell their securities without having to register the securities with the SEC.

21. Securities Regulation

CHAPTER HIGHLIGHTS & NOTES: KEY TERMS, PEOPLE, PLACES, CONCEPTS

A Regulation D offering is intended to make access to the capital markets possible for small companies that could not otherwise bear the costs of a normal SEC registration. Reg D may also refer to an investment strategy, mostly associated with hedge funds, based upon the same regulation.

Accredited investor

Accredited investor is a term defined by various countries' securities laws that delineates investors permitted to invest in certain types of higher risk investments including seed money, limited partnerships, hedge funds, private placements, and angel investor networks. The term generally includes wealthy individuals and organizations such as banks, insurance companies, significant charities, some corporations, endowments, and retirement plans.

In the United States, for an individual to be considered an accredited investor, they must have a net worth of at least one million US dollars, not including the value of their primary residence or have income at least $200,000 each year for the last two years (or $300,000 together with their spouse if married) and have the expectation to make the same amount this year.'

In Canada, the same prerequisites apply, however their net worth must be a minimum of one million dollars not including the value of their principal residence.

Private law

Private law is that part of a civil law legal system which is part of the jus commune that involves relationships between individuals, such as the law of contracts or torts, and the law of obligations (as it is called in civil legal systems). It is to be distinguished from public law, which deals with relationships between both natural and artificial persons (i.e., organizations) and the state, including regulatory statutes, penal law and other law that affects the public order. In general terms, private law involves interactions between private citizens, whereas public law involves interrelations between the state and the general population.

Arbitration

Arbitration, a form of alternative dispute resolution, is a technique for the resolution of disputes outside the courts. The parties to a dispute refer it to arbitration by one or more persons (the 'arbitrators', 'arbiters' or 'arbitral tribunal'), and agree to be bound by the arbitration decision (the 'award'). A third party reviews the evidence in the case and imposes a decision that is legally binding on both sides and enforceable in the courts.

Mediation

Mediation, as used in law, is a form of alternative dispute resolution, a way of resolving disputes between two or more parties with concrete effects. Typically, a third party, the mediator, assists the parties to negotiate a settlement. Disputants may mediate disputes in a variety of domains, such as commercial, legal, diplomatic, workplace, community and family matters.

Issuer

Issuer is a legal entity that develops, registers and sells securities for the purpose of financing its operations.

Issuers may be domestic or foreign governments, corporations or investment trusts.

Public law	Public law is that part of law which governs relationships between individuals and the government, and those relationships between individuals which are of direct concern to the society. Public law comprises constitutional law, administrative law, tax law and criminal law, as well as all procedural law. In public law, mandatory rules (not optional) prevail.
Commission	The payment of commission as remuneration for services rendered or products sold is a common way to reward sales people. Payments often will be calculated on the basis of a percentage of the goods sold. This is a way for firms to solve the principal-agent problem, by attempting to realign employees' interests with those of the firm.
Trade	In professional sports, a trade is a sports league transaction involving an exchange of players' contracts or draft picks between sports clubs. Cash is another commodity that may be packaged together with contracts or draft picks to complete a trade. Typically, trades are completed between two clubs, but there are instances where trades are consummated between three or more clubs.
Tender offer	Tender offer is a corporate finance term denoting a type of takeover bid. The tender offer is a public, open offer or invitation (usually announced in a newspaper advertisement) by a prospective acquirer to all stockholders of a publicly traded corporation (the target corporation) to tender their stock for sale at a specified price during a specified time, subject to the tendering of a minimum and maximum number of shares. In a tender offer, the bidder contacts shareholders directly; the directors of the company may or may not have endorsed the tender offer proposal.
Fraud	Fraud is a deception deliberately practiced in order to secure unfair or unlawful gain (adjectival form fraudulent; to defraud is the verb). As a legal construct, fraud is both a civil wrong (i.e., a fraud victim may sue the fraud perpetrator to avoid the fraud and/or recover monetary compensation) and a criminal wrong (i.e., a fraud perpetrator may be prosecuted and imprisoned by governmental authorities). Defrauding people or organizations of money or valuables is the usual purpose of fraud, but it sometimes instead involves obtaining benefits without actually depriving anyone of money or valuables, such as obtaining a drivers license by way of false statements made in an application for the same.
Securities fraud	Securities fraud, also known as stock fraud and investment fraud, is a deceptive practice in the stock or commodities markets that induces investors to make purchase or sale decisions on the basis of false information, frequently resulting in losses, in violation of securities laws. Offers of risky investment opportunities to unsophisticated investors who are unable to evaluate risk adequately and cannot afford loss of capital is a central problem. Securities fraud can also include outright theft from investors (embezzlement by stockbrokers), stock manipulation, misstatements on a public company's financial reports, and lying to corporate auditors.
Insider	An insider is a member of any group of people of limited number and generally restricted access.

The term is used in the context of secret, privileged, hidden or otherwise esoteric information or knowledge: an insider is a 'member of the gang' and as such knows things only people in the gang know.

In our complicated and information-rich world, the concept of insider knowledge is popular and pervasive, as a source of direct and useful guidance.

Insider trading

Insider trading is the trading of a public company's stock or other securities by individuals with access to non-public information about the company. In various countries, insider trading based on inside information is illegal. This is because it is seen as unfair to other investors who do not have access to the information.

Chiarella v. United States

Chiarella v. United States, 445 U.S. 222 (1980), is a case in which the Supreme Court of the United States held that an employee of a printer handling corporate takeover bids who deduced target companies' identities and dealt in their stock without disclosing his knowledge of impending takeovers, had not violated § 10(b) of the Securities Exchange Act of 1934 (15 U.S.C. § 78j(b)) and SEC Rule 10b-5.

Amendment

An amendment is a formal or official change made to a law, contract, constitution, or other legal document. It is based on the verb to amend, which means to change. Amendments can add, remove, or update parts of these agreements.

Landlord

A landlord is the owner of a house, apartment, condominium, land or real estate which is rented or leased to an individual or business, who is called a tenant . When a juristic person is in this position, the term landlord is used. Other terms include lessor and owner.

Lien

In law, a lien is a form of security interest granted over an item of property to secure the payment of a debt or performance of some other obligation. The owner of the property, who grants the lien, is referred to as the lieneeand the person who has the benefit of the lien is referred to as the lienor or lien holder.

The etymological root is Anglo-French lien, loyen 'bond', 'restraint', from Latin ligamen, from ligare 'to bind'.

Mutual fund

A mutual fund is a type of professionally managed collective investment scheme that pools money from many investors to purchase securities. While there is no legal definition of the term 'mutual fund', it is most commonly applied only to those collective investment vehicles that are regulated and sold to the general public. They are sometimes referred to as 'investment companies' or 'registered investment companies'.

CHAPTER HIGHLIGHTS & NOTES: KEY TERMS, PEOPLE, PLACES, CONCEPTS

Ponzi scheme	A Ponzi scheme is a fraudulent investment operation where the operator, an individual or organization, pays returns to its investors from new capital paid to the operators by new investors, rather than from profit earned by the operator. Operators of Ponzi schemes usually entice new investors by offering higher returns than other investments, in the form of short-term returns that are either abnormally high or unusually consistent. The perpetuation of the high returns requires an ever-increasing flow of money from new investors to sustain the scheme.
Financial Industry Regulatory Authority	In the United States, the Financial Industry Regulatory Authority, Inc. (FINRA) is a private corporation that acts as a self-regulatory organization (SRO). FINRA is the successor to the National Association of Securities Dealers, Inc.
Administration	As a legal concept, administration is a procedure under the insolvency laws of a number of common law jurisdictions. It functions as a rescue mechanism for insolvent entities and allows them to carry on running their business. The process - an alternative to liquidation - is often known as going into administration.
Health Administration	Health Administration or Healthcare Administration is the field relating to leadership, management, and administration of public health systems, health care systems, hospitals, and hospital networks. Health care administrators are considered health care professionals.

CHAPTER QUIZ: KEY TERMS, PEOPLE, PLACES, CONCEPTS

1. A _________ is a state law in the United States that regulates the offering and sale of securities to protect the public from fraud. Though the specific provisions of these laws vary among states, they all require the registration of all securities offerings and sales, as well as of stockbrokers and brokerage firms. Each state's _________ is administered by its appropriate regulatory agency, and most also provide private causes of action for private investors who have been injured by securities fraud.

   a. Cynthia Cooper
   b. Blue sky law
   c. HP Autonomy
   d. James Henry Ting Wei

2. . In the United States under the Securities Act of 1933, any offer to sell securities must either be registered with the United States Securities and Exchange Commission or meet certain qualifications to exempt them from such registration. _________ contains the rules providing exemptions from the registration requirements, allowing some companies to offer and sell their securities without having to register the securities with the SEC. A _________ offering is intended to make access to the capital markets possible for small companies that could not otherwise bear the costs of a normal SEC registration. Reg D may also refer to an investment strategy, mostly associated with hedge funds, based upon the same regulation.

a. Credit Rating Agency Reform Act
b. Fair Fund
c. Regulation D
d. Registration statement

3. _________, the Electronic Data Gathering, Analysis, and Retrieval system, performs automated collection, validation, indexing, acceptance, and forwarding of submissions by companies and others who are required by law to file forms with the U.S. Securities and Exchange Commission (the 'SEC'). The database is freely available to the public via the Internet (Web or FTP).

a. Credit Rating Agency Reform Act
b. EDGAR
c. Financial scandal in the Orthodox Church in America
d. HP Autonomy

4. _________ is a term defined by various countries' securities laws that delineates investors permitted to invest in certain types of higher risk investments including seed money, limited partnerships, hedge funds, private placements, and angel investor networks. The term generally includes wealthy individuals and organizations such as banks, insurance companies, significant charities, some corporations, endowments, and retirement plans.

In the United States, for an individual to be considered an _________, they must have a net worth of at least one million US dollars, not including the value of their primary residence or have income at least $200,000 each year for the last two years (or $300,000 together with their spouse if married) and have the expectation to make the same amount this year.'

In Canada, the same prerequisites apply, however their net worth must be a minimum of one million dollars not including the value of their principal residence.

a. Cynthia Cooper
b. Financial scandal in the Orthodox Church in America
c. Accredited investor
d. James Henry Ting Wei

5. _________ is a practice of protecting the natural environment on individual, organizational or governmental levels, for the benefit of both the natural environment and humans. Due to the pressures of population and technology, the biophysical environment is being degraded, sometimes permanently. This has been recognized, and governments have begun placing restraints on activities that cause environmental degradation.

a. Electronic Signatures in Global and National Commerce Act
b. Environmental Protection
c. Financial scandal in the Orthodox Church in America
d. HP Autonomy

ANSWER KEY
21. Securities Regulation

1. b
2. c
3. b
4. c
5. b

You can take the complete Online Interactive Chapter Practice Test

for 21. Securities Regulation
on all key terms, persons, places, and concepts.

No Additional Costs

http://www.Cram101.com

Register, send an email request to Travis.Reese@Cram101.com to get your user Id and password.

Include your customer order number, and ISBN number from your studyguide Retailer.

22. The International Legal Environment of Business

CHAPTER OUTLINE: KEY TERMS, PEOPLE, PLACES, CONCEPTS

- ______ Law merchant
- ______ Lex mercatoria
- ______ Free trade
- ______ North American Free Trade Agreement
- ______ Trade
- ______ Intellectual property
- ______ Duty
- ______ Corporation
- ______ Administration
- ______ Commission
- ______ International Trade Administration
- ______ Dumping
- ______ Export Administration Act
- ______ Principal
- ______ Tort
- ______ Contract
- ______ Joint venture
- ______ Corruption
- ______ Siemens
- ______ Trust
- ______ Foreign exchange controls

22. The International Legal Environment of Business

CHAPTER OUTLINE: KEY TERMS, PEOPLE, PLACES, CONCEPTS

Letters of credit

Transfer pricing

Alliance

Force majeure

Forum selection clause

Pollution

Arbitration

Confiscation

Expropriation

Nationalization

Overseas Private Investment Corporation

Federal Circuit

Sources of law

Labor relations

National Labor Relations Act

Term	Definition
Law merchant	Lex mercatoria, often referred to as 'the Law Merchant' in English, is the body of commercial law used by merchants throughout Europe during the medieval period. It evolved similar to English common law as a system of custom and best practice, which was enforced through a system of merchant courts along the main trade routes. It functioned as the international law of commerce.
Lex mercatoria	Lex mercatoria is the body of commercial law used by merchants throughout Europe during the medieval period. It evolved similar to English common law as a system of custom and best practice, which was enforced through a system of merchant courts along the main trade routes. It functioned as the international law of commerce.
Free trade	Free trade is a policy in international markets in which governments do not restrict imports or exports. Free trade is exemplified by the European Union / European Economic Area and the North American Free Trade Agreement, which have established open markets. Most nations are today members of the World Trade Organization (WTO) multilateral trade agreements.
North American Free Trade Agreement	The North American Free Trade Agreement is an agreement signed by Canada, Mexico, and the United States, creating a trilateral rules-based trade bloc in North America. The agreement came into force on January 1, 1994. It superseded the Canada-United States Free Trade Agreement between the U.S. and Canada. North American Free Trade Agreement has two supplements: the North American Agreement on Environmental Cooperation (NAAEC) and the North American Agreement on Labor Cooperation (NAALC). In terms of combined purchasing power parity GDP of its members, as of 2013 the trade bloc is the largest in the world as well as by nominal GDP comparison.
Trade	In professional sports, a trade is a sports league transaction involving an exchange of players' contracts or draft picks between sports clubs. Cash is another commodity that may be packaged together with contracts or draft picks to complete a trade. Typically, trades are completed between two clubs, but there are instances where trades are consummated between three or more clubs.
Intellectual property	Intellectual property rights are the legally recognized exclusive rights to creations of the mind. Under intellectual property law, owners are granted certain exclusive rights to a variety of intangible assets, such as musical, literary, and artistic works; discoveries and inventions; and words, phrases, symbols, and designs. Common types of intellectual property rights include copyright, trademarks, patents, industrial design rights, trade dress, and in some jurisdictions trade secrets.
Duty	Duty is a term that conveys a sense of moral commitment or obligation to someone or something. The moral commitment should result in action; it is not a matter of passive feeling or mere recognition.

22. The International Legal Environment of Business

CHAPTER HIGHLIGHTS & NOTES: KEY TERMS, PEOPLE, PLACES, CONCEPTS

Corporation	A corporation is a separate legal entity that has been incorporated either directly through legislation or through a registration process established by law. Incorporated entities have legal rights and liabilities that are distinct from their employees and shareholders, and may conduct business as either a profit-seeking business or not-for-profit business. Early incorporated entities were established by charter (i.e. by an ad hoc act granted by a monarch or passed by a parliament or legislature).
Administration	As a legal concept, administration is a procedure under the insolvency laws of a number of common law jurisdictions. It functions as a rescue mechanism for insolvent entities and allows them to carry on running their business. The process - an alternative to liquidation - is often known as going into administration.
Commission	The payment of commission as remuneration for services rendered or products sold is a common way to reward sales people. Payments often will be calculated on the basis of a percentage of the goods sold. This is a way for firms to solve the principal-agent problem, by attempting to realign employees' interests with those of the firm.
International Trade Administration	The International Trade Administration is an agency in the United States Department of Commerce that promotes United States exports of nonagricultural U.S. services and goods.
Dumping	In economics, 'dumping' is a kind of predatory pricing, especially in the context of international trade. It occurs when manufacturers export a product to another country at a price either below the price charged in its home market or below its cost of production.
Export Administration Act	The Export Administration Act of 1979 (P.L. 96-72) provided legal authority to the President to control U.S. exports for reasons of national security, foreign policy, and/or short supply. However, the 1990 farm bill (P.L. 101-624) provided for contract sanctity by prohibiting the President from restricting the export of any agricultural commodity already under contract for delivery within 270 days from the date an embargo is imposed under the Export Administration Act, except during national emergency or war. With the expiration of Export Administration Act in 1994, the President declared a national emergency and exercised authority under the International Emergency Economic Powers Act (P.L. 95-223; 50 U.S.C. 1701 et seq).
Principal	In commercial law, a principal is a person, legal or natural, who authorizes an agent to act to create one or more legal relationships with a third party. This branch of law is called agency and relies on the common law proposition qui facit per alium, facit per se (Latin 'he who acts through another, acts personally'). It is a parallel concept to vicarious liability and strict liability (in which one person is held liable for the acts or omissions of another) in criminal law or torts.

Tort	A tort, in common law jurisdictions, is a civil wrong that unfairly causes someone else to suffer loss or harm resulting in legal liability for the person who commits the tortious act, called a tortfeasor. Although crimes may be torts, the cause of legal action is not necessarily a crime, as the harm may be due to negligence which does not amount to criminal negligence. The victim of the harm can recover their loss as damages in a lawsuit.
Contract	In common law legal systems, a contract is an agreement having a lawful object entered into voluntarily by two or more parties, each of whom intends to create one or more legal obligations between them. The elements of a contract are 'offer' and 'acceptance' by 'competent persons' having legal capacity who exchange 'consideration' to create 'mutuality of obligation.' Proof of some or all of these elements may be done in writing, though contracts may be made entirely orally or by conduct. The remedy for breach of contract can be 'damages' in the form of compensation of money or specific performance enforced through an injunction.
Joint venture	A joint venture is a business agreement in which the parties agree to develop, for a finite time, a new entity and new assets by contributing equity. They exercise control over the enterprise and consequently share revenues, expenses and assets. There are other types of companies such as JV limited by guarantee, joint ventures limited by guarantee with partners holding shares.
Corruption	In philosophical, theological, or moral discussions, corruption is spiritual or moral impurity or deviation from an ideal. Corruption may include many activities including bribery and embezzlement. Government, or 'political', corruption occurs when an office-holder or other governmental employee acts in an official capacity for personal gain.
Siemens	Siemens AG is a German multinational engineering and electronics conglomerate company headquartered in Berlin and Munich. It is Europe's largest engineering company and maker of medical diagnostics equipment and its medical health-care division, which generates about 12 percent of the company's total sales, is its second-most profitable unit behind the industrial automation division. Siemens' principal activities are in the fields of industry, energy, transportation and healthcare.
Trust	A 'trust,' or 'corporate trust' is a large business. Originally, it was Standard Oil, which was already the largest corporation in the world
Foreign exchange controls	Foreign exchange controls are various forms of controls imposed by a government on the purchase/sale of foreign currencies by residents or on the purchase/sale of local currency by nonresidents.

Common foreign exchange controls include:•Banning the use of foreign currency within the country•Banning locals from possessing foreign currency•Restricting currency exchange to government-approved exchangers•Fixed exchange rates•Restrictions on the amount of currency that may be imported or exported

Countries with foreign exchange controls are also known as 'Article 14 countries,' after the provision in the International Monetary Fund agreement allowing exchange controls for transitional economies. Such controls used to be common in most countries, particularly poorer ones, until the 1990s when free trade and globalization started a trend towards economic liberalization.

Letters of credit

A letter of credit is a document issued by a financial institution, or a similar party, assuring payment to a seller of goods or services provided certain documents have been presented to the bank. 'Letters of Credit' are documents that prove the seller has performed the duties specified by an underlying contract (e.g., the sale of goods contract) and the goods/services have been supplied as agreed. In return for these documents, the beneficiary receives payment from the financial institution that issued the letter.

Transfer pricing

Transfer pricing is the setting of the price for goods and services sold between controlled legal entities within an enterprise. For example, if a subsidiary company sells goods to a parent company, the cost of those goods is the transfer price. Legal entities considered under the control of a single corporation include branches and companies that are wholly or majority owned ultimately by the parent corporation.

Alliance

An alliance is a pact, coalition or friendship between two or more parties, made in order to advance common goals and to secure common interests. It is a Political agreement between countries to support each other in disputes with other countries.

See also military alliance, treaty, contract, coalition (disambiguation) and business alliance.

Force majeure

Force majeure or vis major but seems conceptually synonymous with the common law interpretation of force majeure, comprehending both natural disasters and events such as strikes, civil unrest, and war. However, even in the event of force majeure, liability persists in the face of default by a debtor (Schuldnerverzug, cf. BGB §287 (in German)) or deprivation of property (Sachentziehung, cf.

Forum selection clause

A forum selection clause in a contract with a conflict of laws element allows the parties to agree that any litigation resulting from that contract will be initiated in a specific forum.

There are three types of clause:•the reference might be to a particular court in a jurisdiction agreed upon by the parties (although, if the parties make a mistake as to the power of the nominated court to hear the matter, the civil procedures of the nominated jurisdiction will be applied to identify the appropriate court); or•the clause might refer to a specific kind of dispute resolution process, such as mediation, arbitration, or a hearing before a special referee; or•the clause might refer to both, requiring a specific process to be carried out in a specific location.

A simple forum selection clause covering both the proper law of the contract and the forum for resolving disputes might read:

"This contract is governed by the laws of England and any dispute shall be finally resolved by the English courts."

In many cross-border contracts, the forum for resolving disputes may not be the same as the country whose law governs the contract. And the contract may provide for a staged procedure for resolving disputes.

Pollution

Pollution is the introduction of contaminants into the natural environment that cause adverse change. Pollution can take the form of chemical substances or energy, such as noise, heat or light. Pollutants, the components of pollution, can be either foreign substances/energies or naturally occurring contaminants.

Arbitration

Arbitration, a form of alternative dispute resolution, is a technique for the resolution of disputes outside the courts. The parties to a dispute refer it to arbitration by one or more persons (the 'arbitrators', 'arbiters' or 'arbitral tribunal'), and agree to be bound by the arbitration decision (the 'award'). A third party reviews the evidence in the case and imposes a decision that is legally binding on both sides and enforceable in the courts.

Confiscation

Confiscation i.e. transfer to the treasury' is a legal seizure by a government or other public authority. The word is also used, popularly, of spoliation under legal forms, or of any seizure of property as punishment or in enforcement of the law.

Expropriation

The process of expropriation 'occurs when a public agency takes private property for a purpose deemed to be in the public interest'. Unlike eminent domain, expropriation may also refer to the taking of private property by a private entity authorized by a government to take property in certain situations.

The term appears as 'expropriation of expropriators (ruling classes)' in Marxist theory, and also as the slogan 'Loot the looters!', very popular during the Russian October Revolution.

Nationalization

Nationalization is the process of taking a private industry or private assets into public ownership by a national government or state.

Nationalization usually refers to private assets, but may also mean assets owned by lower levels of government, such as municipalities, being transferred to be the state. The opposite of nationalization is usually privatization or de-nationalization, but may also be municipalization.

Overseas Private Investment Corporation

The Overseas Private Investment Corporation is the U.S. government's development finance institution. It mobilizes private capital to help solve critical development challenges and, in doing so, advances U.S. foreign policy. It also finances projects, including a majority stake such as the 70%, $200m, it provided to Project Salvador, a solar plant in Chile.

Federal Circuit

The United States Court of Appeals for the Federal Circuit is a United States court of appeals headquartered in Washington, D.C.. The court was created by Congress with passage of the Federal Courts Improvement Act of 1982, which merged the United States Court of Customs and Patent Appeals and the appellate division of the United States Court of Claims, making the judges of the former courts into circuit judges. The Federal Circuit is particularly known for its decisions on patent law, as it is the only appellate-level court with the jurisdiction to hear patent case appeals.

Sources of law

Sources of law means the origin from which rules of human conduct come into existence and derive legal force or binding characters.It also refers to the sovereign or the state from which the law derives its force or validity.

Several factors of law have contributed to the development of law. These factors are regarded as the sources of law.

Labor relations

Labor relations is the study and practice of managing unionized employment situations. In academia, labor relations is frequently a subarea within industrial relations, though scholars from many disciplines--including economics, sociology, history, law, and political science--also study labor unions and labor movements. In practice, labor relations is frequently a subarea within human resource management.

National Labor Relations Act

The National Labor Relations Act of 1935 29 U.S.C. § 151-169 (also known as the Wagner Act after NY Senator Robert F. Wagner) is a foundational statute of US labor law which guarantees basic rights of private sector employees to organize into trade unions, engage in collective bargaining for better terms and conditions at work, and take collective action including strike if necessary. The act also created the National Labor Relations Board, which conducts elections that can require employers to engage in collective bargaining with labor unions (also known as trade unions). The Act does not apply to workers who are covered by the Railway Labor Act, agricultural employees, domestic employees, supervisors, federal, state or local government workers, independent contractors and some close relatives of individual employers.

1. A '_________,' or 'corporate _________' is a large business. Originally, it was Standard Oil, which was already the largest corporation in the world

   a. Barriers to exit
   b. Bilateral monopoly
   c. Chamberlinian monopolistic competition
   d. Trust

2. A _________, in common law jurisdictions, is a civil wrong that unfairly causes someone else to suffer loss or harm resulting in legal liability for the person who commits the tortious act, called a tortfeasor. Although crimes may be _________s, the cause of legal action is not necessarily a crime, as the harm may be due to negligence which does not amount to criminal negligence. The victim of the harm can recover their loss as damages in a lawsuit.

   a. Malicious prosecution
   b. superseding cause
   c. Tort
   d. Trespasser

3. _________ is the body of commercial law used by merchants throughout Europe during the medieval period. It evolved similar to English common law as a system of custom and best practice, which was enforced through a system of merchant courts along the main trade routes. It functioned as the international law of commerce.

   a. Commercial law
   b. Lex mercatoria
   c. Bulk sale
   d. Business license

4. A _________ is a separate legal entity that has been incorporated either directly through legislation or through a registration process established by law. Incorporated entities have legal rights and liabilities that are distinct from their employees and shareholders, and may conduct business as either a profit-seeking business or not-for-profit business. Early incorporated entities were established by charter (i.e. by an ad hoc act granted by a monarch or passed by a parliament or legislature).

   a. Bulk sale
   b. Business license
   c. Business method patent
   d. Corporation

5. . _________ rights are the legally recognized exclusive rights to creations of the mind. Under _________ law, owners are granted certain exclusive rights to a variety of intangible assets, such as musical, literary, and artistic works; discoveries and inventions; and words, phrases, symbols, and designs. Common types of _________ rights include copyright, trademarks, patents, industrial design rights, trade dress, and in some jurisdictions trade secrets.

   a. Barriers to exit
   b. Intellectual property

c. Chamberlinian monopolistic competition

d. Competition Commission

ANSWER KEY

22. The International Legal Environment of Business

1. d
2. c
3. b
4. d
5. b

CPSIA information can be obtained
at www.ICGtesting.com
Printed in the USA
BVHW062300120620
581308BV00006B/246